СССР
46
30
96

The Bell P-39 Airacobra and P-63 Kingcobra Fighters

SOVIET SERVICE DURING WORLD WAR II

The Bell P-39 Airacobra & P-63 Kingcobra Fighters

SOVIET SERVICE DURING WORLD WAR II

Yefim Gordon and
Sergey Komissarov
with Dmitriy Komissarov

SCHIFFER MILITARY
4880 Lower Valley Road Atglen, PA 19310

Library of Congress Control Number: 2018959799

Designed by Polygon Press Ltd., Moscow
Type set in Minion Pro/Titan

ISBN: 978-0-7643-5680-3
Printed in China

Published by Schiffer Publishing, Ltd.
4880 Lower Valley Road
Atglen, PA 19310
Phone: (610) 593-1777; Fax: (610) 593-2002
E-mail: Info@schifferbooks.com
www.schifferbooks.com

Contents

Acknowledgments

This book is illustrated with photos by Yefim Gordon and Keith Dexter, as well as from the archives of the M. M. Gromov Flight Research Institute (LII), the ITAR-TASS News Agency, the Bell Aircraft Corporation, the Russian Aviation Research Trust (RART), and the personal archive of Yefim Gordon.

The authors have used the following web sources: www.aex.ru, www.airaces.ru, www.airaces.narod.ru, www.allaces.ru, www.airliners.net, www.airwar.ru, www.justmedia.ru, www.soviet-aces-1936-53.ru, www.forum.warthunder.ru, www.great.victory.ru, www.wp.scn.ru, www.kudago.com, www.rulit.me, www.skytamer.com, www.topwar.ru, www.walkarounds.scalemodels.ru, www.arsenal-info.ru, www.sk16.ru, www.vsponiv.ru, www.waralbum.ru, www.wunderwaffe.narod.ru, www.yaplakal.com, www.warheroes.ru, www.militera.lib.ru, www.betta.vlz.ru, www.dic.academic.ru, www.parnasse.ru, www.military.wikireading.ru, www.tm.ru.net, www.ww2.dk, www.warspot.ru, www.weaponsandwarfare.com, www.veshevoaviatori.narod.ru, www.proza.ru, www.wio.ru, www.pynop.com, www.shkolazhizni.ru, www.forum.evvaul.com, www.gmohist-pkgo.ucoz.ru, www.joebaugher.com, www.kamlib.ru, www.noo-journal.ru, www.pobeda1945.su, www.pirochem.net, www.severpost.ru, www.pravkamchatka.ru, www.vdovgan.ru, www.tinlib.ru, www.710-polk.forumei.org, www.encyclopedia.mil.ru, www.stoletie.ru, www.nevskye.narod.ru, www.e-reading.club, www.ok.ru, and www.pobeda.elar.ru.

Colour artwork by Mikhail Bykov and Andrey Yurgenson.

P-39Qs share a snowbound airfield with a large number of Douglas A-20 Boston bombers while being ferried to the Soviet Union. All the aircraft wear ferry markings on a white background.

Introduction

The story of the Bell P-39 Airacobra and P-63 Kingcobra fighters in Soviet service was chosen as a subject of this book for a number of good reasons. The history of the Second World War, which ended more than seventy years ago, continues to captivate the current generation. In this context, aviation history enthusiasts cannot overlook the significance of the deliveries of combat aircraft from the Allies to the Soviet Union during its war against Germany, and, in particular, the special place occupied by the two Bell fighter types in these deliveries. Moreover, the spectacular success of the Airacobra on the Soviet-German front is in stark contrast with the fairly modest role this fighter played in the air war operations of the Allies. The fighters, which were regarded as disappointing and unsatisfactory by the USAAF and RAF, unexpectedly won acclaim in the Soviet Union as efficient combat aircraft, earning affection and recognition on the part of Soviet airmen. This book is an attempt to explain this phenomenon.

To give a general background of the Soviet episode in the career of the two Bell fighter types, it is necessary to dwell in some detail on the subject of the Lend-Lease deliveries to the USSR.

As far as the Soviet Union was concerned, the Second World War started with the German invasion on 22 June 1941 and developed into a veritable struggle for national survival that came to be termed the Great Patriotic War. Overnight, after 22 June 1941, the Soviet Union, the United States, and Great Britain became allies in the fight against German Nazism. From the outset the US administration declared its intention to give the Soviet Union assistance in its struggle against the common enemy. This assistance found its expression in extending to the Soviet Union the aid given by the United States to a number of countries under the Lend-Lease Act. This aid was of a comprehensive character, comprising deliveries of all sorts of war materiel, transport vehicles, food, strategic raw materials, and other supplies. Aircraft constituted a very substantial part of the Lend-Lease aid reaching the Soviet Union.

Negotiations on Lend-Lease with the USSR were started officially in late September 1941. Prior to that, Harry Hopkins, President Franklin D. Roosevelt's 'Special Assistant' on Lend-Lease matters, was despatched to Moscow in late July 1941 to find out what the Russians wanted as priorities for supplies. The Anglo-American Supply Mission arrived in Moscow on 28 September 1941, and official negotiations started on the following day. The conference with the Soviets resulted in the signature of a protocol setting out the Anglo-American commitments for supplies of war materiel, which could be sent monthly from October 1941 to June 1942. On 1 October 1941 William Averell Harriman, the US president's envoy, signed (together with Lord Beaverbrook, who was then the British Minister of Supply, and the Soviet People's Commissar [that is, Minister] of Foreign Affairs Vyacheslav M. Molotov) the first protocol on deliveries to the Soviet Union, which would amount to one billion US dollars in the course of the following nine months (until the end of June 1942). Yet, it was not before 7 November 1941 that President Roosevelt signed a document extending the Lend-Lease scheme to include the Soviet Union.

The first deliveries to the USSR under the Lend-Lease programme began in October 1941 (but prior to that, there had been some deliveries, also of US-built aircraft, from Great Britain). In 1941 only 256 aircraft were delivered instead of the 600 specified by the protocol. William A. Harriman admitted that the US had fulfilled only a quarter of their obligations under the first protocol.

Subsequently, the volume of aid, including the deliveries of aircraft, began to grow and reached sizeable proportions when it became clear that the Soviet Union was capable of withstanding the onslaught of the German war machine.

The First Moscow Protocol was subsequently followed up by a further three protocols signed consecutively in Washington, DC, London, and Ottawa; their terms of validity were extended respectively to 30 June 1943, 30 June 1944, and 30 June 1945. Officially, the Lend-Lease deliveries were terminated on 12 May 1945; further deliveries until the start of the Soviet offensive against Japanese troops in Manchuria took place under a special agreement. Eventually the deliveries of aircraft under the terms of the abovementioned protocols were effected to the full extent and even surpassed the stipulated obligations by 4.4 percent.

American military aid, including deliveries of aircraft, reached the Soviet Union via several routes. These included the so-called northern route, with its shipping convoys over the North Atlantic to the Soviet ports of Murmansk and Arkhangel'sk; the trans-Iranian route; and the route that came to be widely known by the name of ALSIB (Alaska-Siberia). Their operation will be dealt with in greater detail in chapter 1, with the special emphasis on the deliveries of the Bell P-39 and P-63 fighters.

The three major routes mentioned above were supplemented by a northern air bridge via Iceland. This route was used on a limited scale for the transfer of the Consolidated PBY-6A Catalina amphibians and PBN-1 Nomad flying boats, which travelled from Iceland to northern ports of the Soviet Union. An insignificant number of aircraft (only seventeen machines) were delivered by ships across the Pacific to Vladivostok.

According to calculations made by Russian historians on the basis of archive information, a total of 18,297 aircraft were delivered to the Soviet Union under the Lend-Lease programme during the war; of these, 14,126 came from the US and 4,171 from Britain. These figures presumably exclude the aircraft lost under delivery. (Other sources give slightly differing figures; for example, one

Russian author puts the total of aircraft received under the Lend-Lease programme at 18,763, and the US share of this total at 14,535.) In some publications one may encounter an assertion that the deliveries of Lend-Lease aircraft to the Soviet Union totalled 22,150 aircraft, but this figure does not seem to have wide acceptance.

Coming back to the total of 14,126 American aircraft mentioned above, their deliveries from the US were broken down on a year-by-year basis as follows: 256 aircraft in 1941, 1,485 in 1942, 5,320 in 1943, 5,007 in 1944, and 2,058 in 1945. Distribution by the main aircraft categories gives the following figures: more then 70 percent (9,681 aircraft) were tactical fighters, tactical bombers made up 26 percent (3,632 aircraft), and the remaining 4 percent (813 aircraft) were other types, including flying boats, amphibians, and transport aircraft (the figure of 813 seems to be short of the mark, as will be seen from other calculations below).

Normal operation of the aircraft supplied under the Lend-Lease programme would have been impossible without parallel deliveries of various types of associated materiel. The Soviet Union received more than 15,000 aero engines, as well as aircraft weapons, ammunition, high-grade aviation fuel, spare parts for aircraft, and other items of maintenance equipment.

To get an idea of the importance of the Allied aircraft deliveries to the USSR during the war, one can compare the volume of these deliveries with the volume of Soviet wartime aircraft production. The Soviet aircraft industry manufactured 114,117 combat aircraft of all types, including 59,602 fighters, 37,240 attack aircraft, and

LEFT: P-39Q-20-BE 44-3241 on the ALSIB route. Note the huge 662-litre (175 US gallon) conformal ferry tank; pilots reported that as the fuel was burned off; the remaining fuel sloshing about in this tank made the Airacobra very hard to handle.

BELOW LEFT: Soviet Air Force representative Maj. N. N. Kalinnikov (*left*) and USAAF pilot Flight Officer R. G. Berry stand beside a P-39Q named the 'Hopedale Avenger' at Ladd Field AAF (Fairbanks, Alaska) in 1943. Hopedale was the home town of Robinson Billings, a Bell Aircraft Co. test pilot who flew many of the P-39s destined for the USSR and was good friends with many of the Soviet officers involved in the ferrying effort.

ABOVE RIGHT: A USAAF ferry pilot talks to his Soviet colleague Lt. Pelageychenko while sitting on the wing of a P-39. The aircraft was paid for funds raised by the schoolgirls of School 51 in Buffalo, New York, which explains the name Buffalo Belle and appropriate nose art.

RIGHT: The same aircraft is shown as the same American pilot (with a USAAF ground crewman watching) coaches Lt. Pelageychenko, explaining the positions of the various switches in the cockpit.

17,877 bombers. Allied deliveries totalled 18,297 aircraft of all types, or 16 percent of the Soviet total. If one singles out for comparison the tactical fighters and bombers, the Allied deliveries, totalling 17,484 aircraft, represent 23 percent as compared to the number (77,479) produced by the Soviet industry.

If one takes only the US-produced aircraft, then the tactical fighters delivered made up 16 percent of the number produced by the Soviet industry, and the tactical bombers—20 percent. (All the above figures have been compiled on the basis of archives of the Red Army Air Force Headquarters by Igor' Lebedev, who was a military representative of the Soviet government's purchasing commission in the US between October 1943 and October 1945.)

Let us look at the type-by-type breakdown of US-manufactured aircraft delivered to the Soviet Union (the figures below are based on Russian archive materials and include the aircraft actually delivered).

The following six types made up the bulk of the US aircraft received by the Soviet Union during the war:

Fighters:

- Bell P-39 Airacobra (4,952)
- Bell P-63 Kingcobra (2,400)
- Curtiss P-40 Tomahawk/Kittyhawk/Warhawk (2,134)

Bombers:

- Douglas A-20 Havoc/Boston (2,771)
- North American B-25 Mitchell (861)

Transport aircraft:

- Douglas C-47 Skytrain (705)

Several other types were delivered in smaller numbers or single examples. These included the Republic P-47 Thunderbolt, Consolidated (Naval Aircraft Factory) PBN-1 Nomad, Consolidated PBY-6A Catalina, North American AT-6 Texan, Curtiss O-52 Owl, North American P-51 Mustang, Curtiss C-46 Commando, Vought OS2U Kingfisher, and Consolidated B-24 Liberator.

In addition to these, there were several types that were obtained unofficially—either by collecting aircraft abandoned by the USAAF in eastern Europe, or by appropriating aircraft interned in the Far East. These included the Boeing B-17 Flying Fortress, Boeing B-29 Superfortress, Consolidated B-24, and Lockheed P-38 Lightning.

The Soviet Union did not utilise American engines, parts, and units in aircraft of Soviet manufacture, the only exception being radio sets that were installed in some aircraft.

On the other hand, of great importance for the Soviet war effort and for the development of the Soviet aircraft industry were the deliveries of raw materials, structural materials, and equipment for the aircraft industry. Especially important was the import of aluminium from the US, which started in the spring of 1942—it made up for the loss of aluminium foundries that had been abandoned on the territory occupied by the German forces. One more factor of considerable importance was the import of machine tools for aircraft factories.

To sum up, these deliveries were very substantial and played an important role in enhancing the combat potential of Soviet aviation.

The role played by American aircraft types in Soviet service can be highlighted by the following quotation from an article by the Russian historian Andrey Pochtaryov: *'It should be noted that among the top 100 of the Soviet aces (those with 24 or more claimed air victories), 31 flew and fought on US fighters at various times (a further seven flew British fighters). As for the Soviet pilots who had scored 15 or more 'kills' (601 pilots), 138 of those fought on Lend-Lease aircraft. Among the 62 Soviet pilots who were twice awarded the Hero of the Soviet Union (HSU) title and* [the accompanying] *Gold Star medal, 19 had flown US fighters and bombers at different times (a further three had flown British machines). If one subtracts the attack aircraft pilots—21 persons—from the overall number of Twice HSUs (because* [American] *attack aircraft were not supplied to Soviet attack air units), it appears that roughly 50% of the remaining number of Twice HSUs fought on the Lend-Lease machines.'*

An assessment of the impact the Lend-Lease aid had had on the Soviet war potential was given by Iosif V. Stalin in his letter to President Harry S. Truman, dated 11 June 1945, in which he wrote: *'The agreement, on the basis of which the USA sent strategic materials and food supplies to the Soviet Union under the Lend-Lease programme throughout the war in Europe, has played an important role and has contributed to a considerable degree to the successful end of the war against our common enemy—Nazi Germany.'*

During the Cold War period, guided by ideological considerations, the Soviet government officials and historians tended to play down the importance of Lend-Lease deliveries as one of the factors that had contributed to the Soviet Union's victory in the war. Conversely, Western historians, in the opinion of the Russian side, have tended to go to the opposite extreme, asserting that the Soviet Union would not have held out in the war without the Lend-Lease. Today this view is shared by some so-called liberal (read: pro-Western) historians in Russia, and at the same time is hotly contested by their opponents of the more 'patriotic' (read: anti-Western) observance. Still others adhere to what they consider to be a more balanced and objective view. They insist that the Soviet Union would under all circumstances have been able to repel the German onslaught on its own, but admittedly at the cost of far-greater losses and sufferings; the crucial impact of the Lend-Lease in speeding up the victory cannot be denied. Albeit the war effort of the Soviet Union was primarily based on its own resources, the significant role played by the military aid from the Allies is widely acknowledged and duly noted in Russia today. The Russian people have retained a grateful memory of this cooperation with the Western Allies in the fight against the Nazi threat.

In dealing with the story of testing and operational use of the P-39 and P-63 fighters in the USSR, the authors have made use of structural descriptions and manuals issued by the publishing house of the Soviet People's Commissariat (later Ministry) of Defence, reports prepared by NII VVS (*Naoochno-issledovatel'skiy institoot Voyenno-vozdooshnykh sil*; the Soviet Air Force Research Institute) and by BNT NKAP (*Byuro novoy tekhniki Narodnovo komissariahta aviatsionnoy promyshlennosti*; the Bureau of New Technology of the People's Commissariat of Aircraft Industry). They have also found much useful information in the books and articles on this subject published by many Russian and Ukrainian aviation historians, as well as by some Western authors. Of special value are the memoirs of Soviet pilots who flew the Airacobra and Kingcobra during the war. Some useful information was also gained from various publications on the internet.

The subject of this book has been covered by the authors to a considerable extent in their previous publications, but this time it has been given a far more detailed treatment.

The authors express their gratitude to Sergey D. Kuznetsov for providing some source material and to Dmitriy Komissarov for assistance in preparing the text of this book for print.

CHAPTER 1

The P-39's Introduction into Soviet Service

Airacobras in British Service

The start of the P-39's career in the Soviet air force is connected with this aircraft's initial service with the Royal Air Force. In September 1940 Great Britain ordered the first 386 P-39D (Bell Model 13) fighters in a customised version known as the Model 14, later increasing the order to 675. The Model 14 differed from the P-39D in the armament, featuring a 20 mm (.90 calibre) Hispano-Suiza HS.404 cannon with sixty rounds instead of the 37 mm Browning M4 with only thirty rounds; the two 12.7 mm (.50 calibre) synchronised Browning M2 AN machine guns in the nose were retained, but the four 7.62 mm (.30 calibre) Browning M1919 machine guns in the wings were replaced by a version chambered for the British 7.7 mm (.303 calibre) rounds. In RAF service the Bell Model 14 was initially allocated the name Caribou, but this was changed to the US name Airacobra—to be precise, Airacobra Mk I—by the time deliveries commenced.

The first Airacobra Is arrived in July 1941. They began equipping 601 Squadron (the first—and, as it turned out, the only—RAF squadron to operate the type) in September 1941. The aircraft proved disappointing both to pilots of 601 Squadron and to specialists of the test centres—the Aeroplane and Armament Experimental Establishment (A&AEE) at RAF Boscombe Down and the Air Fighting Development Unit at RAF Duxford. Service tests of the

Two P-39Q-25-BEs (including 44-32648) at a stateside airfield prior to delivery to the Soviet Union (note the USAAF example in the background). The emblem on the nose is that of a high school in East Aurora, New York, whose pupils raised money to pay for the fighters.

ABOVE: Soviet pilot Capt. V. M. Perov from the 1st PAD (Ferry Air Division) in the cockpit of a P-39 on the ALSIB route.

BELOW: P-39Q-10-BEs, including 42-21164, 42-21088, 42-21096, and 42-20996, share a hangar at Ladd Field, Alaska, with A-20Gs destined for the Soviet Union.

RIGHT: Early P-39Q-30-BEs with four-blade propellers (including 44-71446 and 44-71453) at a staging point on the ALSIB route.

BELOW RIGHT: P-39Q-25-BEs with ferry tanks at an Alaskan airfield.

Airacobra I conducted by the British showed that the fighter's speed was 50 km/h (31 mph) less than promised by Bell; the takeoff distance was 686 m (2,250 ft.)—too long, restricting the use of available airfields. During gunnery attacks the gun blast gases penetrated into the cockpit; the weapons' recoil put the gyro out of action, which was regarded as a particularly serious drawback. The Airacobra I was promptly recognised as having inadequate rate of climb and performance at altitude. During trials at Duxford, the Airacobra I was pitted against a Supermarine Spitfire Mk V and a captured Messerschmitt Bf 109E; mock combat sessions showed that the American aircraft matched them both for speed and manoeuvrability at altitudes below 4,570 m (15,000 ft.). However, because of the lack of a supercharger, the performance fell off rapidly above 6,100 m (20,000 ft.), which rendered the Airacobra I useless as an interceptor. The British felt that with its 20 mm cannon the Airacobra might be well suited for antishipping and ground-strafing duties. A very limited number of combat sorties of this kind were flown in the English Channel and Dunkirk area with rather modest results, and by mid-October 1941 the operational career of the Airacobra I in British service came to an end. The RAF ended up accepting only eighty Airacobra Is. Two hundred Airacobras from the British order were diverted to the USAAF after the Japanese attack on Pearl Harbor and the US entry into the Second World War, seeing action on the South Pacific and European theatres of operations. To discern them from regular US-standard P-39Ds, these aircraft were given the designation P-400, reflecting the advertised 400 mph (644 km/h) maximum speed.

471465
471446

471353

In the severe frost typical of Alaska in the winter it was necessary to preheat the cockpit and the engine before flight. P-39Q-15-BE 44-2091 (complete with 662-litre ferry tank and underwing machine gun pods) is seen here at Ladd Field with a lot of warm air hoses connected.

Disenchanted with the Airacobra, by December 1941 the British withdrew this type from RAF service and sent all the delivered P-39s to the Soviet Union. According to a published British account, they also offered to divert to the Soviet Union a further 200 aircraft from the British order for Airacobras. Not surprisingly, the offer was readily accepted because the Red Army Air Force had already drawn up some plans concerning the acquisition of the P-39. In September 1941 the Soviet military had come to the conclusion that the Bell fighter was among the types that best suited the Soviet requirements. A report prepared by the Intelligence Department of the General Staff as a background for negotiations with the Allies stated that *'the Airacobra meets the requirements posed to a modern fighter and can be employed in the Red Army Air Force.'*

This attitude was further reinforced after a group of Soviet pilots paid a familiarisation visit to RAF Duxford. A Russian publication states that this visit took place in October and that on 7 October a Soviet pilot was even given permission to perform two flights in an Airacobra I belonging to 601 Squadron. A British account states that *'on 8th November 1941 a delegation of Soviet officers visited Duxford for the purpose of assessing the Airacobras for use in the USSR.'* The Soviet pilot's comment on his impressions was favourable.

A British account states that 266 Airacobras were transferred to the USSR from the RAF; 44 of these were lost en route when the ships of the Arctic convoys carrying them were sunk by the Germans. One may also come across other figures—according to some sources, 212 (or 265) Airacobra Is were diverted to the Soviet Union, fifty-four of that number being lost in transit.

Airacobra I Initial Deliveries and Testing in the USSR

Thus, the first P-39s to reach the USSR were the ex-RAF Airacobra Is (Model 14) with a 20 mm Hispano-Suiza HS.404 (Hispano Mk 1) cannon firing through the propeller hub, two .50 Browning machine guns in the nose, and two .303 Brownings in each wing.

The first Airacobra I from RAF stocks delivered to the USSR was serialled AH628 (construction number 14-59); it was despatched with the first batch to Arkhangel'sk in November 1941. It was evaluated at Kol'tsovo airfield near Sverdlovsk (now renamed back to Yekaterinburg), where NII VVS had been temporarily relocated after the outbreak of the Great Patriotic War (the airbase later became the city's international airport), and twenty more aircraft were taken on charge for training purposes by the 22nd ZAP (*zapasnoy **aviapolk***; Reserve Air Regiment) based at Kineshma (Ivanovo Region), northeast of Moscow. This unit, sometimes referred to as the 22nd ZIAP (*zapas**noy** istre**bitel'nyy** **aviapolk***; Reserve Fighter Regiment), was part of the 6th ZAB (*zapas**naya** aviabri**gada***; Reserve Air Brigade) and was an operational conversion unit tasked with training fighter units on US and British types before they were sent into battle. According to one source, by the end of 1941 eleven Airacobra Is had been delivered to northern seaports of the USSR; a different source states that the first twenty P-39s (Airacobra Is) arrived in the Soviet Union in January 1942. The crated fighters were unloaded at the ports of Murmansk and, to a smaller extent, Arkhangel'sk. Many of the Airacobras reassembled in Murmansk were delivered directly to Soviet air force units operating on the nearby Karelian Front, or to the naval aviation (specifically the North Fleet's air arm), but most were flown to Ivanovo, where they joined the 22nd ZAP. The same was the case with the machines assembled in Arkhangel'sk. They were flown to Ivanovo via Vologda from an improvised airfield built in the woods 25 km (15 miles) south of the city. Actually, this was a wood-planked airstrip!

An interesting episode is associated with their delivery. As related by the Russian military historian Viktor A. Bakurskiy, in late December 1941, when the 22nd ZAP was receiving Hawker Hurricanes supplied by Great Britain under the Lend-Lease agreement, a crate arrived. Inspection revealed it contained a dismantled Airacobra without any supporting documents (manuals and the like). The British technicians seconded to the regiment to help in reassembling the Hurricanes were unfamiliar with the Airacobra and refused to assemble it. Then the Soviet engineers and technicians, moved by the desire to save the machine for frontline use, set to work and, guided by their experience and common sense, assembled the aircraft. What surprised them was the absence of armament. To test the machine, they invited an NII VVS test pilot, Captain Vladimir Ye. Golofastov. He took the machine into the air and started gaining altitude when suddenly the engine cut;

Golofastov managed an emergency landing in a snow-covered field. Later it turned out that the crate contained not an aircraft intended for assembly but a set of spare parts, which, for some reason, had arrived earlier than the aircraft themselves. That explained the absence of documents and weapons. The episode bears testimony to the skill and enthusiasm of the Soviet engineers and technicians.

The Airacobra Is entered service in May 1942 with the Soviet Air Force's 19th GvIAP (*Gvar**deys**kiy istre**bitel**'nyy **a**via**polk*** – Guards Fighter Regiment) at Afrikanda, near Murmansk. They retained their RAF serials and dark-green/dark-earth camouflage but wore Soviet red stars in place of the RAF roundels.

Airacobras from the US: Routes of Delivery

The bulk of the P-39 fighters received by the Soviet Union came directly from the US. Like other types of aircraft supplied by the US under the Lend-Lease programme, they were delivered via two main routes. One of them was the so-called southern route via Iran, usually called 'the Persian corridor' in the West. Aircraft were shipped to Abadan, which became the main base for the reassembly of crated aircraft, as well as their testing and transfer to the custody of Soviet acceptance teams responsible for the further ferrying to the USSR.

The crated Airacobras (initially these were of the P-39D-2 version, also known as Bell Model 14A-1) were sent via Iceland or directly from ports on the eastern coast of the US. The ships followed two alternative routes: through the Mediterranean or around the Cape of Good Hope. In the former case the main points on the route were Gibraltar, the Suez Canal, the Red Sea, the Sea of Arabia, the Persian Gulf, and Abadan. The distances to be covered by the ships were truly big: 15,600 nm (28,860 km) between New York and Abadan via Gibraltar, and 23,500 nm (43,475 km) on the route round the Cape of Good Hope. The use of such long routes was necessitated by the great losses suffered by Allied northern convoys; the new routes that came into operation in late 1942 afforded a much-greater degree of security, but at the cost of a considerable delay of delivery (the maritime part of the journey alone took thirty-five to sixty days, depending on the weather).

Practical operation of the 'southern route' became possible thanks to the joint political and military action undertaken by Great Britain and the Soviet Union. In September 1941, British and Soviet troops occupied Persia (Iran), eliminating the danger of that country being involved in cooperation with Nazi Germany. The British pioneer troops built up the necessary infrastructure by improving port and railroad facilities, as well as the network of airfields.

As far as aircraft were concerned, the 'southern route' came into operation from June 1942. The first types to be delivered were Douglas A-20 Boston bombers and Hawker Hurricane IIs; in November they were joined by Airacobras, Supermarine Spitfires, and Curtiss P-40 Kittyhawks.

For the Airacobras the procedures were as follows: crated aircraft delivered by sea were unloaded at Abadan; there they were assembled by Soviet specialists and test flown by Soviet pilots. Then they were ferried to Quali-Margi airfield near Tehran, where they underwent approval and acceptance by Soviet military representatives. Thereupon the aircraft were ferried to a pilot conversion training centre in Adzhikabul (in Soviet Azerbaijan) or to ferrying airfields in the vicinity of Kirovabad (the one in Azerbaijan; now called Gyandzha).

ABOVE: P-39Qs lined up at Ladd Field in 1943, awaiting the next leg of the journey to the Soviet Union. The nearest aircraft has had the name 'Mouse the Louse' applied in chalk by the US technicians.

RIGHT: This P-39Q-15-BE (44-22 . . .) came to grief while staging through Nome, Alaska, when the undercarriage collapsed or was prematurely retracted on takeoff. A pool of gasoline spreads from the ruptured conformal ferry tank while the pilots and ground crew decide what to do next.

LEFT: Soviet pilots of the 2nd PAP pose with a P-39Q-30-BE (44-7 . . .) at Seymchan, one of the first Soviet staging points on the ALSIB route, in 1944. Note that the aircraft is a later example with a three-blade propeller. The variance in the pilots' headdress is also noteworthy.

BELOW: Col. Il'ya P. Mazuruk, commander of the 1st PAD (Ferry Air Division) and one of the first Heroes of the Soviet Union, in the cockpit of a P-39 on the ALSIB route.

OPPOSITE PAGE, TOP: A P-39L destined for the Soviet Union is prepared for departure from Ladd Field. A technician pokes his head through the open port window to give the pilot last-minute instructions.

The fighter regiments designated for reequipment with the Airacobra underwent conversion training at the facilities of the 25th ZAP (again, sometimes referred to as the 25th ZIAP) in Adzhikabul. In fact, this unit acted not only as a conversion training centre but also as a kind of depot responsible for distributing the newly delivered aircraft directly to combat air units at the southern sector of the Soviet-German front. Later it was joined in this role by several other ZAPs.

The second main route used for the delivery of Airacobras to the Soviet Union was the route that later became widely known as ALSIB (Alaska-Siberia). It came into being as the result of efforts to find a route that would be both safe and speedy.

The idea of organising this route was put forward by the US at an early stage. It was mentioned by President Franklin D. Roosevelt in a conversation with the then-current Soviet ambassador Konstantin A. Umanskiy on 1 August 1941. During the second half of 1941 and the first half of 1942, the US raised this question several times, but the official attitude of the Soviet side was lukewarm, with no tangible progress in the discussions. Yet, the Soviet side grasped from the outset the advantages of the proposed route and started preparations. In fact, as early as July 1941 the State Defence Committee (GKO: *Gosudarstvennyy komitet oborony*) adopted a resolution ordering the start of explorations on the tracing of the eventual route that would provide the shortest air link between the USSR and the US. On 9 October 1941 the GKO adopted a resolution ordering the commencement of construction of ferrying airfields.

A change in the Soviet attitude came in June 1942. On 17 June, Roosevelt wrote to Stalin: '*Ambassador* [Maksim M.] *Litvinov has informed me that you have approved the ferrying of American aircraft via Alaska and North Siberia to the western front, and I am glad to learn this*' [translated back from Russian]. On 2 July 1942, Stalin wrote back: *'I fully share your opinion about the expediency of an air route for transferring American aircraft through Alaska and Siberia to the western front.'*

Practical steps were immediately taken by the Soviet authorities. On 3 August 1942 the GKO issued a directive establishing the Krasnoyarsk Air Route of the Red Army Air Force. Having considered several possible versions of tracing the route, the Soviet government opted for the one that ran from Uel'kal' on the Chukotka coast to Krasnoyarsk in the south of western Siberia, the staging points on this route being Seymchan (Magadan Region), Yakutsk (Yakutian ASSR), and Kirensk (Irkutsk Region, eastern Siberia). Tremendous effort was put into this work. By June 1942 the construction of the main airfields was completed. Some fifteen main and auxiliary airfields were constructed along the huge stretch of the 6,000 km (3,728 mile) route. The complete lack of roads, the mountainous terrain, and impassable thickets of taiga, coupled with the severe frost, put the physical and moral capacities of the men engaged in this unprecedented project to a cruel test.

In the US the new air route was called ALSIB, while in the Soviet Union it was officially known as the Krasnoyarsk Air Route because its final point was in Krasnoyarsk. The overall command of the Krasnoyarsk Air Route was initially entrusted to the Main Directorate of the Air Force, then for a brief period it was under the control of the Long-Range Aviation, and from 15 June 1943 it was transferred to the Main Directorate of the Civil Air Fleet (GU GVF: ***Gla**vnoye oo**p**ravl**en**iye Grazh**dahn**skovo voz**doosh**novo **flota***)—that is, the Soviet airline Aeroflot.

In early August 1942 Col. Il'ya P. Mazuruk, an experienced polar aviation pilot, was appointed chief of the Krasnoyarsk Air Route, with headquarters at Yakutsk. At the same time he commanded the 1st PAD GVF (*pere**gon**ochnaya **a**viadi**vee**ziya Grazh**dahn**skovo voz**doosh**novo **flota***; Ferry Air Division of the Civil Air Fleet), which was specially established for the purpose of ferrying Lend-Lease aircraft from the US. The division comprised five ferry air regiments (PAP: *pere**gon**ochnyy **a**via**polk***) and one airlift regiment catering for the needs of the division. The ferry air regiments were each responsible for a specific section of the route, acting on the principle of a relay race. The 1st PAP was based at Ladd Field in Fairbanks, Alaska, delivering aircraft to Uel'kal' in Chukotka. There the resident 2nd PAP took over, and the pilots of the 1st PAP returned to Alaska aboard the airlift regiment's Lisunov Li-2 transports (a Soviet licence-built derivative of the Douglas DC-3).

The 2nd PAP delivered the aircraft to Seymchan. From there the aircraft were flown by pilots of the 3rd PAP to Yakutsk. That was the most dangerous part of the route because it passed over a region of high mountain ridges that, into the bargain, was known as the coldest spot on earth in the winter season—temperatures in Oimyakon, Yakutia, which is one of the contenders for the title of the Northern Hemisphere's Pole of Cold, could go as low as –70°C (–94°F).

In Yakutsk the 4th PAP took over on the stretch to Kirensk. Finally, the 5th PAP delivered the aircraft received from the US to Krasnoyarsk; thence they were transported further by rail.

The US part of ALSIB, known as the Northwest Staging Route, functioned as follows. A base was organised at Fairbanks as the final point of the American stretch, where Soviet acceptance teams and Soviet pilots took over the Lend-Lease aircraft from US pilots after appropriate checks and eventual repairs. US pilots were responsible for the transfer of the P-39s (as well as other types) from Great Falls, Montana, to Fairbanks. Great Falls was the airfield near the Canadian border that was the focusing point of delivery routes from different US aircraft manufacturers supplying

ABOVE RIGHT: P-39s arrive at Uel'kal', the first airfield on the Soviet side. The officer on the radio is A. Mel'nikov, who directs the next group of fighters coming in from Fairbanks, Alaska, while Il'ya Mazuruk (in his flying outfit) sits on the right.

RIGHT: A P-39Q is refuelled at a staging point on the ALSIB route, with three others waiting their turn.

P-39Q-30-BEs with wings, horizontal tails, and rudders detached are transported by rail from Krasnoyarsk to Moscow.

the machines to be transferred. Flights on the Great Falls–Fairbanks stretch were operated by the USAAF 7th Ferrying Group. The United States constructed seven airfields in central Alaska; several airfields were built by Canada on its territory.

As mentioned above, the necessary repairs and the final delivery of aircraft to the Soviet acceptance team were conducted at the Ladd Field base near Fairbanks. It was in November 1942 that P-39 fighters were for the first time included into the groups flying from Ladd Field to Uel'kal' on the Soviet side of the Bering Strait. The fighters were usually ferried in groups of eight to twelve machines, with a B-25 or A-20 bomber as the leader aircraft.

For a long time the P-39 Airacobra remained the most numerous type of aircraft ferried along the ALSIB route. In all, 2,618 machines of this type were accepted in Alaska; 2,593 of them safely reached their destination at Krasnoyarsk. Deliveries from Fairbanks consecutively included P-39s of the D, K, L, M, N, and Q models. The last five P-39Qs were accepted and ferried to the Soviet Union in January–February 1945.

In the early summer of 1944 the first batches of the Bell P-63 Kingcobra fighters arrived at Fairbanks. By the end of 1944 their number exceeded the number of the P-39s, and in early 1945 they became more numerous than the machines of all other Lend-Lease types taken together. More will follow concerning this in chapter 6, dealing with the P-63.

Ferrying operations on the ALSIB route were dangerous for the pilots involved. Russian archives declassified in the 1990s suggest that 113 Soviet pilots lost their lives while flying ferry missions over that vast and desolate area. Even now, wrecks of Lend-Lease planes that crashed in Siberia during the war are still discovered in the taiga from time to time. Here are just a few examples. On 24 March 1943, pilot V. I. Kovalyov from the 7th PIAP (*pere**gon**ochnyy istre**bitel**'nyy **avia**polk*; Ferry Fighter Regiment) was lost with his P-39N-BE, serialled 42-4962, en route from Seymchan to Yakutsk. The wreckage was found in 1945. On 6 June 1943, A-20G-1-DO 42-53721, flown by a crew from the 3rd PAP, was lost when flying a weather reconnaissance sortie between Seymchan and Yakutsk. The wreckage was not discovered until 1973. On 24 October 1943 a P-39Q-5-BE (42-20519) piloted by Grigoriy Chuiko from the 5th PAP went missing en route from Kirensk to Krasnoyarsk. The wreckage and the pilot's remains have not been found to this day. On 7 May 1943, a B-25C-15-NA (42-32519) with six crew captained by squadron commander Maj. A. M. Boronenko crashed into the Lena River immediately after takeoff from an airfield in Yakutsk. The wreckage was found in 1986; the crew's remains were given a dignified burial. This mournful list can be expanded.

Equally self-sacrificing was the job done by USAAF pilots on their 3,000 km (1,860 mile) stretch of the ALSIB. American pilots had to endure the same sort of hardships as their Soviet colleagues. An American author wrote: *'Winter ground temperatures of –50° Fahrenheit* [–45.5°C], *the threat of being forced down in remote wilderness, hazardous flying weather, Spartan living conditions and a lack of sufficient hangar space, which sometimes forced mechanics to work outside under cruel winter conditions, made life difficult for the personnel assigned to duty along the ALSIB route.'*

In the same vein, a Russian historian (Andrey Pochtaryov) states: *'Flying in the harsh conditions of the High North, over tundra and vast expanses of forests, with no properly equipped radar ground stations, and in ambient temperatures dropping as low as –70°C* [–94°F], *Soviet and American aviators worked miracles of bravery and courage. The USAAF lost 133 aircraft and nearly as many pilots on its stretch of the ferrying route which the Americans dubbed ALCAN (Alaska-Canada). The losses of the 1st KPAD* (*Krasnozna**myon**naya pere**gon**ochnaya **aviadi**veeziya* – Red Banner Ferry Air Division) *amounted to 44 aircraft. The sites of some crashes remain unknown to this day.'*

In October 1992, on the fiftieth anniversary of the opening of the ALSIB air bridge, a monument was unveiled at Yakutsk-Tuimaada airport to pay homage to the aviators who lost their lives on that hazardous route. With the blessing of the then principal leader of the Russian Orthodox Church, Patriarch of Moscow, and All Russia Aleksiy II and with the approval of the president of the Russian Federation, Vladimir V. Putin, a memorial flight along that historic route was carried out in 2000. On 27 August 2006, the official opening of the Lend-Lease Monument took place at Fairbanks to commemorate the interaction between the Allies in the war against Nazism.

It remains to be noted that the ALSIB air bridge not merely fulfilled a very important mission during the war; it also had some influence on the postwar development of the Soviet Union. The pilots who became masters of flying under the conditions of extreme hardships on this route formed the core of the flying personnel of the Soviet Polar Aviation, supporting both the Soviet Arctic/Antarctic research effort and the functioning of remote settlements beyond the Arctic Circle. Their invaluable experience proved useful when Soviet Li-2s (C-47s) came to fulfill transport duties in Antarctica. A part of the flying personnel of the 1st KPAD was incorporated into the Krasnoyarsk Civil Aviation Directorate. During the postwar years the airfields built on this route proved useful for the development of northern Siberia and the eastern parts of Russia; for the exploitation of natural gas, oil, and gold deposits; and for establishing scheduled air transportation in these regions.

CHAPTER 2

Testing and Mastering the Airacobra

As was the usual practice with Lend-Lease aircraft, the type was subjected to thorough study, testing, and evaluation; these were conducted primarily by NII VVS. Engineers and test pilots of this test centre started studying the aircraft in January 1942 at the base of the 22nd ZAP in Kineshma, to which two machines from the first British contract had been delivered in dismantled condition. The aircraft were reassembled directly on the airfield; the Russian personnel were aided by British engineers, and technicians seconded to the regiment. The team of specialists from NII VVS was headed by the very competent and experienced engineer Izrael' G. Rabkin; it included engineers V. I. Usatov, P. S. Ivanov, and V. F. Nikishin and test pilot Vladimir Ye. Golofastov.

Rabkin recalled later: *'The very first days of service in January–February 1942 revealed a very serious shortcoming in the Airacobra's oil system. The engine oil could not be emptied fully. The oil left in the engine sump, propeller reduction gearbox, oil cooler, and certain oil lines would freeze, and all of these required lengthy warming-up with hot air before the engine could be*

Still wearing full RAF insignia, Airacobra I AH628 from the first lot is seen during trials at NII VVS.

AH628

AH628

OPPOSITE PAGE: Two more views of the same aircraft at NII VVS. Note the yellow surround to the roundels, the Sky Type S quick-identification band around the rear fuselage, and the characteristically upswept colour division line on the nose.

RIGHT: A close-up view from the NII VVS test report, which was probably meant to accentuate the tricycle landing gear, since the Airacobra was one of the first tricycle-gear aircraft tested at the institute.

BELOW: Airacobra I AH644 was also tested at NII VVS, although this photo was taken earlier. The RAF fin flash is still in place, but the roundels have been painted out with green and Soviet insignia applied on top.

started. We had to install de-oiling cocks in the oil lines and invent a special manifold which led hot air to all the necessary locations at once. This gadget was tested successfully and recommended for all units operating the type.'

Golofastov started his familiarisation with the new type, which featured an unfamiliar tricycle landing gear, by making a 40-minute taxiing session. He was impressed by the excellent view from the cockpit and the aircraft's ability to taxi at high speed over all types of surface available at the airfield, including a snow-covered flight line. There was virtually no risk of the aircraft standing on its nose.

The first flights around the airfield and in its immediate vicinity gave the test pilot much useful information complementing what was written in the American flight manual. All the valuable

information thus obtained was immediately brought to the knowledge of the pilots and technical personnel of the 22nd ZAP, who joined in mastering the operation of the new fighter.

The initial familiarisation that had started in the 22nd ZAP was followed by more-extensive tests of the Airacobra I at NII VVS facilities. One of the test aircraft with the RAF serial AH628 (c/n 14-59) operated from Kol'tsovo AB, near Sverdlovsk, which as already mentioned was the new temporary base of NII VVS. Another (AH644, c/n 14-75) was based at Chkalovskaya AB (the institute's home base), near Moscow. These two aircraft were flown by Col. Andrey G. Kochetkov (AH628) and Col. Aleksandr A. Avtonomov (AH644); they were joined by Aleksey G. Kubyshkin, Vladimir Ye. Golofastov, and Aleksandr F. Moshin. The pilots' impressions of the aircraft's handling were favourable. They reported that the Cobra was fairly nimble, with light control forces. The aircraft's stability during turns with the normal CG position was also satisfactory. If the stick was pulled too far back, the aircraft shuddered and tried to straighten out but showed no inclination to spin.

Upon completion of the testing, lead engineer Izrael' G. Rabkin drew up a report that stated: *'At flight levels above 3,000 m* [9,840 ft.] *the Airacobra is superior to the Yak-1 and LaGG-3 fighters; it is one of the best aircraft as regards manoeuvrability in the horizontal plane.'* Field performance and range in economical cruise also received a favourable assessment.

There were some critical comments too. It was noted that the V-1710 engine lacked a constant-pressure valve regulating turbo pressure. This could cause the engine to become overpressurised in low-level flight, disintegrating as a result. It was stressed in the report that *'the Airacobra demands correct treatment in service, and special attention has to be paid to knowing the engine's limits and the cockpit layout during conversion training.'*

A further example of the Airacobra I from the third British contract (BX382, c/n 14-623) was ferried to the NII VVS airfield, where the state acceptance trials were conducted in April–May 1942. During these tests the aircraft's performance figures were determined. Furthermore, NII VVS specialists evaluated the functioning of the armament and equipment. An assessment was made of the machine's strengths and weaknesses and of the peculiarities of its maintenance.

The overall assessment of the fighter was positive. NII VVS test pilots praised the Airacobra's manoeuvrability, field performance, potent armament, and good equipment.

When comparing the performance of several types of US, British, and German fighters tested at NII VVS, this centre's specialists noted that *'among the fighters under review the types with the best handling qualities are the Airacobra and the Me-109F'* (the types involved in the comparison were the Hawker Hurricane II, Curtiss P-40C Tomahawk, P-40E Kittyhawk, Airacobra I, North American P-51B Mustang, and Messerschmitt Bf 109F).

Here is a brief summary of a report on the P-39's handling qualities in an NII VVS document: *'The aircraft taxies steadily on an even surface. The view from the cockpit is good. On a snow-covered airfield with the snow not rolled smooth well enough, steering is hampered by the tendency of the nosewheel to dig in. The take-off run presents no difficulties even in a crosswind. The take-off procedure is much simpler thanks to the tricycle undercarriage, control forces are negligible. The unstick speed is 187 km/h* [116 mph]. *During horizontal flight with the average operational CG position of 27% MAC, the aircraft is statically and dynamically stable and is neutrally trimmed with hands off the stick within a considerable range of speeds. The banking turns are steady. The loop and the combat turn are performed normally. The height gained in a combat turn is 400 m* [1,310 ft.] *versus the Tomahawk's 700 m* [2,300 ft.]. *The aircraft is steady in a dive, which enhances gun aiming accuracy. Thanks to the tricycle undercarriage the landing procedure is considerably simplified and does not require an unduly large airfield. The good view from the cockpit makes the landing easier. The tricycle undercarriage ensures a good view during the landing run. In common with other US aircraft, the P-39 requires smooth movement of the controls when performing aerobatic manoeuvres. As compared to other US types, the Airacobra is more sensitive to jerky movements of the controls; it reacts to these by a jolt followed by dropping a wing.'*

Test pilot Vladimir Ye. Golofastov, who flew the Airacobra I at NII VVS.

OPPOSITE PAGE: A third Airacobra I tested at NII VVS, BX382, was an aircraft from the third lot and was painted differently. Here, full Soviet insignia have been applied (with no surround, as per then-current standards).

Performance characteristics of the ex-RAF Airacobra I determined during state trials at NII VVS in April-May 1942

	Standard configuration	Lightened configuration
Engine type	Allison V-1710-35 (V-1710-E4)	
Maximum rating	1,105 hp	
Propeller type	Curtiss Electric 3-blade prop	
Propeller diameter	3.136 m (32 ft 3 3/16 in)	
Take-of weight	3,556 kg (7,841 lb)	3,263 kg (7,195 lb)
Maximum speed:		
at sea level	493 km/h (306 mph)	n.a.
at 4,200 m (13,780 ft)	585 km/h (364 mph)	n.a.
at 5,000 m (16,400 ft)	577 km/h (359 mph)	n.a.
Landing speed	145 km/h (90 mph)	n.a.
with flaps at 43°	140 km/h (87 mph)*	n.a.
Landing approach speed (IAS):		
without flaps	175 km/h (109 mph)	n.a.
with flaps	150 km/h (93 mph)	n.a.
Take-off run:		
without flaps	350 m (1,150 ft)	270 m (886 ft)
with flaps	300 m (980 ft)	220 m (722 ft)
Take-off run time:		
without flaps	15.0 seconds	n.a.
with flaps	12.0 seconds	n.a.
Landing run:		
without flaps	400 m (1,310 ft)	250 m (820 ft)
with flaps	300 m (980 ft)	150 m (490 ft)
Service ceiling	9,600 m (31,490 ft)	10,000 m (32,810 ft)
Range:		
at 550 m (1,800 ft) altitude with 10% fuel reserves	993 km (617 miles)	n.a.
at 1,000 m (3,280 ft)	1,100 km (684 miles)	n.a.
at 3,000 m (9,840 ft)	1,040 km (646 miles)	n.a.
at 5,000 m (16,400 ft)	960 km (597 miles)	n.a.
at 7,000 m (22,965 ft)	800 km (497 miles)	n.a.
Time of 360° banking turn	19 seconds	n.a.
	17.7-18.7 seconds*	n.a.
Dimensions		
Wing span	10.363 m (34 ft 0 in)	
Wing area	19.8 m² (213.13 sq ft)	
Length	9.195 m (32 ft 5¾ in)	
Height	3.37 m (11ft 0¾ in)	
	3.78 m (12 ft 4 13/16 in)†	

Armament

Type	Number	Ammunition
7.62-mm Colt machine-gun	4	1,000 rpg
12.7-mm Colt machine-gun	2 (synchronised)	270 rpg
20-mm Hispano cannon	1	60 rounds

Allison V-1710-E4 engine (additional data)

Mode	Altitude	Power rating	RPM
Take-off rating	0	1,150 hp	3,000
Continuous rating	0	900 hp	2,600
Continuous rating	3,310 m (10,860 ft)	1,000 hp	2,500
Combat rating	0	1,040 hp	3,000
Combat rating (5 minutes)	3,650 m (11,970 ft)	1,150 hp	3,000

*From an NKAP statistical file; † In level attitude with the undercarriage extended

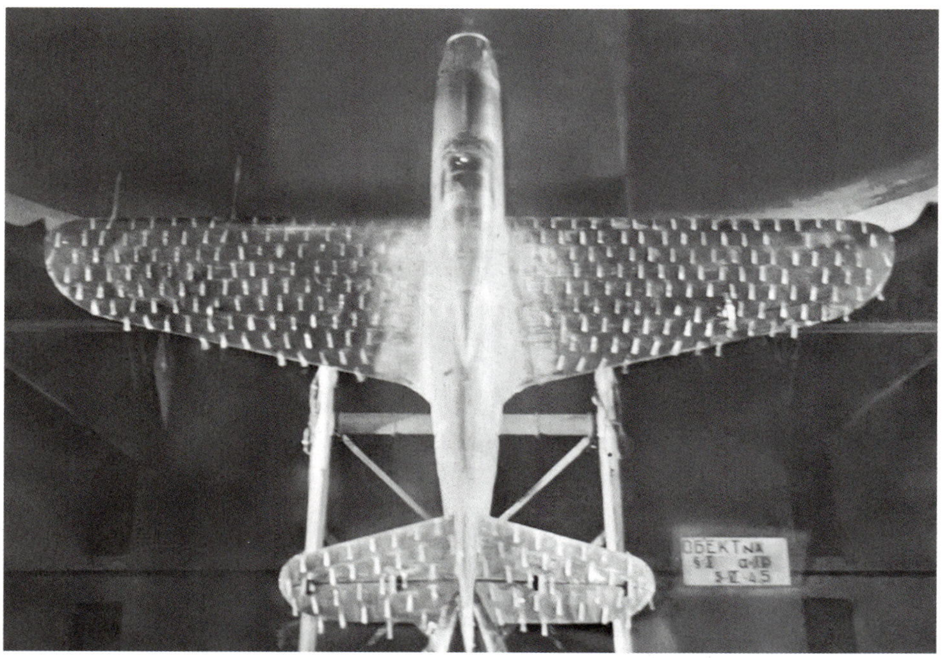

An Airacobra in TsAGI's T-101 full-size wind tunnel in the course of the type's Soviet trials. The wings and horizontal tail are covered with wool tufts for airflow visualisation; the propeller has been removed and the spinner refitted.

One of the Airacobras subjected to static tests at TsAGI. This particular airframe was use to check the strength of the wings.

RIGHT: A P-39 with 1942-style white-outlined insignia during static tests of the tail unit at TsAGI. The USAAF serial is almost obliterated but appears to be 42-4972, making it a P-39N-0-BE.

BELOW: Partly dismantled Airacobra I AH725 in the BNT NKAP display hall, in company with a P-51 Mustang, a P-40C Tomahawk, and a captured Bf 109G-2. The aircraft were studied by Soviet specialists.

LEFT: Here Airacobra I AH725 is shown in more complete condition. As can be seen, the aircraft is trestled, not sitting on its undercarriage, which may have been removed for study.

BELOW AND BELOW LEFT: Two views of AH725 with the gun bay cowls and the annular forward fairing removed, exposing the propeller reduction gearbox. The armament has also been removed for study.

BOTTOM: Another view of the Airacobra, Mustang, and Tomahawk at BNT TsAGI.

RIGHT: The same hall at a later date; the Airacobra has an La-7, an La-5F, a Yak-9, and a Yak-7 for company. On the other side are a Tu-2 bomber, a Pe-2 dive bomber, and an Il-2 attack aircraft.

Testing revealed that the performance advertised by the Bell Aircraft Company was clearly higher than the real figures. The speed at 4,200 m (13,780 ft.) was a mere 585 km/h (363 mph), falling short of the figure promised by the manufacturer.

According to some assessments, the Airacobra I's speed, rate of climb, and manoeuvrability at low and medium altitudes were inferior to those of Soviet fighters. Nevertheless, on the whole the fighter demonstrated good performance at low altitudes. This allowed the P-39 to be used for escorting the Ilyushin Il-2 attack aircraft, for destroying the enemy's dive bombers, and for close-air-support missions.

The overall conclusion was that the P-39's performance was roughly on a par with that of Soviet and German mass-produced fighters of the same class. The P-39 was pronounced capable of being used for aerial combat with all types of German aircraft and for strikes against ground targets.

A feature appreciated by Soviet pilots was the comfortable cockpit, which, into the bargain, was provided with heating (a luxury unheard of on Soviet fighters of that period).

Among the examples of the Airacobra I tested in the Soviet Union, mention must be made of the machine serialled AH725 (c/n 14-156). The test status of this particular example is evident from the fact that it was displayed as a sample at the BNT (Bureau of New Technology, a branch of NKAP) in Moscow in 1943, together with various Soviet and foreign aircraft.

As P-39s of later models began to reach the Soviet Union, they were also subjected to testing at NII VVS and other test establishments. They included examples of the P-39L-1-BE (USAAF serial 42-4666), P-39M-1-BE (42-4750), P-39N-BE, P-39Q-5-BE, P-39Q-10-BE (42-20561) and P-39Q-25-BE (44-32467) (both tested at NII VVS), and a P-39Q-5-BE (42-1988 . . .) subjected to wind tunnel tests at the Central Aero- & Hydrodynamics Institute, named after Nikolay Ye. Zhukovskiy (TsAGI: *Tsentrahl'nyy aero-ghidrodinamicheskiy institoot*). In January 1943 BNT issued a document titled 'Technical description no. 113: Handling qualities of foreign aircraft according to test results.' It contained a detailed appraisal of handling qualities of several types of Lend-Lease aircraft (including the Tomahawk, Kittyhawk, Airacobra, and Hurricane fighters) and a single war booty aircraft—the Bf 109F. The appraisal was based on the results of tests at NII VVS. The document stated that *'among the fighters under review it is the Airacobra and the Me-109F* [sic] *that possess the best handling qualities.'* At the same time it was noted that all US aircraft required smooth control inputs during the execution of manoeuvres and that the Airacobra was more sensitive than other types to abrupt inputs, to which it reacted by shuddering and dropping a wing. Surprisingly, the document did not make any critical comments on the spinning characteristics of the Airacobra.

Interestingly, another BNT document—a description of structural design of the Airacobra issued in April 1943 (Doc. no.

a
б

BRAKE CYLINDER
ACCESS DOOR

LEFT AND ABOVE LEFT: P-39L-1-BE 42-4666 during trials at NII VVS.

BELOW LEFT: The gun bay of 42-4666 with the cowl removed, showing the breeches of the M4 cannon and the M2 AN machine guns, as well as the forward armour plate. Note the message: 'Airplane must not be flown without guns, armor or equivalent ballast.'

BELOW, FAR LEFT: The cockpit of P-39L-1-BE 42-4666.

ABOVE: P-39M-1-BE 42-4750 was also tested at NII VVS.

RIGHT: The cockpit of 42-4750.

BELOW RIGHT: The gun bay of 42-4750. Note the oxygen bottle.

123)—gave an appraisal the Airacobra's key feature—the centrally placed engine. This layout was considered to be 'unquestionably rational,' among other things, because it facilitated the use of the very advantageous tricycle undercarriage.

The P-39's Vices and Deficiencies Discovered by Soviet Test Pilots and First-Line Pilots

Experience gained by the Soviet air force command with the service use of the Hurricane, Tomahawk, and Kittyhawk prompted a cautious attitude to the service introduction of the P-39 Airacobra. The command decided not to send the newly delivered aircraft to service units immediately. A special group was formed in the air force for the assembly and flight testing of the machines received. The group was tasked with thoroughly studying the machines' performance characteristics and rectifying any faults that cropped up.

LEFT AND ABOVE LEFT: Another Airacobra tested in the T-101 wind tunnel was this P-39Q-5-BE. Note the wool tufts on the wings and the aileron deflection sensors. The serial is presented as 42-1988 (which was actually a Vultee BT-15), but the last digit is obliterated for some reason; the real identity is either 42-19881, 42-19882, 42-19885, 42-19887, or 42-19889.

ABOVE: An unidentified P-39 during tests at LII (the Flight Research Institute).

ABOVE RIGHT: A different P-39, which was also tested by LII. The curious number '30' on the tail probably had no connection with the serial.

RIGHT: A P-39Q-15-BE (44-2xxx; the serial is unfortunately not clearly legible) during tests at NII VVS. The white spiral painted on the propeller spinner is unusual.

220561

LEFT AND BELOW LEFT: P-39Q-10-BE 42-20561 during tests at NII VVS, with a 175 US gal (662 litre) ferry tank and underwing pods with 12.7 mm machine guns.

ABOVE AND BELOW: Two more aspects of the same aircraft, accentuating the size of the ferry tank.

ABOVE AND BELOW: The same aircraft after modifications for spinning trials at NII VVS.

OPPOSITE PAGE: This view shows the truss-mounted spin recovery parachute and the motion sensors on the tail control surfaces.

Despite all its merits, the Airacobra had its share of deficiencies. The biggest of these was the US fighter's vicious spinning behaviour, which was caused by the aircraft's excessive sensitivity to changes in the CG position. For example, with the ammunition expended, the CG position shifted aft considerably, causing the fighter to enter a spin at the slightest provocation. The same could happen as a result of minor piloting errors, especially excessive aft movement of the stick or excessive pedal inputs. This peculiarity of the P-39 grew into a serious problem, having caused several fatal crashes. Not only 'green' service pilots fell victim to it, but test pilots lost their lives as well. For example, on 2 February 1943 Maj. Konstantin A. Groozdev, one of the best pilots of NII VVS, failed to recover from a spin when testing the abovementioned Airacobra I serialled AH628 at Kol'tsovo airfield. On 3 January 1944 another NII VVS test pilot, Aleksandr A. Avtonomov, was killed when his P-39N entered a spin from which he could not recover. Yet another NII VVS test pilot, Lt.-Col. Konstantin I. Ovchinnikov (former air force attaché to the Soviet Embassy in Washington, DC), was killed in a crash of P-39Q-10-BE 42-20563 on 27 April 1944. Attempts to bail out in the event of an uncontrollable spin frequently ended in the pilot being struck by the horizontal tail, with heavy injuries or even death as a result. The pilot had to be extra careful and follow certain procedures when abandoning the aircraft—notably, to bend his knees in a proper fashion. Among the pilots who suffered heavy injuries in such situations were Heroes of the Soviet Union Nikolay M. Iskrin (on 16 May 1943) and Boris B. Glinka (on 14 July 1944), for both of whom the injuries put an end to their flying careers.

Even if the pilot managed to recover from a spin, there was another danger in store for him: high g-loads deformed the tail unit, causing the control surfaces to jam. Special investigations showed that abrupt manoeuvres sometimes led to warping of the P-39's rear fuselage.

The spin caused numerous accidents and crashes in frontline units. This had its effect on the morale of the pilots, some of whom became panic stricken at the thought of performing aerobatic manoeuvres on the P-39.

The Bell Aircraft Company was forced to take urgent measures. In the spring of 1943 a special team of Bell specialists arrived in Moscow to deal with the situation. They visited service units, examining the causes of accidents and failures on-site. Subsequent discussions with the specialists of NII VVS and representatives of the aircraft industry management helped evolve the measures designed to rectify the situation.

A comprehensive programme intended to overcome the abovementioned problems was devised in the Soviet Union. Test engineer Izrael' G. Rabkin recalls the effort taken at NII VVS to deal with the spin recovery problems of the P-39. A special series of flights were conducted to investigate the problem. Prior to starting the flights, Rabkin received a consultation from Professor A. N. Zhuravskiy at TsAGI. Zhuravskiy strongly recommended the use of a spin recovery parachute during these flights to make them as safe as possible. A P-39Q-10-BE serialled 42-20561 was fitted with such a parachute mounted behind the rudder on a curved truss attached to the rear fuselage underside, in addition to an unusually rich complement of test equipment that recorded the

inputs of control surfaces, the pitch, yaw and roll rates, the smallest changes of g-load on all axes, the aircraft's angle relative to the horizon, and, of course, the speed and altitude. The flights were performed by test pilot Vladimir Ye. Golofastov, while Rabkin, as an observer, watched some of these flights from a North American AT-6 Texan trainer piloted by test pilot Viktor G. Masich. The flights yielded much useful information.

Careful testing helped identify pilot inputs that were liable to make the aircraft enter a spin. NII VVS test pilots evolved a series of recommendations to service pilots in regard to the piloting of the P-39; experienced pilots were sent to the air force units to demonstrate the safe techniques of flying the aircraft. Notably, a team of specialists and test pilots from NII VVS were sent to the 6th IAK (*istrebitel'nyy aviakorpus*; Fighter Corps) commanded by Maj.-Gen. Ibragim M. Dzoosov and to the 1st GvIAD (*Gvardeyskaya istrebitel'naya aviadiveeziya*; Guards Fighter Division), where a number of serious accidents had taken place. (The Guards units were the elite of the Soviet armed forces, and this status was conferred for gallantry in combat.) With Dzoosov's consent, the NII VVS team organised a series of theory courses for the pilots, who received much useful information on the peculiarities of the P-39's aerodynamics and the most-rational ways of using the aircraft's capabilities. In addition, a demonstration flight was arranged to show the proper spin recovery techniques. In this flight test, pilot Vladimir Ye. Golofastov performed the upright and inverted spin, commenting on his actions during recovery,

his comments being transmitted over the radio and via loudspeakers to the pilots who watched his evolutions. Strict limits were imposed on the CG location; it was prohibited to perform aerobatic manoeuvres without weapons and ammunition or equivalent ballast in the nose.

The structural-strength problems of the P-39 came to the fore in March 1944, when NII VVS received information about a series of accidents and crashes in the 11th IAK committed to action at the North-Western Front. A team of specialists headed by test engineer Izrael' G. Rabkin were sent to deal with the matter on-site. Investigation led to the conclusion that the crashes were

TOP AND ABOVE: P-39Q-25-BE 44-32467 seen during trials at NII VVS. These views show the four-blade Aeroproducts propeller. The fighter still wears ferry markings with a white background as applied at the Bell Aircraft factory; in first-line units the white background was deleted as too catchy, being a liability in air combat (not to mention the fact that it was nonregulation).

RIGHT AND ABOVE RIGHT: 44-32467 was also used for spinning trials and accordingly was fitted with the same type of spin recovery parachute and sensors as P-39Q-10-BE 42-20561.

FAR RIGHT: A NII VVS test pilot checks 44-32467 before a flight.

caused by insufficient strength of the rear fuselage. Warping and failure of this part of the airframe under high g-loads during violent manoeuvres inevitable in air combat made the aircraft uncontrollable and sealed its fate. Inspection of the fighters in the corps's inventory revealed fifteen machines with the first signs of warping that might prove fatal in the course of the further operation. The team's verdict was clear: a reinforcement of the rear fuselage was necessary. Urgent measures were taken to this effect. An experimentally modified machine with reinforcement strakes on the rear fuselage was tested at NII VVS, whereupon similar field modifications were made to the Airacobras directly in the fighter regiments.

The Airacobra had also a fair share of minor deficiencies that had to be dealt with. For example, the bulletproof glass pane protecting the pilot's head from the rear had a tendency to fall out of its frame during violent manoeuvres. Fortunately, putting it back in place presented no problems.

One more nuisance was caused by the inward-opening direct-vision panel incorporated into the port side of the cockpit windshield. At high flight speeds the airstream pressed this panel into the cockpit, popping it off the hinges, and the transparency came flying straight at the pilot, hitting him violently in the face. Cases were on record when this caused loss of control and cost the pilot his life.

The cockpit heaters on the P-39s delivered from Britain proved troublesome. These were gasoline stoves provided with ignition plugs, and the latter didn't get along with the radio, creating an unbearable noise in the pilot's earphones. The problem was eliminated on the P-39Q-5 and subsequent versions where the cockpit was heated by air bled from the engine's cooling system.

In addition to the problems arising from the peculiarities of the P-39's design, some difficulties were encountered in the course of routine maintenance. As already mentioned, winter operations were hampered by oil congealing in the oil lines and in various units (oil coolers, propeller reduction gearbox, and so on). Soviet

TOP: 44-32467 had a cine camera mounted on the canopy to record control surface movements during spin recovery.

ABOVE: The same aircraft before a test mission. These two pictures are stills from an NII VVS documentary.

engineers were forced to devise urgent measures for rectifying this deficiency. Extra drain cocks were added to the piping to ensure complete draining of oil from the oil system; a special manifold was used to distribute hot air to all the places that had to be warmed up before starting the engine.

The Allison V-1710 engine added its share of headaches. It could use only imported fuel with an octane rating not less than 95; furthermore, it was very sensitive to oil quality, accepting only the best grades of oil. Too-frequent application of the highest permissible rpm and supercharging values led to engine failures. Having logged less than half of the designated service life, the engine began to disintegrate: the connecting rods broke and caused havoc, puncturing the crankcase and the fuselage skin and severing the linkage to the elevators. It cost much effort to overcome these problems during the first months of the Airacobra's operation.

A fair share of the troubles experienced with the engines were admittedly due to the propensity both of pilots and technicians to neglect or forget about some important points of operation and servicing. For example, pilots tended to overindulge in the use of boosted mode. The condition of the oil system was not properly checked; sometimes indigenous fuel and oil of unsuitable grades were used for want of the required ones. Also, as one Russian author put it, *'back on the P-40 the Soviet technicians had found out that the good American V-1710 engine is capable of a lot more than its designers had imagined—if you tweak it a bit. This reduced engine life from 150 to 50 hours, but it's better to have a 50-hour engine life and kick the Messerschmitts' asses than to have a 150-hour engine life and have them kick your ass.'*

Some problems with the engines arose from the fact that the V-1710 was very sensitive to the dust and sand that was ingested into the carburettor during operations from unpaved airfields. The highly abrasive dust and sand found their way into the cylinders and the oil system, ruining the crankshaft bearings, with engine failure as a consequence.

There were cases of the fuel lines failing due to vibration. A broken fuel line could lead to an in-flight fire and the loss of the aircraft, and probably the pilot as well. To prevent this, Soviet technicians sometimes replaced the fuel system's original duralumin tubes with annealed copper tubes. Other minor improvements included the use of plastic rollers in the flight control system instead of the original aluminium ones—this helped reduce the wear and tear on the cable linkage.

In the course of operational service, one more deficiency came to the fore: the insufficient strength of all three undercarriage legs. On numerous occasions, one of the main gear legs broke off when the aircraft landed at a somewhat excessive speed on an unprepared airfield. This defect was characteristic of the early versions of the P-39—the Airacobra I and the P-39D-2. Later versions of the fighter had their undercarriage strengthened.

The nose leg, while offering some obvious advantages, tended to vibrate as the aircraft moved on the rough surface of unpaved airfields; this compelled the pilot to reduce the taxiing speed. NII VVS engineer Izrael' G. Rabkin recalls in his memoirs his visit to the 6th IAK in which five accidents with the nose gear leg had taken place. The pilots ignored the warning, increasing the taxiing speed to 60–70 km/h (37.2–43.5 mph). The NII VVS group actually witnessed one such accident during its stay in the air unit. A young pilot, elated after a successfully accomplished mission, grew careless while taxiing and increased the speed inadvertently. A less-than-perfectly-executed ground manoeuvre then caused the nose gear unit to collapse, and when the propeller struck the ground the aircraft swung abruptly, colliding with another Airacobra and putting it out of operation. Two aircraft damaged on the ground! That was a scandalous affair to which the commander of the unit reacted with understandable harshness.

To conclude this chapter, it should be noted that in the course of its service in the Soviet air force, the P-39 was constantly refined by the concerted efforts of Soviet test pilots and specialists in close and fruitful cooperation with the Bell Aircraft Company, which promptly and positively reacted to NII VVS recommendations and requests coming from frontline pilots.

CHAPTER 3

Versions of the P-39 in Soviet Service

The total number of Airacobras of different models delivered directly from the US to the Soviet Union during the war amounted to 4,719 machines (some sources put this number at 4,746). They were supplemented by 212 aircraft transferred or diverted from Great Britain (of these, 158 reached their destination). The breakdown of the deliveries by the different basic P-39 models can be established only on the basis of the (American) reports on military aid; they give the following figures: 108 P-39Ds, 40 P-39Ks, 137 P-39Ls, 157 P-39Ms, 1,113 P-39Ns, and 3,291 P-39Qs.

The P-39 was supplied to the Soviet air force in several successive production versions, which were sometimes subjected to modification by the technical personnel of the Soviet air force's operational air units. To start with, here is a list (possibly incomplete) of these versions, partly compiled on the basis of flight and maintenance manuals prepared by the Red Army Air Force: Airacobra 1 (Model 14, P-400), P-39D (P-39D-2), P-39K (P-39K-1), P-39L-1, P-39M-1, P-39N-0, N-1, N-5, P-39Q-1, Q-5, Q-10, Q-15, Q-20, Q-21, Q-25, Q-30, and TP-39 trainer (not supplied).

The following brief review of these variants focuses on the testing of these aircraft at NII VVS and other test establishments, on the assessment passed by Soviet engineers, and on the procedures for the technical operation and piloting of these aircraft recommended on the basis of these tests.

Early-model Airacobras (note the small nosewheel) in service with the North Fleet air arm in early 1943. The fighters have had temporary winter camouflage applied, rendering them unidentifiable by their USAAF serials.

Airacobra I AH619 / '34 White' was one of the first delivered to the Soviet Air Force's 19th GvIAP; the outlined star insignia are superimposed on the painted-out RAF roundels. This aircraft was shot down on 19 July 1942 while flown by Lt. (JG) Vladimir V. Gabrinets.

Airacobra I (Model 14, P-400)

A 'Brief description and flight manual of the Airacobra I aircraft' prepared by NII VVS was endorsed on 11 July 1942. It was apparently based on the results of the tests conducted at NII VVS with this version. The manual was supplemented by a 'Technical description of the Airacobra aircraft powered by the Allison V-1710-E4 engine,' which was endorsed on 11 November 1942 (apparently also referring to the Airacobra I).

This version, as described above, was an export model—the RAF equivalent of the P-39D—and was turned over to the Soviet Air Force. As mentioned earlier, 212 ex-British machines were shipped to the Soviet Union; of these, 158 reached their destination. They were armed with a 20 mm Hispano-Suiza HS.404 (Hispano Mk 1) cannon firing through the propeller hub, two 12.7 mm (.50) Browning M2 AN machine guns in the nose, and two 7.7 mm (.303) Browning M1919 machine guns in each wing. A recognition feature of the Airacobra I was the rather long cannon barrel protruding from the propeller spinner and, on some aircraft, the twelve exhaust stubs on each side instead of the six stubs on later versions. Ex-British machines in Soviet service retained their RAF serials. Interestingly, like the undelivered Aircobra Is taken over by the USAAF, these fighters are referred to by some Russian sources as P-400s. Also, one Western source refers to the fighters built for the RAF (with no USAAF serials)

P-39D-2-BE 41-38442, 22nd ZAP/6th ZAB, Kineshma, March 1942. The USAAF insignia are painted out but not the 'U.S. Army' titles.

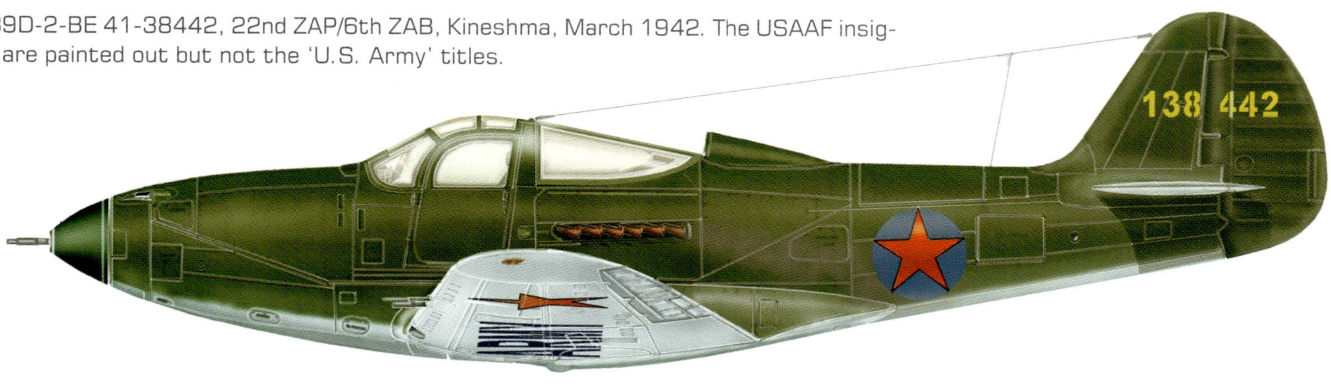

P-39D-2-BE 41-38442 in service with the 22nd ZAP in Kineshma, March 1942. The aircraft was delivered via Abadan, Persia; note the 'U.S. Army' titles on the wing underside. Ace Innokentiy V. Kuznetsov flew this particular aircraft while mastering the Airacobra.

as Airacobra IA, using the designation Airacobra I for three stock P-39Cs that were evaluated by the RAF and did have USAAF serials in addition to RAF serials.

The Airacobra Is delivered from RAF stocks or reassigned to the USSR from the British Lend-Lease account came from all three RAF delivery contracts. They were serialled AH570, AH571, AH575, AH577, AH584, AH586, AH599, AH604 to AH608, AH610 to AH613, AH615 to AH620, AH622 to AH628, AH630 to AH636, AH638 to AH647, AH649 to AH655, AH658 to AH660, AH662 to AH671, AH673 to AH692, AH694, AH695, AH697, AH699, AH700, AH702 to AH711, AH713 to AH731, AH733, AH734, and AH739 from the first contract; AP264, AP265, AP271, AP272, AP275, AP276, AP279, AP282, AP283 to AP286, AP288, AP293, AP296, AP298, AP299, AP301 to AP303, AP306 to AP308, AP311 to AP318, AP320, AP321, AP323, AP324, AP358, AP384, BW106, BW109, BW131, and BW149 from the second contract; and BX176, BX178, BX179, BX182, BX184, BX185, BX188, BX190, BX191, BX206, BX207, BX212, BX214, BX221, BX225, BX226, BX228, BX229, BX232 to BX237, BX239, BX240 to BX242, BX246, BX254, BX255, BX257 to BX259, BX261, BX263, BX264, BX266 to BX268, BX271, BX275, BX277, BX282, BX284, BX285, BX289 to BX291, BX295, BX296, BX298, BX300, BX301, BX305, BX315, BX316, BX319, BX321, BX322, BX324, BX328, BX332, BX334, BX336 to BX338, BX340 to BX342, BX346, BX347, BX349 to BX352, BX355 to BX357, BX359 to BX364, BX370 to BX372, BX379, BX381, BX382, BX384, BX387, BX394, BX396, BX403, BX404, BX408, BX410, BX419, BX420, BX425, BX427, and BX431 from the third contract.

Fifty-four of the above Airacobras were lost when the British Merchant Marine ships delivering them as part of the Arctic convoys were sunk by German U-boats or Luftwaffe aircraft. These include AH651, AH662, AH699, AH722, AH727, AH729, AH731, AH734, AH739, AP276, AP283, AP296, AP302, AP303, AP306 to AP308, AP311 to AP313, AP317, AP323, BW106, BX179, BX188, BX190, BX191, BX212, BX221, BX232, BX239, BX241, BX244, BX263, 264, BX290, BX296, BX298, BX316, BX319, BX321, BX328, BX334, BX337, BX340, BX341,BX356, BX357, BX364, BX371, BX372, BX410, and BX427, with one more aircraft unaccounted for.

It should be noted that some Russian sources mention Airacobra Is AH621, AH712, AH737, AP281, AP289, AP292, AP294, AP310, AP325, BX168, BX231, BX265, BX272, BX279, BX318, and BX320 as delivered to the USSR, sometimes with details of a specific aircraft's unit, Soviet tactical code, and pilot. However, the Russian list is rather incomplete, and the aircraft serialled AH623, AP265, AP276, AP283, BX176, BX178, BX179, BX185, BX188, BX190, BX191, BX207, BX212, BX214, BX221, BX225, BX226, BX229, BX233, BX236, BX239, BX241, BX242, BX246, BX255, BX259, BX261, BX263, BX267, BX277, BX284, BX289 to BX291, BX295, BX296, BX300, BX315, BX319, BX322, BX328, BX332, BX334, BX337, BX340, BX341, BX346, BX347,

BX349 to BX351, BX356, BX357, BX360 to BX364, BX371, BX372, BX381, BX382, BX387, BX394, BX396, BX403, BX404, BX408, BX410, BX419, BX420, BX425, BX427, and BX431 all are omitted.

As mentioned earlier in chapter 2, an Airacobra I underwent state acceptance trials at NII VVS in April–May 1942. Immediately upon completion of these tests, in May 1942, two Airacobras from the very first shipment, serialled AH628 and AH644, were transferred to NII VVS. There they served both as a test object and as a tool for all sorts of experiments with the purpose of eradicating the Airacobra's numerous faults and problems discovered in the course of the type's operational service in frontline units. Sadly, AH628 eventually crashed 2 km (1.24 miles) northeast of Kol'tsovo AB on 2 February 1943, killing NII VVS test pilot Lt.-Col. Konstantin A. Groozdev. The cause of the accident could not be determined with certainty, but the most likely reason was structural deformation of the rear fuselage caused by g-loads during spin recovery, which rendered the aircraft uncontrollable. The other machine, AH644, was sent back to the 22nd ZAP in May 1943.

The manual endorsed on 11 July 1942 stated that the nosewheel undercarriage of the Airacobra simplified the takeoff and landing procedure, and that the mastering of this aircraft would present no difficulties to pilots flying contemporaneous Soviet fighter types—the Yakovlev Yak-1, Mikoyan/Gurevich MiG-3, and Lavochkin/Gorbunov/Gudkov LaGG-3. At the same time it contained a number of warnings and recommendations on the operation of the aircraft.

P-39D (D-1, D-2)

A Soviet manual for Airacobra pilots issued in July 1943 stated that *'along with the P-39D (Model 14) Airacobras powered by Allison V-1710-35 (V-1710-E4) engines, Airacobras of the following models powered by different versions of the V-1710 were supplied and put into service with air units in 1943.'* The first to be mentioned among these was the P-39D-2 (Bell Model 14A-1); no mention was made of the P-39D-1 (Bell Model 14A). The manual called the pilots' attention to the fact that on the P-39D-2 and subsequent models of the Airacobra (P-39N-1, N-0, L-1, M-1, Q-1, N-5—listed in that order), the manual petrol pump was replaced by an electric pump (used primarily during takeoff). Another change was the deletion of mechanical landing-gear position indicators (rods popping up above the wing surface to show the gear was extended)—a red signal lamp in the cockpit was now used for that. Also deleted was the petrol heater for the cockpit and the armament bay; warm air for heating them was now bled from the coolant radiator.

The P-39D was powered by the 1,150 hp V-1710-35 engine (V-1710-E4 in the Allison Engine Company's nomenclature). The armament was identical to that of the Airacobra I—the 37 mm cannon firing through the propeller hub was replaced by a 20 mm cannon and supplemented by two 12.7 mm machine-guns in the nose and four 7.7 mm machine guns in the wings. The P-39D-2 subtype differed in being powered by the V-1710-63 (V-1710-E6) engine, delivering up to 1,325 hp and reverting to the 37 mm cannon. To reduce the all-up weight, the ammunition complement was reduced and the hydraulic device for cocking the cannon was deleted.

Of the 1,000 or so examples built, 108 were delivered to the Soviet air force. These included three P-39D-1-BEs (serialled 41-28257, 41-38287, and 41-38563) and 105 P-39D-2-BEs (41-38414 to 41-38464 and 41-38516 to 41-38562).

Further models included the experimental XP-39E (Bell Model 23, the immediate precursor of the P-63—see chapter 6) and the production P-39F (Bell Model 15B), with an Aeroproducts hydraulically operated constant-speed propeller instead of the original Curtiss Electric propeller (the latter was not available in sufficient numbers because Curtiss produced it primarily for its own P-40 fighter). This model was not supplied to the Soviet Union.

The P-39G (Bell Model 26), intended to be identical to the P-39D-2, was never completed as such (part of the production run was redesignated P-39K, and the remaining machines became P-39Ls).

The designations P-39H and P-39I were never assigned. The designation P-39J was applied to a total of twenty-five P-39Ds modified to take the 1,100 hp V-1710-59 engine with automatic boost control; again, this version was not supplied to the Soviet Union.

P-39K (P-39K-1)

Soviet manuals for P-39 pilots issued in 1943 and 1944 mention the P-39K-1 (not the P-39K) among the Airacobra models supplied to the Red Army Air Force units. The P-39K (Bell Model 26A; originally ordered as the P-39G but renamed in the course of production) was powered by the V-1710-63 engine. The type was basically identical to the P-39D-2 except for the Aeroproducts propeller. Of the 210 P-39K-1-BEs built, forty were delivered to the Soviet air force on the UK Lend-Lease account. These were serialled 42-4396, 42-4397, 42-4399, 42-4401 to 42-4429, and 42-4445 to 42-4452.

P-39L

The P-39L (Bell Model 26C) was similar to the P-39K but fitted with the older Curtiss Electric propeller of 3.14 m (10 ft. 3⅝ in.) diameter. Of the 250 machines built, 140 were allocated to the Soviet air force on the UK Lend-Lease account. According to the British aviation historian Phil Butler, these were P-39L-1-BEs 42-4504, 42-4507, 42-4511, 42-4525, 42-4526, 42-4529, 42-4531, 42-4537, 42-4552, 42-4564 to 42-4613, 42-4615 to 42-4629, 42-4631 to 42-4644, 42-4646 to 42-4673, 42-4675 to 42-4677, 42-4679, 42-4681 to 42-4686, 42-4688 to 42-4692, 42-4696 to 42-4700, 42-4702, and 42-4703. Five of the above aircraft (42-4488, 42-4497, 42-4633, 42-4672, and 42-4682) crashed on US territory during the delivery flight, while 42-4624 force-landed in Canadian territory and was possibly a write-off as well. US aviation researcher Joe Baugher gives a somewhat different picture, omitting the examples serialled 42-4537 and 42-4615 to 42-4629.

In the summer of 1943, one example of this version, P-39L-1-BE 42-4666, powered by a V-1710-63 and armed with the 37 mm cannon, was delivered to NII VVS for testing. The flight testing took place between 25 July and 23 August 1943. The aircraft proved capable of attaining a speed of 596 km/h (370 mph) at an

ABOVE: P-39M-1-BE 42-4725 with a 284-litre (75 US gal) drop tank fitted; note the large nosewheel and the cannon barrel shroud.

BELOW: P-39M-1-BE '14 White' (42-4939, c/n 26D-236) with the North Fleet's 255th IAP at Vayenga-1 AB in late 1943, flown by Lt. (SG) Pyotr A. Rassadkin. Note the seven 'kill' stars; the white spinner and fin cap are quick-recognition markings.

ABOVE: Two P-39Ns (including (P-39N-0-BE 42-4983/'43 White') take off on a mission.

BELOW: P-39N-1-BE 42-9266 / '11 White', probably an aircraft from the same unit as the two pictured above.

A P-39N from the 7th Air Army; the serial has been painted out before applying the star insignia to the tail, making more accurate identification impossible. Note the individual emblem on the nose near the tactical code and the damage to the star on the fuselage.

altitude of 3,250 m (10,660 ft.). In this respect it was on a par with Soviet fighters of that period—the Yak-1B, Yak-7B, Yak-9, and Lavochkin La-5, while being inferior to them in vertical speed above 3,000 m (9,840 ft.). On the other hand, the P-39L was superior to them in range and in the armament.

At NII VVS the P-39L-1 underwent thorough testing with a view to investigating the g-loads to which the fighter was subjected in aerobatic manoeuvres. The purpose was to determine the causes of the numerous accidents in service units when Airacobras entered a spin and suffered deformation of the rear fuselage, often with fatal consequences. While the propensity for entering a spin was fairly obviously caused by the excessive aft position of the CG, the structural deformations were due to the insufficient strength of the tail. Measures devised to rectify this situation included strengthening the rear fuselage with the help of reinforcing plates (straps) and sections.

P-39M and P-39M-1

The P-39M (Bell Model 26D) was similar to the P-39L but was powered by a new version of the engine, the 1,200 hp V-1710-73 (or, according to some sources, an identically rated V-1710-67/V-1710-E8), which was replaced by the generally similar V-1710-83 (V-1710-E18) engine on the P-39M-1. The P-39M-0 again used the Aeroproducts propeller, but this gave way to the Curtiss-Electric propeller on the P-39M-1.

Of the 240 machines built, 157 were allocated to the Soviet air force, most of which (130 aircraft) were delivered on the UK Lend-Lease account. According to Phil Butler, they were serialled 42-4707, 42-4709, 42-4711, 42-4713, 42-4715 to 42-4717, 42-4719 to 42-4722, 42-4725 to 42-4728, 42-4730 to 42-4732, 42-4735, 42-4736 to 42-4738, 42-4744, 42-4747, 42-4749, 42-4750, 42-4753 to 42-4755, 42-4757 to 42-4763, 42-4765 to 42-4769, 42-4771 to 42-4792, 42-4794, 42-4796 to 42-4806, 42-4808 to 42-4810, 42-4859 to 42-4865, 42-4867 to 42-4885, 42-4887 to 42-4909, 42-4911, and 42-4913 to 42-4943, all of them listed as P-39M-1-BEs; seven of these were lost on the US/Canadian section of the ferrying route. Again, Joe Baugher gives slightly different data, not listing five of the above aircraft (42-4730 to 42-4732, 42-4737, and 42-4749) as intended for the Soviet Union.

An example of the P-39M-1 (42-4750) was tested at NII VVS.

P-39N

The P-39N (variously reported as the Bell Model 26F or Mo-del 26N) was a version powered by the 1,325 hp V-1710-85 (V-1710-E19) engine, with a lower gearing ration driving a new Aeroproducts propeller of 3.52 m (11 ft. 6³⁷⁄₆₄ in.) diameter. It often lacked the aerial mast. 2,095 P-39Ns in blocks 0, 1, and 5 were built.

Again, most of the P-39Ns supplied to the Soviet air force were delivered on the UK Lend-Lease account. In this case there is a significant discrepancy between available figures. Phil Butler lists the P-39N-BEs assigned to the USSR as 42-4945 to 42-4948, 42-4950, 42-4952, 42-4980, 42-4985 to 42-4987, 42-4996, 42-4997, 42-5000, 42-5002 to 42-5005, 42-5007, 42-5013, 42-5016, 42-5017,

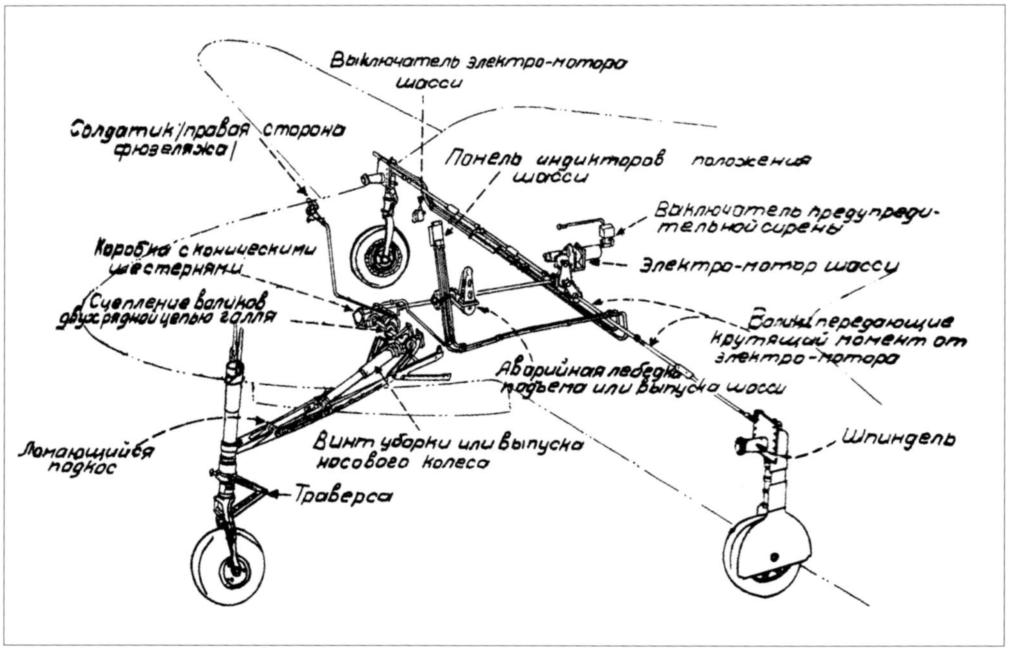

In the Soviet Union the P-39 was rigorously tested at NII VVS, and Russian manuals were prepared to assist Soviet pilots in mastering the type. This drawing from such a manual shows the landing-gear design.

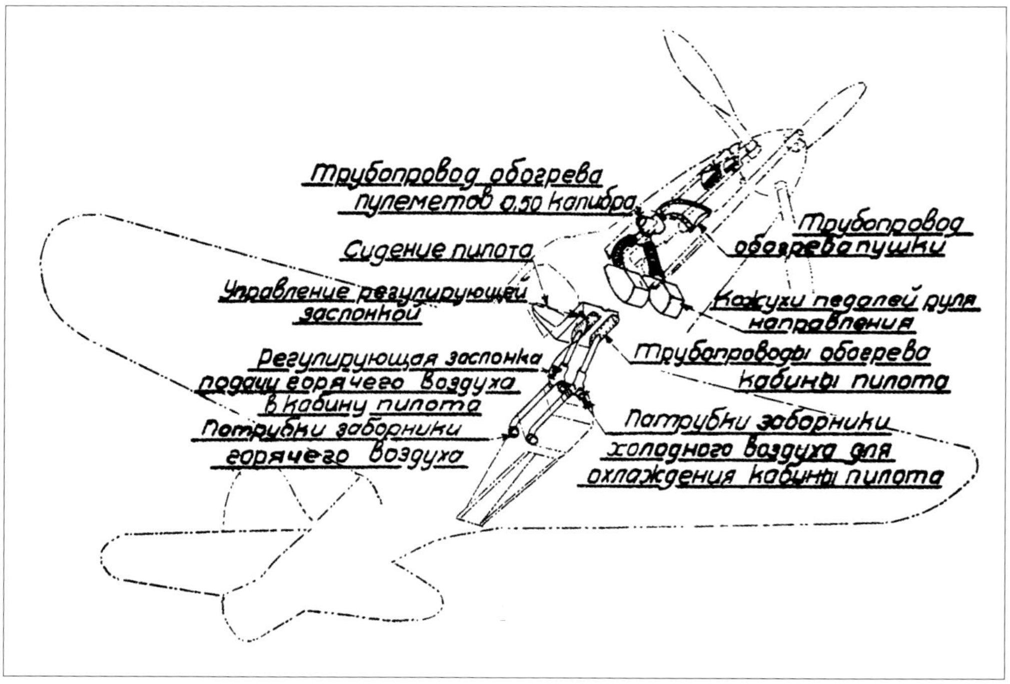

Another drawing from the same manual showing the P-39's heating and ventilation system.

BELOW: P-39 '24 White' of the 191st GvIAP (reporting to the 8th Air Army in action on the Leningrad Front) is refuelled by a BZ-35 fuel bowser on a ZiS-6 6x4 truck chassis (military ID number B-3-63-18) in 1944. Note the white spinner and white rudder, which are unit markings.

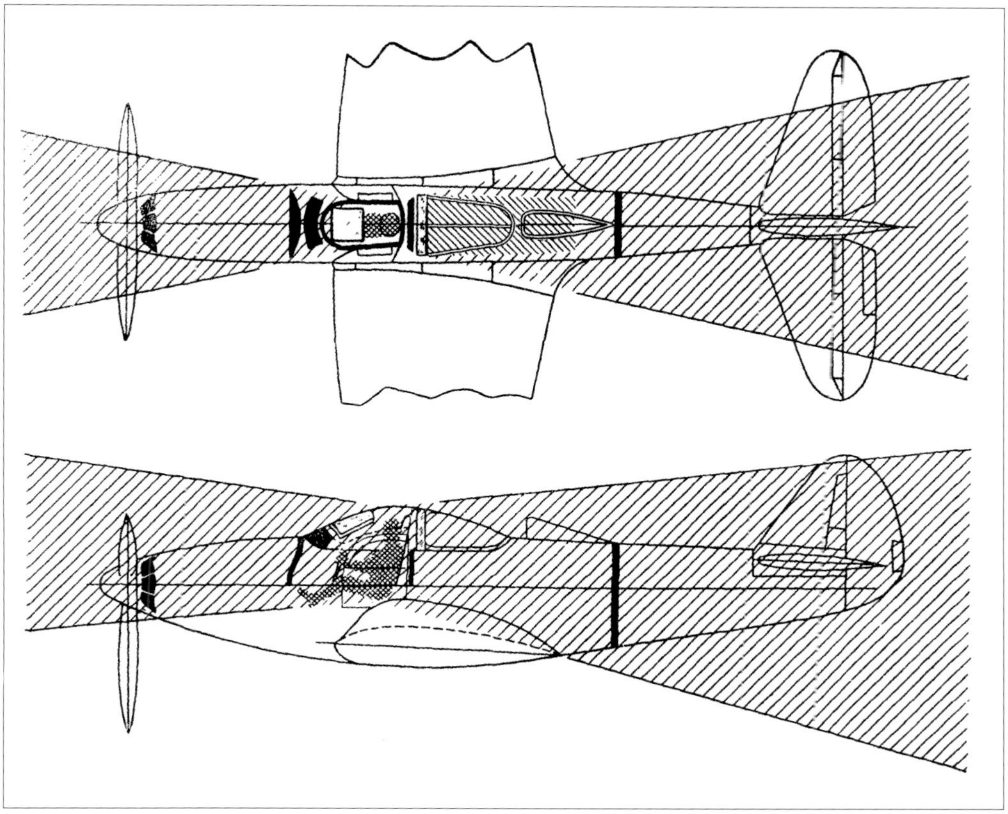

RIGHT: A drawing of the P-39's armour plating from a Soviet manual prepared by NII VVS. The shaded areas show the sectors in which protection for the pilot against enemy fire was ensured.

BELOW: P-39 '10 White' taxies out for takeoff, with another one close behind.

42-5020, 42-5021, 42-5024 to 42-5043, 42-8727 to 42-8805, 42-8807, 42-8912 to 42-8961, and 42-8980 to 42-9079 (though 42-5032 crashed before delivery, while 42-8740 is reported as crashed in Papua New Guinea and thus must be a USAAF aircraft). Joe Baugher additionally mentions 42-4954 to 42-4957, 42-4959 to 42-4963, 42-4965 to 42-4969, 42-4971 to 42-4979, 42-4981 to 42-4984, 42-4988, 42-4990, 42-4992 to 42-4995, 42-4998, 42-4999, 42-5001, 42-5006, 42-5008, 42-5010, 42-5012, 42-5014, 42-5015, 42-5018, 42-5019, and 42-5023 as delivered to the USSR.

The P-39N-1-BE featured internal changes to adjust the CG position when the nose guns were fired. According to Phil Butler, the P-39N-1-BEs assigned to the USSR were 42-9127 to 42-9140, 42-9142 to 42-9144, 42-9146, 42-9147, 42-9149, 42-9155 to 42-9184, 42-9215 to 42-9246, 42-9249 to 42-9254, 42-9256 to 42-9287, 42-9289 to 42-9336, 42-9437 to 42-9543, 42-9545 to 42-9574, 42-9576 to 42-9594, 42-9596 to 42-9641, 42-9643 to 42-9666, 42-9713, and 42-18301. Conversely, Joe Baugher further includes 42-9544, 42-9575, and 42-9595, while 42-9216 is listed as a

USAAF aircraft and 42-9713 as a Free French Air Force aircraft. P-39N-1-BEs 42-9258, 42-9290, 42-9291, 42-9299, 42-9305, 42-9311, and 42-9325 were lost before delivery.

The P-39N-5-BE version had the weight of the armour reduced from 105 to 88 kg (from 231 to 193 lb.), a new SCR-695 identification friend-or-foe (IFF) radio set, and a new oxygen system. Phil Butler lists the P-39N-5-BEs assigned to the USSR as 42-18546 to 42-18623, 42-18625 to 42-18675, 42-18682 to 42-18711, 42-18941 to 42-18985, 42-19046 to 42-19132, and 42-19134 to 42-19240. Joe Baugher also includes 42-18624 and 42-19133 but omits 42-18547. The aircraft serialled 42-18578, 42-18584, and 42-18624 crashed on the Canadian section of the delivery route, while 42-18547 is reported as crashed in Papua New Guinea and thus was a USAAF aircraft.

According to military historian Viktor A. Bakurskiy, the renowned Soviet ace Aleksandr I. Pokryshkin flew a P-39N with the tactical code '100 White' (albeit some sources assert that this machine was a P-39Q, Bakurskiy insists on his identification). A colour profile of Pokryshkin's Airacobra coded '100 White' was published by a Russian magazine with comments by A. Kanevskiy. The profile is captioned 'Pokryshkin's Bell P-39N-0 Airacobra'; it shows the USAAF serial 42-9004, which is indeed a P-39N-0-BE. Moreover, a US website confirms this identity, listing P-39N-BE 42-9004 as *"White 100," flown by Alexander Pokryshin* [sic], *top Allied ace.'*

In the middle of August 1943, one P-39N was transferred to TsAGI for static testing. The tests showed that the airframe of this aircraft did not meet the Soviet structural-strength standards then in force. The tail section of the fuselage obviously required strengthening.

A P-39N was tested at NII VVS, operating from Chkalovskaya airbase near Moscow. On 3 January 1944 it crashed in the Noginsk District of the Moscow Region, killing the test pilot Aleksandr A. Avtonomov. The mission objective that day was to check the fuel burn per mile. Thirty minutes into the mission, the engine quit; Avtonomov attempted a forced landing in an open field but suddenly noticed a farmhouse ahead. As the pilot made a sharp manoeuvre to avoid a collision, the aircraft stalled at 50–100 m (164–330 ft.) and crashed inverted in a 15–20° nose-down attitude, exploding on impact.

P-39Q

On 14 July 1943, chief engineer of the Red Army Air Force, Engineer-Colonel-General Aleksandr K. Repin, endorsed the 'Pilot's manual on the operation and piloting techniques of the P-39 Airacobra aircraft powered by Allison V-1710-63, -83, and -85 engines.' The manual contained an enumeration of the following subtypes: P-39D-2, P-39K-1, P-39L-1 (V-1710-E6/V-1710-63 engine version), P-39M-1 (V-1710-E18/V-1710-83 engine version), P-39N-0, P-39N-1, P-39N-5, P-39Q-1, P-39Q-5, and P-39Q-10 (V-1710-E19/V-1710-85 engine version). Just over a year later, on 6 September 1944, Repin endorsed an updated version of the same manual titled 'Pilot's manual on the operation and piloting techniques of the P-39 Airacobra aircraft powered by Allison V-1710-35, 63, 83 and 85 engines,' which covered the P-39D, P-39K-1, P-39L-1, P-39M-1, P-39N-0, P-39N-5, P-39Q-1, P-39Q-5, P-39Q-10, P-39Q-15, and P-39Q-20 subtypes. Thus, it may be regarded as a generalised document referring to all these versions in Soviet service.

The P-39Q (variously reported as the Bell Model 26E or Mo-del 26Q), the final main production model of the Airacobra, entered production in 1942. It, differed from the preceding models in having the four wing-mounted 7.62 mm (.30) Browning M1919 machine guns replaced by two 12.7 mm (.50 cal.) Colt-Browning M2 AN machine guns with 300 rpg in underwing pods. However, the armament fit of the P-39Q (including the 37 mm

Colt-Browning M4 cannon) was considered excessive for the needs of air-to-air combat, and the underwing machine guns were removed in many cases. In Soviet service the P-39Qs normally lacked the aerial mast that can be seen on examples in USAAF service.

There is no confirmation that the P-39Q-0 and P-39Q-1 were actually delivered to the Red Army Air Force. The Soviet Union received P-39Qs in the -5, -10, -15, -20, -21 (?), -25, and -30 production blocks. The P-39Q-5-BE had the weight of the armour reduced from 105 to 88 kg (from 231 to 193 lb.) and an increased fuel supply (416 litres / 110 US gallons). According to Phil Butler, the examples assigned to the USSR were 42-19596, 42-19598 to 42-19602, 42-19604, 42-19605, all even-numbered aircraft from 42-19696 to 42-19726, 42-19726 to 42-19838, 42-19840 to 42-19852, 42-19854 to 42-19873, all odd-numbered aircraft from 42-19875 to 42-19911 (except 42-19903), 42-19915, 42-19917, 42-19919, 42-19923, 42-19925, 42-19926, 42-19948, 42-19954, 42-19958, 42-19964, 42-19974, 42-20042, 42-20072, 42-20086, all even-numbered aircraft from 42-20124 to 42-20326 (except 42-20166), all even-numbered aircraft from 42-20330 to 42-20356, all even-numbered aircraft from 42-20360 to 42-20408, all even-numbered aircraft from 42-20414 to 42-20422, 42-20444, 42-20471, 42-20473, 42-20475, and 42-20486. Joe Baugher also includes 42-19839, 42-19853, 42-20166, 42-20167, 42-20171, and 42-20442 but does not mention 42-19875, starting the odd-numbered batch from 42-19877. Eight aircraft (42-19602, 42-19735, 42-19819, 42-19855, 42-19871, 42-19915, 42-20222, and 42-20374) crashed on the US/Canadian section of the delivery route.

The P-39Q-10-BE had both heavier armour (103 kg / 228 lb.) and an even-greater fuel capacity (454 litres / 120 US gallons). Examples assigned to the USSR were serialled 42-20546 to 42-20624, 42-20626 to 42-20650, 42-20652, 42-20654 to 42-20690, 42-20693, 42-20694, and 42-21038 to 42-21187, though eight aircraft (42-20576, 42-20586, 42-20599, 42-20626, 42-20646, 42-20661, 42-20690, and 42-21122) crashed in the US whilst on delivery.

The P-39Q-15-BE introduced various structural reinforcements to prevent fatigue cracking and had a reduced oxygen supply. A total of 654 P-39Q-15-BEs were eventually assigned to the Soviet Union, including 343 aircraft delivered on the UK Lend-Lease account. Phil Butler lists them as 44-2011 to 44-2142, 44-2144 to 44-2147, 44-2149 to 44-2264, 44-2468 to 44-2629, 44-2631 to 44-2716 and 44-2751 to 44-3000. Joe Baugher further includes 44-2630 but incorrectly lists 44-2142 as 44-2162 (which is included all right) and omits 44-2144 to 44-2147. One of the above aircraft (44-2485) crashed in northern Canada on delivery.

The P-39Q-20-BE featured minor equipment changes and sometimes lacked the underwing machine-gun pods. A total of 310 P-39Q-20-BEs were assigned to the Soviet Union, including 246 aircraft delivered on the UK Lend-Lease account. According to Phil Butler, they were serialled 44-3113, 44-3114, 44-3146 to 44-3148, 44-3156, 44-3159, 44-3162, 44-3166, 44-3167, 44-3173, 44-3177, 44-3188, 44-3191, 44-3203 to 44-3452, 44-3551, 44-3552, 44-3603 to 44-3644, 44-3646 to 44-3834, and 44-3836 to 44-3849. Joe Baugher also includes some of the intervening serials (44-3453 to 44-3550 and 44-3645).

The P-39Q-21-BE was a conversion with a four-blade Aeroproducts propeller. In addition to the direct deliveries on the Soviet and UK Lend-Lease accounts (44-3941 to 44-4000), a few such aircraft were transferred to the USSR from a Free French air force order after sitting in storage in North Africa; they were delivered via Abadan, Iran. None of these have been identified, although Phil Butler lists 44-3855 to 44-3858 from one of the French batches as delivered on the UK Lend-Lease account.

The P-39Q-25-BE was a new-build version that also had the four-blade Aeroproducts prop, differing from the -21 in having a reinforced rear fuselage and stabiliser structure. A total of 666 were assigned to the Soviet Union, including 401 aircraft on the UK Lend-Lease account. According to Phil Butler, they were serialled 44-32167 to 44-32431, 44-32437 to 44-32446, 44-32457 to 44-32483, 44-32485 to 44-32660, 44-32665, 44-32666, 44-70618 (?), 44-70620 (?), 44-70905 to 44-70916, 44-70921 to 44-70934,

OPPOSITE PAGE: 44-2567 / '67 White,' a 68th GvIAP P-39Q-15-BE pictured in the winter of 1944–45, shows off its unit markings—a fuselage band (probably red) edged in white. The spinner appears to be red as well.

RIGHT: Ground crewmen hook up a bomb to the centreline hardpoint of P-39Q-25-BE 44-32512. Again, the aircraft has a differently coloured spinner and a stripe on the tail as quick-identification markings.

44-70939 to 44-70952, 44-70956 to 44-71008, 44-71010 to 44-71053, 44-71055 to 44-71059, and 44-71061 to 44-71104. Joe Baugher also includes 44-71054 and 44-71060, but not 44-32665/44-32666 (which are listed as delivered to the Free French air force) and 44-70618/44-70620 (which reportedly never existed, the serials being assigned to contracts that were later cancelled). Could these be 44-70918 and 44-70920?

The P-39Q-30-BE was similar to the -25; early aircraft likewise had four-blade props, but later ones reverted to the three-blade propeller. Block 30 was entirely destined for the Soviet Union, numbering 400 aircraft (44-71105 to 44-71504), 164 of which were delivered on the UK Lend-Lease account; Phil Butler lists them as 44-71105 to 44-71453 and 44-71455 to 44-71504, which makes 399 aircraft. All of them were delivered except 44-71122, which crashed fatally near Bismarck, North Dakota, on 11 June 1944 during delivery.

At some point in time a P-39Q-5-BE was tested in TsAGI's T-101 wind tunnel. The available photo shows the serial as '21988,' but since 42-1988 was a Vultee BT-15 basic trainer, the serial was obviously 42-1988*, with the last digit obliterated for some reason (it was 1, 2, 5, 7, or 9). The aircraft was mounted on three V-struts, one of which was attached to the rear fuselage; the propeller was removed but the spinner was fitted and the gap between it and the fuselage was taped over. Wool tufts were applied to the starboard wing, and the control surfaces were fitted with deflection sensors rigged to recording equipment.

A P-39Q-10 fitted with a conformal ferrying fuel tank was tested at NII VVS. It carried the poorly discernible serial 42-205 . . ., the last two digits being illegible on the available photo.

P-39Q-10-BE 42-20561—possibly the same aircraft—was tested at NII VVS in October 1943 in connection with a series of crashes of the P-39Qs in frontline units, which occurred when the aircraft failed to recover from a spin. According to the test report, this machine had two 12.7 mm machine guns 'in the wings' (presumably in underwing pods). The purpose of the testing was to investigate the aircraft's spin behaviour with different load configurations, to determine the possibility of spin recovery at the extreme aft CG position, and to prepare instructions for pilots on handling the P-39Q. The tests were conducted by test pilots Konstantin I. Ovchinnikov and Vladimir Ye. Golofastov between 16 and 19 October 1943. In twelve flights the aircraft was put into a spin 115 times and made a total of 180 turns. The flights were performed with five different payload configurations and a CG position ranging from 28.4 to 30.9 percent MAC. The test pilots' verdict was as follows: the P-39 of the Q series can reliably recover from a spin at all operational CG positions, but this requires resolute and correct control inputs. Too-smooth and incomplete inputs can delay recovery or even prove insufficient for recovery. This, generally speaking, optimistic conclusion was accompanied by a number of warnings. For example, it was stated that moving the CG aft adversely affected the P-39's longitudinal stability and made the aircraft sensitive to the slightest piloting errors. Therefore it was necessary to be vigilant when loading the aircraft, so as to prevent any excessive aft movement of the CG. Placing heavy objects in the rear fuselage, filling an excessive amount of oil in the oil tank, and removing the weapons from the forward fuselage without appropriate weight compensation were absolutely inadmissible.

It was also noted that excessive aft movement of the stick or a too-generous bootful of rudder during aerobatic manoeuvres could cause the aircraft to flick into a spin. The same faulty movement of the stick during vertical manoeuvres could result in an inverted spin.

The final conclusion was as follows:

'1. Spin on the P-39 Airacobra of the Q series presents no danger, and recovery from the spin can be effected at all operational CG positions, provided the pilot makes complete and resolute control inputs for recovery and there is a sufficient altitude margin.

2. To prevent inadvertent spin entry in the course of aerobatic manoeuvres, first-line air units should be given the following instructions:

a) pilots must study thoroughly the "Additional instructions on the piloting of the P-39Q Airacobra";

b) vigilance must be exercised during the loading of the aircraft so as to avoid a shift of the CG beyond the aft operational CG limit.'

The test report was endorsed on 10 November 1943.

Despite the seemingly encouraging test results, the problems with spin recovery remained on the agenda. In the spring of 1944 a different P-39Q-10 (42-20563) was flown by Konstantin I. Ovchinnikov in further tests concerned with the aircraft's spinning characteristics. On 27 April 1944 the tests ended in a crash when the tail unit started disintegrating during a maximum-speed run at 7,000 m (22,965 ft.). When the elevators jammed, the Airacobra entered a steep dive; as Ovchinnikov attempted to pull out, the starboard elevator separated at 1,500 m (4,920 ft.) due to high g-loads. The P-39 then entered an irrecoverable flat spin and impacted near Rakhmanovo village (Moscow Region), the pilot losing his life.

The results of the abovementioned testing of the P-39Q-10 and some other tests of the Q model were reflected in instruction no. 105 endorsed by the chief engineer of the Red Army Air Force on 23 July 1944. It was titled 'On measures for improving the CG location of the P-39 (Airacobra) aircraft.' The document stated:

'The aft CG location and insufficient longitudinal stability are characteristic for all models of the P-39 (Airacobra) aircraft. The latest models (Q-10, Q-15, and Q-20) have the CG location shifted further aft; flying these aircraft requires the use of compensating loads (ballast).

Reinforcement of the fuselage and tail unit, which is being conducted on the P-39 aircraft at present, shifts the CG location still further aft (the CG is moved to aft by 0.47% MAC), and any unwarranted deletion or relocation of these loads, without taking into account the influence of this factor on the CG location of the aircraft, can lead to grave consequences.

The CG position at 30% MAC is to be regarded as the utmost aft limit, ensuring normal operation of the P-39 aircraft of all models.

For the purpose of ensuring normal operational CG location on the P-39 (Airacobra) aircraft I hereby order:

1. The P-39 aircraft of all versions are to be loaded as follows:

A North Fleet air arm P-39 coded '22 White' and sporting a diagonal tail stripe as quick-identification markings takes off from a frozen lake in 1942.

a) armament – three weapons (one 37 mm cannon and two synchronised 12.7 mm machine guns);

b) ammunition – 30 rounds for the 37 mm cannon and 400 rounds for two 12.7 mm machine-guns;

c) fuel – both tanks filled to full capacity (120 US gallons on the D-2, K-1, L-1, M-1, Q-10, Q-15, and Q-20 models; 87 US gallons on the N-0, N-1, N-5 models; 110 US gallons on the Q-5 model);

d) oil – not more than 7.5 US gallons (28.5 litres) in the engine oil tank, 2.0 US gallons (7.6 litres) in the reduction gear housing;

e) radio equipment: [three versions are detailed, the main one comprising one BC-454A receiver, one BC-457 transmitter, and the MN-26M (U) direction finder].

2. The following armour plates are to be removed from the P-39 aircraft: [specific plates are indicated—one plate on models up to the P-39Q-5 and six plates on the Q-10, Q-15, and Q-20 models].

3. For the purpose of retaining normal operational CG position, ballast must unconditionally be placed ahead of the storage battery [the weight of the ballast is specified for different models, ranging from 21.0 kg (46.3 lb.) on the P-39Q-5 and earlier models to 56.0 kg (123.46 lb.) on the P-39Q-15 and P-39Q-20].

4. [. . .]

5. Removal of the ballast and any relocation of the loads without special permission is strictly prohibited because the stipulated location of loads and ballast ensures, after the depletion of ammunition, fuel, and oil, the 29.25% MAC aft limit of the operational CG location.'

The testing of the P-39Q-10 at NII VVS was concerned, among other things, with the use of external fuel tanks. As noted in one of the Soviet manuals, the P-39s could use the following types of centreline drop tanks:

- a duralumin tank holding 75 US gallons (284 litres);
- a tank made of vulcanised fibre holding 150 US gallons (568 litres);
- a duralumin tank holding 175 US gallons (662 litres).

The tests at NII VVS showed that the performance of the P-39Q-10 fitted with the 175-gallon tank deteriorated in comparison with the 'clean' configuration: the maximum speed fell by 45 km/h (28 mph), and time to 3,000 m (9,840 ft.) was increased by 2.3 minutes. The increase of the AUW due to the drop tank made it necessary to increase the minimum speed of the aircraft. During flights with a drop tank it was forbidden to fly at speeds less than 274 km/h (170 mph), to make sustained turns with the undercarriage retracted at speeds less than 290 km/h (180 mph), to make sustained turns with the undercarriage extended, to exceed a bank angle of 40°, and to perform aerobatics.

An example of the P-39Q-25-BE serialled 44-32467 was also tested at NII VVS. In particular, it was tested for spin behaviour and was fitted with a spin recovery parachute attached to the fuselage by a special truss similar to the one fitted to 42-20561. Additionally, this aircraft had a cine camera installed on top of the canopy frame, suggesting that one of the wings (or the horizontal tail) was covered with wool tufts for airflow visualisation.

The P-39Q was produced in greater numbers than any other version of the Airacobra. According to US Lend-Lease statistics, 3,291 P-39Qs were sent to the Soviet Union. They included machines of different subtypes that incorporated various modifications, sometimes directly inspired by the Soviet operational experience. For example, on the P-39Q-10 the oil system was modified to improve reliability in the Russian winter conditions. As already mentioned, the P-39Q-25 (featuring a four-blade propeller) came with reinforced rear fuselage and stabilisers.

It is interesting to summarise the comments, warnings, and recommendations on the operation and piloting of the different Airacobra models, which can be found in Soviet manuals and which were obviously based largely on the results of tests at NII VVS. Many of these recommendations were applicable to all P-39 models.

Describing the handling qualities of the P-39, the manuals give a generally positive assessment. They note that the aircraft is easily balanced in flight with the help of trim tabs, and a well-trimmed aircraft can fly hands-off for quite some time.

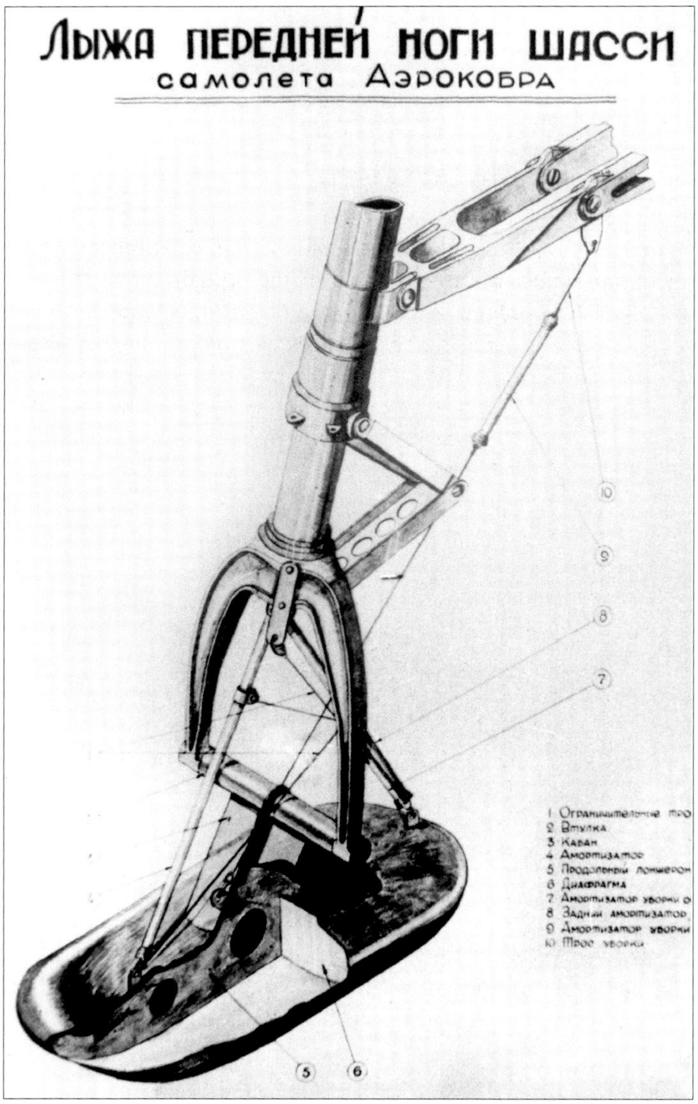

A drawing from a Soviet manual showing how the Airacobra could be fitted with retractable skis.

Speaking about piloting techniques, the manuals always stress that due to the relatively high AUW and aft CG location, jerky control inputs lead to aerobatic manoeuvres characterised by violent and uneven rotation. Manoeuvres based on the principle of autorotation cause buffeting of the tail unit; in consequence, the execution of such manoeuvres is forbidden.

Particular attention is paid in the manuals to the spinning characteristics of the P-39. The aircraft was prone to flicking into a spin as a result of piloting errors; this could happen during banked turns in the case of poor coordination of controls and loss of speed. However, a manual published in July 1943 also noted that *'if, after snapping into a spin, the controls are immediately, resolutely and fully set into the position for recovery, the aircraft recovers from the spin without delay.'*

A special section in one of the manuals was devoted to the influence of the Airacobra's CG position on longitudinal stability and piloting techniques. It was noted that the normal position of the CG with the undercarriage retracted was 28.5 percent MAC, which corresponded to a full complement of armament in the fuselage and 7.5 US gallons (28.3 litres) of oil in the engine's oil tank. With this CG position the aircraft was longitudinally stable, entering a spin only in the case of a grossly excessive backward movement of the stick during aerobatic manoeuvres.

If the ammunition load is absent and the oil tank is filled with 11.5 US gallons (43.5 litres) of oil, the CG with the undercarriage retracted moves aft to 31.5 percent MAC. With this CG position the aircraft becomes longitudinally unstable and easily snaps into a spin after even a minor error on the part of the pilot. Hence, a recommendation was made: before every flight the pilot must make sure that the amount of oil in the engine oil tank does not exceed 7.5 US gallons; during training flights he must make sure that a full ammunition load is in place.

It was strictly forbidden during redeployment of air units to place an excessive load (tools, coverings) into the rear fuselage, which might cause a shift of the CG to more than 30 percent MAC.

A special note was made of the spinning characteristics of the P-39Q-1, P-39Q-5, and P-39Q-10 models. The manual stated that these versions of the Airacobra *'recover from a spin freely at all operational locations of the CG, provided that the pilot makes confident and correct control inputs.'*

The manual contained a warning: *'Due to the highly effective elevators on the P-39 Airacobra an abrupt pulling of the stick causes high G-loads. The G-load arising after an abrupt pulling of the stick at high flight speeds can make the pilot suffer G-loc (gravity-induced loss of consciousness) and even cause structural deformation of parts of the airframe. Therefore, when performing aerobatic manoeuvres, the longitudinal stick movements shall be moderate and smooth.'*

Soviet Modifications of the P-39 Airacobra

Airacobras in Soviet service were sometimes subjected to locally devised modifications. As already noted, some of them were of minor character and were intended to improve the fighter's serviceability, especially in winter conditions. Small alterations were introduced in the oil system and water-cooling circuit. Single

The flight line of the air defence force's 103rd GvIAP of the 2nd GvIAK on 18 September 1943, the day when the regiment and the corps received Guards status (formerly 158th IAP/7th IAK). Note the Guards badge on the cockpit doors and the all-white vertical tails.

examples featured some 'customised' items of equipment. For example, one P-39 serving with the 1st Ferrying Air Division was fitted with a Soviet RPK-10 direction finder (*rahdiopolukompas*, or DF) and was used as a lead ship for groups of single-engined aircraft during their ferrying flights from the US to the Soviet Union. Some machines were fitted in the field with Soviet bomb racks, enabling them to carry bombs of Soviet types. There were also modifications of a more substantial nature.

P-39 as Photoreconnaissance Aircraft

Attempts were made in the Red Army Air Force to use the P-39 as a short-range photoreconnaissance aircraft. Various subtypes of the Airacobra had been adapted by the Bell Company for this role; for example, some P-39D-3-BE and P-39D-4-BE machines, as well as 27 P-39Fs, were converted into reconnaissance fighters. Likewise, cameras were installed in some P-39Ls and P-39Ms. The P-39N served as the basis for two photoreconnaissance versions—the P-39N-2-BE and P-39N-3-BE. A number of P-39Q fighters were fitted with Kodak K-24 and K-25 aerial cameras. However, there is no evidence of these photoreconnaissance versions reaching the Soviet Union. Instead, indigenous photo equipment had to be installed locally. In the spring of 1943, several machines were operated in this role in the 118th RAP (*razvedyvatel'nyy aviapolk*; Reconnaissance Air Regiment); they were fitted with AFA-I cameras (*aerofotoapparaht istrebitelya*; aerial camera for fighters) for vertical photography. However, they were operated in this role only for a brief period and were replaced by Kittyhawks, which were considered more suitable for reconnaissance duties. As related by the Russian historian Vladimir R. Kotel'nikov, the 4th DRAP (*dahl'niy razvedyvatel'nyy aviapolk*; Long-Range Reconnaissance Air Regiment) formed the 3rd Reconnaissance Squadron, which was equipped with six P-39Ds. They were fitted with AFA-I or AFA-B (*aerofotoapparaht bombardirovshchika*; aerial camera for bombers) vertical cameras. The guns in the wings were usually removed. In the course of five months these aircraft made more than 100 sorties. Similarly equipped Airacobras flew reconnaissance missions in one of the squadrons of the 98th GvDRAP (*Gvardeyskiy dahl'niy razvedyvatel'nyy aviapolk*; Guards Long-Range Reconnaissance Air Regiment). Single examples of the P-39 were retrofitted with aerial cameras in fighter regiments as well. One source states that a P-39D equipped with an AFA-I camera was used by the 4th Reconnaissance Air Regiment of the Supreme Command. However, the use of the P-39s for photoreconnaissance was practised only on a limited scale by the Soviet air force.

P-39 with a Ski Undercarriage

Attempts were made to equip the Airacobras serving with naval aviation units of the Baltic Fleet and the North Fleet with a retractable ski undercarriage. According to Vladimir R. Kotelnikov, in April 1944 one of the versions of ski undercarriage was developed and manufactured by Rakov, a skilled workman in the aircraft repair shop of the White Sea Flotilla's air force. All three undercarriage legs were fitted with retractable skis. The main skis stood some 150–170 mm (5²⁹⁄₃₂ to 6¹¹⁄₁₆ in) proud of the wing undersurface. The undercarriage was tested in April 1944 with good results. Retraction and extension of the skis proceeded faultlessly; taxiing on snow-covered surfaces posed no problems. Nevertheless, the ski undercarriage failed to gain wide acceptance, and the P-39s continued to be operated on wheels all the year round.

P-39 with a Starter Dog

Experience showed that during severe Russian winters with strong frost, the electric inertia starter of the V-1710 engine often failed. The remedy was found in the use of the starter truck (a widespread practice in the Red Army Air Force since the 1920s and 1930s),

which could transmit the rotation of its engine's crankshaft to the aircraft's propeller via an articulated extension shaft; the latter could be set at different angles to adapt it to a particular type of aircraft. To ensure the coupling of the extension shaft with the propeller hub, the latter had to be provided with a starter dog, which was absent on the US-produced machines. According to Vladimir R. Kotel'nikov, in response to a Soviet request the Bell factory installed these starter dogs on several P-39Ks; three of them were handed over to the Soviet acceptance team in Fairbanks in July 1943. They were supposed to be subjected to service tests in the units of the 7th Air Army, but no corroborating documents have yet been found.

Nevertheless, the testing of the starting procedure described above did actually take place in the Soviet P-39-equipped units in November 1943. It turned out that the diameter of the starter dog did not match that of the shaft on the Soviet starter trucks, nor did the standard angle of their extension shaft match the angle of the propeller axis on the P-39. The problem was solved by the use of specially manufactured adapters. There is no evidence as to further deliveries of P-39s equipped with starter dogs.

P-39s with Klimov Engines

Several dozen P-39s were reengined with Soviet 1,100 hp Klimov M-105P (VK-105P) engines in the aircraft repair shops of the Leningrad Front due to the lack of spare Allison engines. The reengining was made possible by the fact that the M-105 and the V-1710 were closely comparable in layout and overall dimensions. However, the Soviet engine differed from its American counterpart in one important respect: it incorporated a gearbox as standard to reduce the propeller shaft's rpm, which meant the output shaft was placed higher than that of the V-1710-E tailored for the Airacobra. Available sources give no clue as to how the Soviet engineers managed to circumvent this problem and adapt the M-105 to the American airframe, but, in any case, it appears that the reengining did not involve any radical structural changes.

UTI P-39N Trainer (Soviet Analogue of the TP-39)

One of the versions of the P-39 developed by Bell was the TP-39—a two-seat trainer. Produced as a modification of the P-39F, and then of the P-39Q-5, it featured a second cockpit for the instructor installed ahead of the existing one, supplanting the gun bay (the trainer had no armament). The forward cockpit canopy was blended into the existing one and opened sideways. The vertical tail area was increased by adding a ventral strake to compensate for the extra area ahead of the CG.

As far as is known, no TP-39s were delivered to the USSR, but the type served as an inspiration for a similar conversion undertaken by the Soviet air force.

Single-seat P-39s were converted into two-seat trainers in various units of the Soviet air force on the basis of technical drawings prepared in TsNEB VVS (*Tsen**trahl**'naya naoo**chno**-eksperimen**tahl'**naya **bah**za Vo**yen**no-voz**doosh**nykh sil*; the Air Force's Central Scientific & Experimental Base) in the town of Lyubertsy (Moscow Region). (TsNEB VVS was later renamed

NII ERAT VVS, *Nao**och**no-is**sled**ovatel'skiy insti**toot** eksplua-**tah**tsiï i re**mon**ta aviatsi**on**noy **tekh**niki Vo**yen**no-vozdooshnykh sil*; the Air Force Research Institute for Operation and Repair of Aviation Materiel.) These machines had a second cockpit installed in front of the standard one, in similar fashion to the US-manufactured TP-39. Externally they differed from their American counterpart in having some additional elements of the new cockpit's canopy framing. Individual aircraft had subtle differences in regard to the shape of the additional ventral strake and the shape and size of the additional fin fillet. Some sources refer to them (somewhat incorrectly) as TP-39, but one may encounter the local designation UTI P-39N (*oo**cheb**no-treni**ro**-vochnyy istre**bi**tel'*; fighter-trainer), rendered rather strangely as 'УТИ P-39N,' with a mix of Cyrillic and Roman letters. At least one such converted two-seater was tested at NII VVS. This version was not exactly popular with the pilots, as witnessed by the comments of V. P. Voronov, who flew this machine in the 6th GvIAP after the war. He reminisced: *'The "hybrid" coped with its task, but the pilot felt very uncomfortable in the front cockpit: the propeller was rotating at a distance of some 40 centimetres* [1 ft. 3¾ in.] *from your face. Should you have to bail out in an emergency, there was every chance of being struck by the propeller.'* In reality, this apprehension proved to be unfounded. Vladimir R. Kotel'nikov cites an episode in which the instructor occupying the front seat successfully bailed out from the two-seat UTI P-39 in an emergency, while the trainee pilot did not manage to do the same and was killed.

ABOVE: A P-39 (42-91 . . .) retrofitted with a Bendix MN-26Y direction finder in the Soviet air force's 4th Reserve Air Brigade.

OPPOSITE PAGE: A TP-39Q-20-BE trainer (44-3879) that was demonstrated to Soviet test pilots Aleksey G. Kochetkov and Fyodor P. Suprun at Bell's factory airfield in Buffalo, New York, in April 1944. Similar trainer conversions were undertaken in the Soviet Union as part of the effort to deal with the Airacobra's dangerous spin characteristics.

BELOW: A drawing illustrating a technical proposal by a Soviet engineer to equip the P-39 with rocket-assisted takeoff boosters.

P-39 with Soviet Guns

During the fairly long postwar service of the P-39 in the Soviet air force, the original US armament eventually became

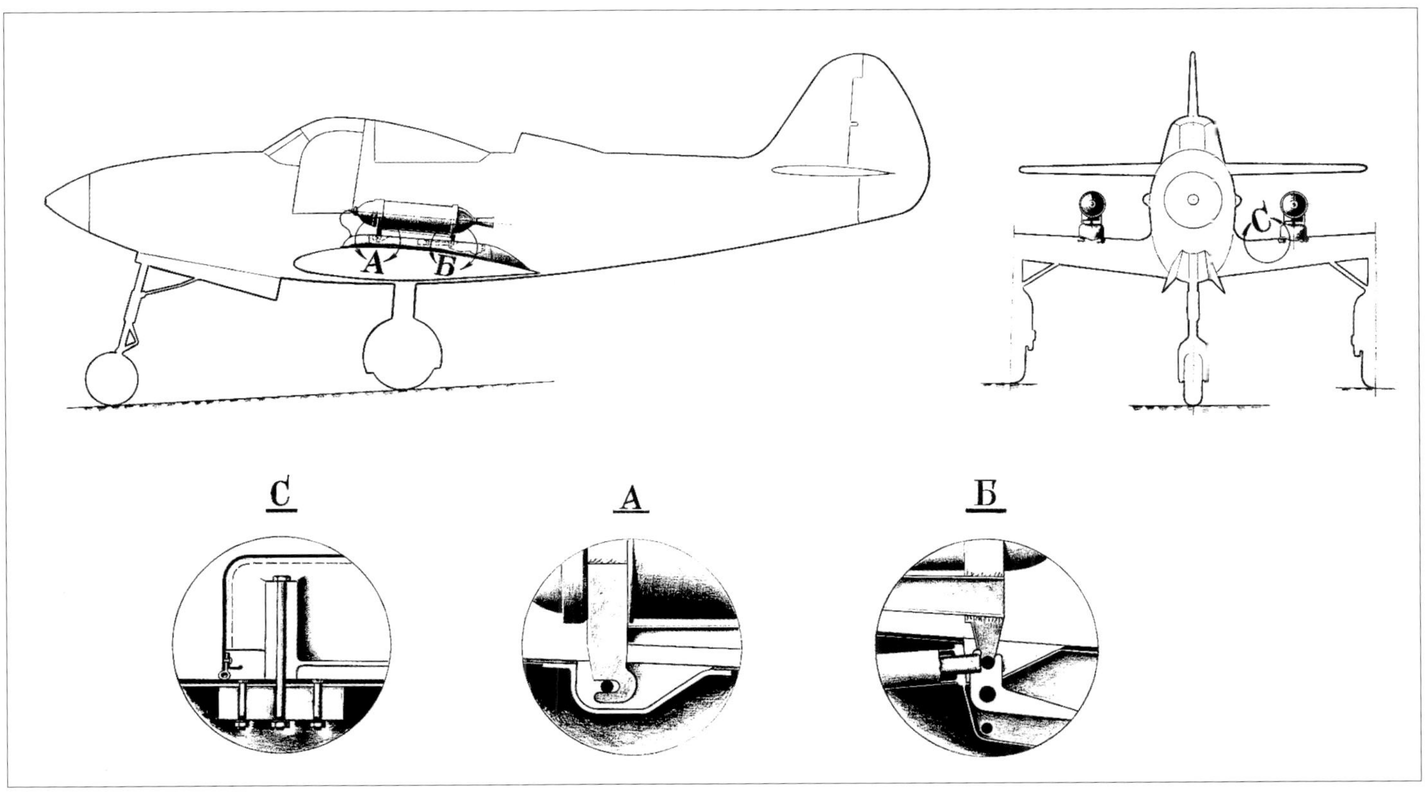

unserviceable. It was then replaced by a Soviet 20 mm (.78 calibre) Berezin B-20 cannon and 12.7 mm Berezin UBS machine guns (*ooniver**sahl'**nyy [poole**myot**] Be**re**zina, sin**khron**nyy*; versatile machine gun designed by Mikhail Ye. Berezin, synchronised).

P-39 (Airacobra I) with Soviet Drop Tanks

The ex-RAF Airacobra Is in Soviet service were occasionally fitted with Soviet 350-litre (92.4 US gallon) PLGB-350 drop tanks. These tanks were introduced on the P-39 in the North Fleet air arm from April to May 1943—first in the 255th IAP, and then in the 2nd GvIAP. The PLGB-350 tanks had a bigger capacity in

LEFT: A P-39 converted to a two-seat trainer in the Soviet Union (the so-called UTI P-39). It is shown here during trials at NII VVS. The shape of the additional ventral strake is similar to that of the US-built TP-39.

BELOW LEFT: Close-up of the tandem cockpits with the instructor's canopy open; note the inset direct vision window on the port side. The design of the canopy frame makes an interesting comparison with the TP-39Q on page 54.

BOTTOM LEFT: Three-quarters front view of the same aircraft. The propeller spinner is somewhat blunter than on the TP-39Q.

RIGHT AND ABOVE RIGHT: Front and rear views of the UTI P-39.

BELOW: Three-quarters rear view of the same aircraft.

The same aircraft as on page 57 is pictured here during a different series of tests at NII VVS. Note the distinctive hexagonal concrete slabs of the hardstand at Chkalovskaya AB, near Moscow, which hosted NII VVS.

This side view shows that the vertical tail area has been further increased by adding a small dorsal fin.

comparison with the standard 284-litre (75 US gallon) drop tank of the Airacobra, making it possible to increase the fighter's endurance to 1.5 hours.

P-39s with Soviet Direction Finders

According to Kotel'nikov, one of the P-39s belonging to the 1st Ferrying Air Division was equipped with a Soviet-made RPK-10 direction finder (***rah**diopolu**kom**pas*; DF). This machine was used as a lead aircraft during the ferrying of groups of single-engined aircraft. Some Airacobras were fitted with direction finders in the US, but apparently the number of such machines delivered to the USSR was very small. A photo shows one such machine (P-39M-1-BE 42-4805) that was fitted with a DF in the US prior to ferrying to the Soviet Union; the DF loop aerial was mounted under the rear fuselage. Another photo shows a similarly equipped P-39Q-10-BE (42-20561) tested at NII VVS. At least one P-39 was fitted with the US-made Bendix MN-26 direction finder in the 4th ZAB.

Rocket-Assisted Takeoff for Soviet Airacobras (Proposal)

An archive drawing shows the installation of two rocket-assisted takeoff boosters (presumably solid-fuel rockets) on the P-39. Unfortunately no accompanying text is available. The cylindrical boosters are mounted above the wing roots on platforms standing proud of the wing upper surface, with electric ignition cables connected to the hemispherical front ends, and are attached by tandem struts fitting into lugs on the platforms. The boosters were to be jettisoned after burnout; an actuating rod was to move an L-shaped lever that secured the booster's rear fitting, releasing the latter, whereupon the spent booster would slide aft under the pressure of the slipstream, and the hooked front fitting would part company with the lug.

Since no mention of this modification has ever appeared in print, there is every reason to surmise this was just a proposal that remained a paper project. On reflection, this is no surprise; judging by the way the boosters were mounted, there was a strong probability of them striking the horizontal tail as they were jettisoned.

CHAPTER 4

Airacobras in Combat

The P-39's Combat Record at the Soviet-German Front

The P-39 provides a classic example of how the same aircraft could earn a totally different assessment from its operators at different theatres of operations. The Allies dismissed the Airacobra as a mediocre aircraft hardly suitable for combat and chose to turn it over to the Soviet Union in large numbers, selecting other fighter types for service with the USAAF and the RAF. Conversely, in the hands of the Soviet air force the Airacobra unexpectedly proved a success. Soviet fighter pilots regarded the P-39 as an aircraft of advanced design meeting that period's combat requirements.

This discrepancy in assessments was in no small measure due to the different tactical environment on the Soviet-German front and on the theatres where the Allies waged war against Germany and Japan. The USAAF and the RAF placed much emphasis on the high-altitude performance of their fighter aircraft, which were often called upon to provide escort for the big bombers used on a mass scale. In contrast, air combat on the Soviet-German front was conducted mostly at altitudes below 5,000 m (16,400 ft.). In

Lt. (JG) V. V. Gabrinets (North Fleet / 19th GvIAP) watches as armourers reload the ammunition boxes of his Airacobra I at Shongui airfield near Murmansk in the spring of 1942.

Airacobra I '60 Red' (serial unknown) in temporary winter camouflage, 28th GvIAP / 239th GvIAD, North-Western Front, the winter of 1942–43.

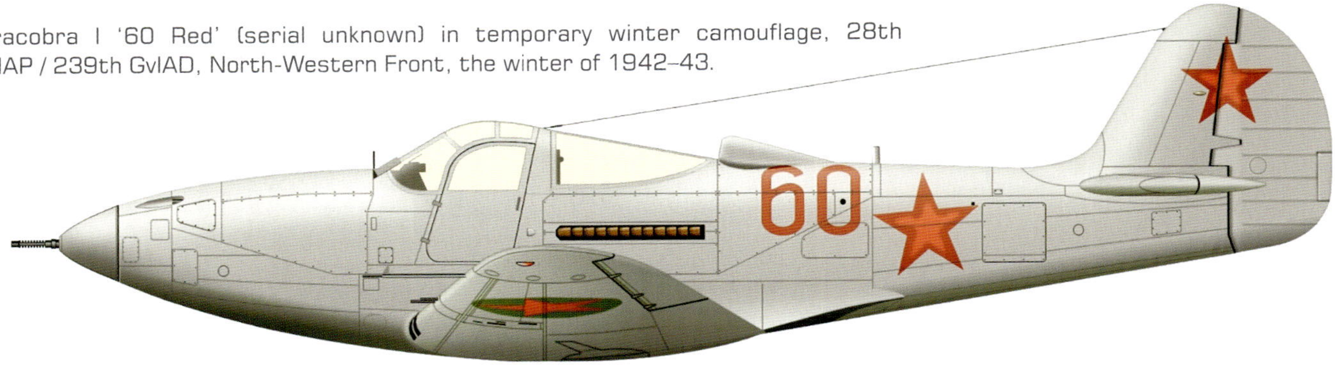

LEFT: This early-model Airacobra (an Airacobra I or a P-39D) appears to wear winter camouflage. Note the mechanic taking a ride on the wing.

BELOW: A Soviet pilot poses with his Airacobra I, coded '12 White.' The white-outlined stars show that the picture was taken in 1942.

these conditions the P-39 was more than a match for the opposing German fighters. Soviet pilots showed their ability to use to their advantage the P-39's strengths: sturdy construction, reliable radio gear, and adequate firepower.

The Red Army Air Force used the Airacobra in several roles. The most common role was to cover or protect ground forces. This entailed patrolling in a zone above a specific Red Army formation and preventing the penetration of German bombers and their escort fighters into that zone. In the course of the war the methods of performing this mission underwent considerable changes. For example, the introduction of air defence radar stations (albeit on a small scale) permitted the fighters to stay on the ground instead of loitering over the area, and to scramble only after receiving notification about an approaching group of enemy bombers.

A second mission for the P-39 was to escort Ilyushin Il-2 attack aircraft or Petlyakov Pe-2 dive bombers during their raids against German troops and installations. The P-39s were intended to protect the Il-2s and Pe-2s from German fighters or to suppress German AA defences. Naturally, the escort missions, as a rule, led to encounters with German fighters and to dogfights in which the fighter versus fighter combat capabilities of the P-39 were put to the test. Interdiction of German bombing attacks led to fighter versus bomber air engagements. Disrupting enemy air transport operations and aerial reconnaissance activities was also among the duties fulfilled by the P-39s.

The two missions described above gave rise to the strategic task of gaining air superiority, initially over certain specific regions, with the overall goal of achieving total air superiority as the war entered the closing phase. This presupposed new methods of air war operations.

One of these was 'free chase' (attacking targets of opportunity), a method that was widely practiced by German aces but initially much less common in the Red Army Air Force. Aleksandr I. Pokryshkin recalled that 'free chase' was initially directed especially against ground targets; steam locomotives were particularly popular as targets for such missions. In 1941–42, elements of 'free chase' were incorporated even into reconnaissance missions—on the way to the assigned area, the pilots tried to attack the enemy. In 1942 Pokryshkin began to practice 'free chase' against aerial targets as well. He recalled: *'We began to employ "free chase" on a particularly wide scale over the Kuban' area, but that was against ground targets. But in the same year of 1943, in the Donbass area, we did the same against aerial targets—the "messers"* [Soviet slang for the Messerschmitt Bf 109s] *and bombers.'*

'Free chase' became popular among Soviet fighter pilots, but Pokryshkin was well aware of the limitations inherent in this method. He stressed that 'free chase' could not exercise a decisive influence on ground operations; in his opinion it was to be regarded as an auxiliary element of gaining air superiority. The decisive role, in his opinion, *'belonged to the total mass of aviation.'*

Yet another mission for the P-39s was reconnaissance, both visual and photographic, although this kind of activity apparently was not practiced on a wide scale.

Finally, an important task for the P-39 was ground attack. Actually, at one time the authors of many Western publications considered this to be the prevalent type of missions for Airacobras on the Soviet-German front. This was not true; yet, undeniably,

ABOVE: Lt. (JG) S. F. Bogatskiy with his Airacobra I.

BELOW: A Soviet pilot looks at his tactical map in front of his early-model P-39. The latter has a light-coloured (unpainted?) cannon bay access panel bearing the unusual tactical code '022 Black.'

Airacobra I AH669 (c/n 14-100), 22nd ZAP/Sqn 1, Kineshma, the first half of 1942; on 20 July 1942 it was wrecked in a landing accident.

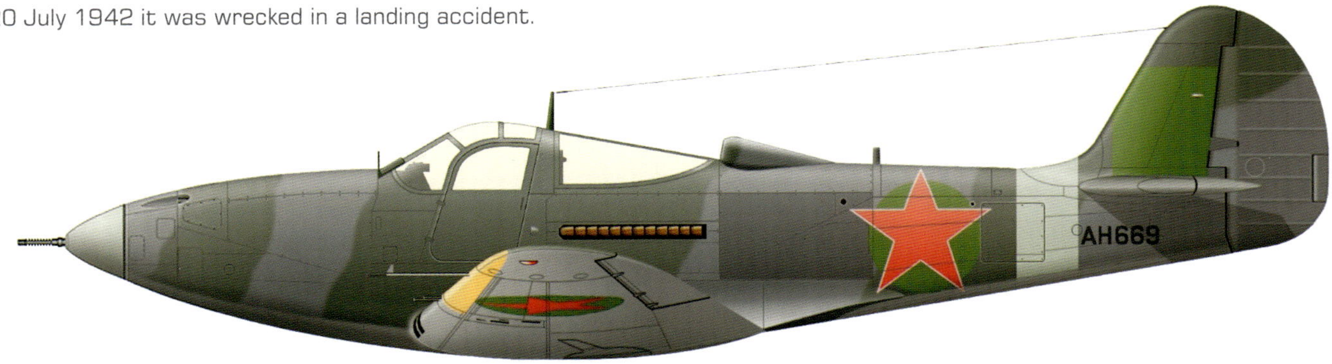

LEFT: Two Airacobra Is are prepared for a mission in a winter setting.

RIGHT: An Airacobra from an unidentified Guards fighter regiment, with the appropriate Guards emblem on the cockpit door. Note the Yakovlev fighter in the background 'photobombing' the picture.

BELOW: Four North Fleet Airacobra Is seen in November 1942; the nearest one is in the BX serial block. In spite of the snow, none of the fighters wear winter camouflage.

Airacobra I AH679 / '35 White'
(c/n 14-110), 19th GvIAP.

This Airacobra I coded '24 Blue' (exact RAF serial unknown) was flown by Lt. (SG) I. V. Polyakov in the 28th IAP / 6th IAK PVO, protecting Moscow and based at Moscow-Vnukovo in the spring of 1942.

LEFT: Airacobra I AH674 / '74 White' (c/n 14-105) lies on its belly after collapsing the undercarriage in a crash landing. The unusual (for an Airacobra, that is) location of the Soviet tactical code is noteworthy.

BELOW: AH669, an Airacobra I of the 22nd ZAP that came to grief when landing at Kineshma on 20 July 1942 with Maj. K. A. Groozdev at the controls. The nose section is wiped out, with the propeller gearbox being separated from the rest of the airframe, and the aircraft looks like a write-off.

the P-39s were used for ground attack or strafing on a fairly large scale. The targets were mainly troop concentrations, road convoys or trains, and airfields. In the naval aviation air units the P-39s were used with considerable success against the enemy's shipping (small warships and transport vessels). However, one of the American researchers, James Gebhardt, makes the following point: *'Contrary to the popular myth, the P-39 was not employed as a "tank-buster" for two very good reasons: the M-4 37 mm cannon was slow firing and had only 30 rounds of ammunition, and the Soviets never received M80 Armor Piercing Shot ammunition through Lend-Lease.'*

It is interesting to cite the judgment passed by the prominent Russian aviation historian Vladimir R. Kotelnikov. He points out: *'In our country* [Russia] *as well, the value of the Airacobra as a*

RIGHT: Airacobra I '12 White' (the RAF serial ends in a '7') overran into a ditch when landing after a training flight at a base near Arkhangel'sk. The unusually small size of the star insignia is noteworthy.

BELOW: This P-39 has 'neither head nor tail,' having lost its propeller and snapped off the tail section in a crash landing. However, the cockpit section is intact, suggesting that the pilot may have walked away from this accident.

ground attack weapon was never contested. As early as the second half of 1943 the P-39s begin to depart from the role of "pure" fighter and become increasingly involved in attacks against surface targets on the ground and in the sea. That can be testified, for example, by the results of combat activities of the 9th GvIAP during February 1944: the losses inflicted on the enemy included 13 aircraft shot down, and the destruction of 110 trucks, 100 horses, five locomotives, and "a large number of the enemy's military personnel."'

The Airacobra packed a powerful punch, which prompted the Air Force Command to use it for ground attack—a role in which the P-39 was very effective. From the second half of 1943 onwards, a growing part of the sorties flown by Airacobras were directed against ground targets. The P-39s were good at disrupting the

enemy's railway traffic, busting locomotives with armour-piercing cannon shells.

Still, it must be emphasised again that the P-39 also proved eminently suitable for air-to-air combat and was used extensively by the Soviet air force against a variety of German aircraft, including Bf 109s, Focke-Wulf Fw 190s, Junkers Ju 87s, and Ju 88s. The renowned Soviet ace Aleksandr I. Pokryshkin flew the P-39 from late 1942 to the end of the war. On the P-39, Soviet pilots scored the highest number of individual 'kills' attributed to any US fighter type in Soviet service.

ABOVE: A 225th IAP signal man waves a flag, clearing a pair of Airacobras for takeoff. The unit's aircraft sported white spinners and white fin caps for quick identification.

BELOW: A row of P-39s at a snowbound airfield. Most are being worked on, but the nearest one appears to be dead and cannibalised for spares. The second aircraft in the row is a P-39Q-25-BE, as the four-blade propeller indicates.

BELOW RIGHT: '02 White,' a North Fleet / 2nd GvIAP P-39M with a drop tank; note the seven 'kill' stars. It later became '14 White' in the 225th IAP.

P-39M-1-BE '02 White', North Fleet/2nd GvIAP, May-June 1943.

Introduction of the P-39 into the Soviet frontline units started in 1942. From 1942 to 1943 the Red Army Air Force alone sent to the front twenty-five air regiments equipped with Airacobras; they were supplemented by air units belonging to the air defence force and the naval aviation. Initially the Airacobras were committed to action on secondary sectors of the Soviet-German front: in the High North and the extreme South. Units based in the northern areas received Airacobra Is, while the units in the Caucasus area started to be equipped with P-39Ds and Ks. In 1942 it was common practice to equip two squadrons of a regiment with the Bell fighters and the third squadron with P-40s. This not only gave no tactical advantages but also created problems with ammunition replenishment, maintenance, and repairs. Hence, in 1943 this practice was abandoned and all three squadrons were equipped with the same type.

From the summer of 1943 onwards, Airacobras were used on practically all fronts of the Great Patriotic War—from the Arctic to the Caucasus. Here are a few episodes of the P-39's combat career at the Soviet-German front.

Several units operating the P-39 were deployed in Karelia and the Murmansk area. For example, one (or more) air regiments of the 6th Fighter Brigade of the North Fleet air arm ensured protection of the Murmansk area and the northern convoys. In the course of 1943, Airacobras were delivered to the 255th IAP and the 2nd GvIAP of the North Fleet. That same year one more large air unit of the Karelian Front—the 258th Composite Air Division—was equipped with P-39s and P-40s. The 19th GvIAP, armed with Airacobra Is, was likewise deployed on the Karelian Front.

The first Soviet Air Force unit with which the Airacobra I saw action was the 145th IAP, which fought on the Karelian Front. In recognition of the valour displayed by the regiment's pilots in that combat, the regiment was given Guards status on 4 April 1942, being transformed into the 19th GvIAP. Its conversion to the Airacobra started in late April 1942, when sixteen Airacobras

P-39D-2-BE 41-38555 / '27 White,' flown by Lt. (SG) Nikolay M. Iskrin (HSU), 16th GvIAP.

16th GvIAP P-39D-2-BE 41-38428 / '37 White,' flown by Vadim I. Fadeyev (see chapter 5) and shot down on 5 May 1943.

arrived in crates at Afrikanda airfield in the vicinity of Arkhangel'sk. Within the next month they were assembled under the supervision of the unit's engineer Maj. P. Gol'tsev. Three weeks after the first training flight performed by Capt. Pavel S. Kutakhov (a future ace and eventually air marshal), on 15 May 1942, Soviet air force 'Cobras had their first encounter with Luftwaffe aircraft, in which neither side scored any 'kills.' The following day, Airacobra I AH660 (c/n 14-91) engaged in a dogfight and was damaged, being declared a total loss after a forced landing. Luckily, the pilot, Lt. (SG) I. D. Gaidayenko, walked away. A month later, on 15 June, it was the Airacobras' turn to draw blood. A group of six Ju 88s, with sixteen Messerschmitt Bf 110s flying top cover, were approaching Murmansk. Six Airacobras scrambled to intercept them. In the ensuing fight, nine German aircraft were shot down, according to reports of the Soviet pilots. The Germans acknowledged the loss of one Ju 88A-4 coded 4D+DR (W.Nr. 0242) of III/KG 30.

On 9 September 1942, one of the pilots of the 19th GvIAP, Lt. (SG) Yefim A. Krivosheyev, gave an example of heroism in performing the first ramming attack on the P-39. Soviet pilots resorted to such attacks in extreme situations—usually after running out of ammunition and when the enemy had to be destroyed at all cost. In the air combat on that day, Krivosheyev, flying Airacobra I BX320 (c/n 14-561), shot down a Bf 109 and then saw that another Messerschmitt was about to attack his squadron commander Pavel Kutakhov from the rear. At that moment Krivosheyev's Airacobra had not a single round in the ammunition boxes. He directed his machine at the enemy fighter and rammed it, saving his commander at the price of his own life. Yefim Krivosheyev was posthumously awarded the title of Hero of the Soviet Union.

The activities of the 19th GvIAP in the Murmansk area were supplemented by the actions of another Airacobra unit, the 20th GvIAP. This regiment (formed on 4 April 1942 by reorganising the 147th IAP) was armed originally with MiG-3s and P-40Es, which were superseded by P-39s. The regiment received the first two Airacobras in April 1943; it is believed that they were either lost or damaged in accidents because they were not listed in the inventory as per 1 August 1943. Introduction of the new type started in earnest with the delivery of 30 P-39N Airacobras in August 1943. Conversion to this type was completed in February 1944, and the regiment retained Airacobras in its inventory until the summer of 1945, when it received late-model Yak-9s. The regiment ensured air protection for Murmansk and the Kirov Railroad between Murmansk and Leningrad in 1942–44, operating from Murmashi AB near Murmansk. In October 1944 the regiment took part in the Petsamo-Kirkenes operation (northern Norway), providing air cover for the Soviet ground troops on the offensive and for the ground attack and bomber aircraft. The P-39Ns were used by the regiment in combat until 13 January 1945, when it was withdrawn from the front. Among the pilots serving in the 20th GvIAP, one may single out Pavel Kutakhov, who fought in the ranks of this regiment between June 1944 and June 1945. He was one of the Soviet fighter pilots who were awarded the title of Hero of the Soviet Union two times (more is said about him in chapter 5).

OPPOSITE PAGE: P-39L-1-BE 42-4608 / '14 White,' flown by ace Ivan P. Stepanov. The rendering of the '4' in the tactical code is a bit odd.

TOP: A pilot explains combat tactics to his buddy beside P-39 '22 White' still wearing ferry markings with a white background.

ABOVE: 129th GvIAP pilot Lt. (JG) Sergey V. Akinshin poses on the wing of his P-39 in 1944. Note the unusual white cannon bay cowl bearing the code '15.' Akinshin became an ace with seven 'kills' but was killed in action over Iassy, Romania, on 30 May 1944.

LEFT: An Airacobra I with 1942-style insignia coded '11 White' (the serial is unfortunately illegible).

RIGHT: A 298th IAP P-39 with the serial ending in '97' undergoes maintenance prior to a sortie on the North Caucasian Front on 12 June 1943.

BELOW RIGHT: A different perspective of the same aircraft. Note the padded walk-way placed by the mechanic on the wing to avoid scuffing the skin.

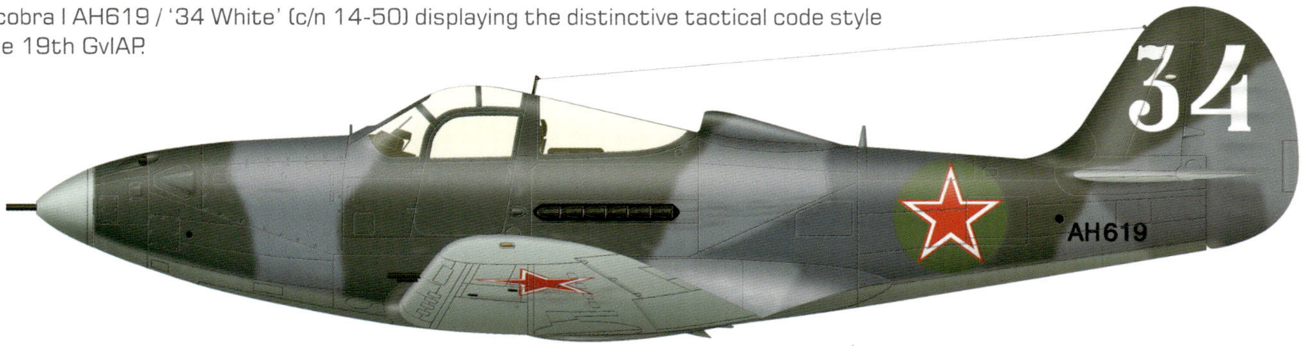

Airacobra I AH619 / '34 White' (c/n 14-50) displaying the distinctive tactical code style of the 19th GvIAP.

P-39D-2-BE 41-38427 / '39 White,' 16th GvIAP, Germany, April 1945.

An early-model P-39 with the USAAF serial painted out, North Fleet / 2nd GvIAP, Vay-enga, the summer of 1943. The aircraft was flown by an ace; the eighteen red stars denote individual 'kills,' and the seven white ones may indicate shared 'kills.'

97

LEFT: An armourer checks that a bomb is securely attached to the centreline rack of a P-39.

BELOW: The command staff of the 20th GvIAP (*left to right*: Chief Political Officer P. G. Grimov, three squadron commanders, and regiment CO Maj. M. V. Semyanistyy) pose with one of the unit's P-39s at Murmashi airfield near Murmansk (now the city's airport) in 1943.

RIGHT: This 57th GvIAP P-39 was seriously damaged in an off-field forced landing.

BELOW RIGHT: Finnish army officers and technicians examine the wreckage of a P-39 that crashed 1 km (0.62 miles) south of Kanneljärvi railway station, Karelia.

LEFT: Soviet pilots serving with an Airacobra unit enjoy a brief lull between sorties, posing with a P-39 coded '55 White.'

BELOW: 102nd GvIAP pilots *(left to right:* Lt. (JG) Zhileostov, Lt. (JG) Anatoliy G. Ivanov, Lt. (JG) Boldyrev, Lt. (SG) Nikolay P. Aleksandrov, Lt. Dmitriy A. Shpigoon, N. A. Kritsyn, and Vladimir Gorbachov) pose with P-39 '33 White.' The lines from a Soviet song ('photographer, position yourself in the middle and take a picture of us all embracing: we could be together for the last time in this photo') held true: Ivanov, Aleksandrov, and Shpigoon all were killed while ferrying a batch of P-39s, crashing in beastly weather when the weather forecast turned out to be wrong.

At the same time, the Kineshma-based 22nd ZAP remained the main unit handling the P-39. This regiment had developed into a major training centre with a well-established training programme and good technical facilities. The unit had four assembly teams, one of which was tasked with assembling 'Cobras.

The 508th IAP was the first unit to start Airacobra conversion training at the 22nd ZAP. However, on completing the training course it was ordered to convert again—this time to the LaGG-3. The reason behind this decision is hard to guess. Later the 508th IAP did convert to the P-39—more on this follows later in this chapter.

A further two regiments that had converted to Airacobras were the 153rd and the 185th IAPs, which were included into the 3rd Strike Group (later reorganised as the 244th Air Division). They were sent to the Voronezh Front, where violent fighting was going

RIGHT: Soviet pilots in heavy winter clothing pose with a P-39 wearing nose art in the shape of a wild cat. Such nose art was not welcome in the Soviet air force, but in wartime conditions the command could stretch a point!

BELOW: The entire flight and ground personnel of the 25th Red Banner IAP pose with one of the unit's Airacobras.

on. The units arrived on the scene of action on 29 June 1942 and joined the fray immediately. In the days that followed, Airacobra pilots claimed sixteen 'kills,' including eleven Ju 88s. There were losses, too—two Airacobras were shot down and one went missing.

The 185th IAP flew 'Cobras only briefly. It underwent conversion to Airacobras at the 22nd ZAP in Ivanovo between 7 April and 9 June 1942 and received twenty machines, forming two squadrons. On 30 June 1942 it was sent to the front and was deployed to Lipetsk, where it was tasked with providing top cover for A-20 Boston bombers and with ensuring the air defence of Lipetsk. In August 1942 it was disbanded and the personnel moved to the 1st PAD (Ferry Air Division), which was to play an important role in the functioning of the ALSIB ferrying route for Lend-Lease aircraft.

19

LEFT: A P-39Q-5-BE coded '19 White' pictured on the point of becoming airborne. The serial is only partly readable (42-201*6) because of the quick-identification stripe.

BELOW LEFT AND FAR LEFT: Usually it was the pilots who got the limelight on wartime publicity photos, but sometimes the photographers felt (quite rightly) that the humble technicians should not be left out either. Here we see an armourer at work on the guns of a P-39; the access panels are off, giving a good view of the nose-mounted 12.7 mm Brownings and their ammunition boxes.

ABOVE RIGHT: A P-39 undergoing engine maintenance.

RIGHT: Not only the lateral cowling panels but also the rear section of the canopy could be detached to provide excellent all-around access to the Allison V-1710 engine, which is clearly visible in this view.

RIGHT: The mechanics seem to be taking their job with a touch of humour here. The open starboard door (the one used for normal cockpit access) gives a view of the interior, including the gunsight and the map case on the inside of the door.

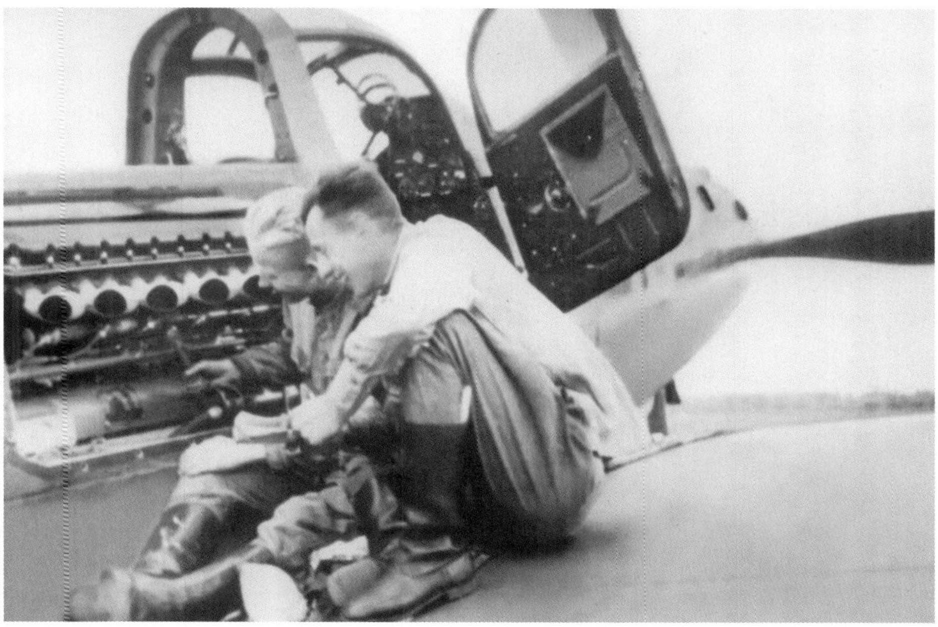

СССР
46
30
96

The 153rd IAP, on the other hand, moved to Lipetsk and continued operations until 25 September 1942. The regiment had received twenty Airacobra Is, including BX182, BX184, BX206, BX228, BX234, BX235, BX240, BX254, BX266, BX268, BX305, BX338, and BX379. Conversion training had taken place at the 22nd ZAP in Ivanovo. On 29 June 1942 the regiment's Airacobras arrived at the Voronezh Front, and on the following day they flew their first combat mission. One group was tasked with providing top cover for Soviet bombers performing a bombing raid; another group was sent on a 'free chase' mission. Detecting a group of some seventeen German bombers, the Airacobras rushed into attack; in the ensuing engagement they downed seven enemy aircraft without loss to their own number.

On 1 July 1942 the 153rd IAP's full complement (twenty aircraft) was committed to action, repelling a raid of fifty German aircraft that attempted to bomb the regiment's airfield near Voronezh. Two days later the Germans made a further bombing raid against Voronezh. In both cases the P-39s attacked the bombers and scored several 'kills'; some of the 'Cobras suffered battle damage and made forced landings. The group's own combat losses amounted to two Airacobras shot down and two pilots severely wounded. One pilot and one Airacobra were lost for noncombat reasons.

The regiment's pilots flew 1,070 sorties on the Voronezh Front, claiming the destruction of sixty-four German aircraft; eight Airacobras were shot down and three pilots were killed in action, three more aircraft were lost, and one pilot was killed in accidents. *'The fact that combat losses are so few is due to the high skill of the pilots and the high performance of the Airacobra fighter,'* the unit's CO Col. Sergey I. Mironov wrote in his report.

On 7 August 1942, in response to a special order of the Red Army Air Force command, the 153rd IAP detailed a task group of eight pilots and twenty-eight technicians who were transferred to the Western Front. In the period between 8 August and 11 September this group operated from several airfields near Moscow, performing 167 combat sorties and conducting sixty-eight aerial engagements in which thirty enemy aircraft were shot down or damaged. This score included nine Ju 88 bombers and four Bf 109 fighters.

At the end of September 1942 the regiment was withdrawn for reorganisation and replenishment; it became a three-squadron unit, with thirty-two Airacobras in its inventory. On 22 November 1942 the 153rd IAP was given Guards status and redesignated as the 28th GvIAP. On 30 October 1942, two of the three squadrons were committed to action, the third squadron joining them in December. Between October 1942 and September 1943 the regiment flew combat missions for the North-Western Front, escorting Il-2 ground attack aircraft, Sukhoi Su-2 short-range bombers, and Pe-2 dive bombers.

On 28 December 1942, a highly unusual episode took place in the unit's combat record. Five Airacobras led by Captain Kislyakov were escorting a Tupolev Tu-2R on a strategically important reconnaissance mission when they were attacked by eight Bf 109s. Despite the Germans' numerical superiority, their attack was a dismal failure—four Messerschmitts were shot down and three more damaged, for no loss to the 'Cobras. Three of the German pilots, after bailing out, were taken prisoners. The pilots of the Aircobras were duly rewarded, but they did not escape being reprimanded for having forgotten in the heat of the skirmish about their primary duty—protecting the Tu-2 (fortunately, it safely returned to base).

Later, in the course of the war, the 28th GvIAP took part in major offensive operations on the territories of Belorussia, the Baltic Sea area, and East Prussia, including the Königsberg operation. Its Airacobras soldiered on until the end of the war and remained in the inventory until 1948.

ABOVE LEFT: The war is nearly over. 19th GvIAP Deputy Commander Lt.-Col. A. A. Boroday addresses the unit's personnel at Salmijärvi (near Petrozavodsk, Karelia) in April 1945.

LEFT: The personnel of the 158th IAP PVO take the Guards oath on 18 September 1943, when the unit became the 103rd GvIAP.

RIGHT: Two lieutenants junior grade pose for a photo with a P-39.

21

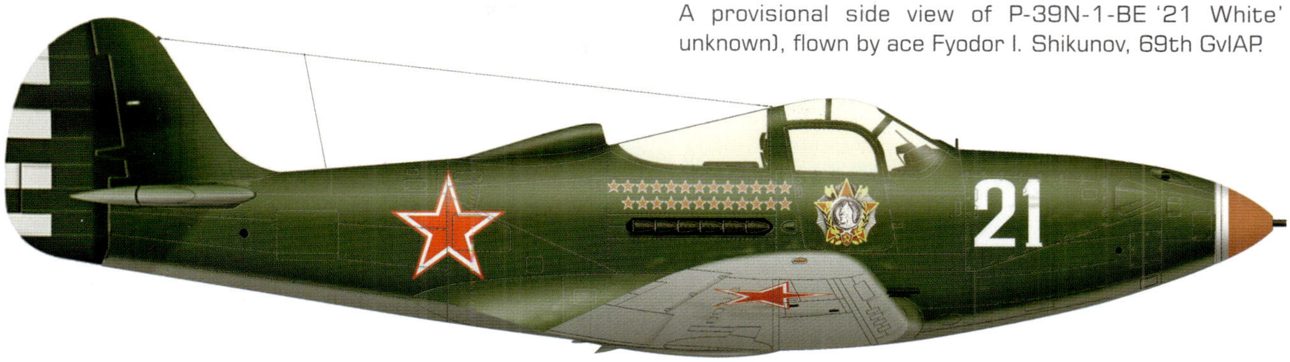

A provisional side view of P-39N-1-BE '21 White' (serial unknown), flown by ace Fyodor I. Shikunov, 69th GvIAP.

Despite initial combat successes, the 'Cobras were scarce on the Soviet-German front in 1942. This was partly due to the cautious approach of the air force command to introducing the newly received P-39s. At that time these were mainly the ex-RAF Airacobra Is, but also a number of P-39Ds that the USSR had ordered directly; only 193 machines were received in 1941–42.

Predictably, the Soviet air force command followed with keen interest the reports from the fronts on combat experience of Soviet pilots flying foreign aircraft. One such report, sent from the Karelian Front by engineer Lt.-Col. Andrey G. Kochetkov in late September 1942, stated that in comparison with other US fighters *'the Airacobra clearly shows the best combat results. Even young pilots flying it successfully oppose Bf 109E and Bf 109F fighters.'* The air force command requested that deliveries of the Curtiss P-40B Tomahawk and P-40E Kittyhawk be reduced and that deliveries of the Airacobra be increased instead.

Stalin's reaction to these recommendations was prompt. On 7 October 1942 he addressed President Franklin D. Roosevelt with a message in which he spoke of an urgent need to increase the deliveries of up-to-date fighters, *'notably the Airacobra.'* Stalin went on to request that deliveries of P-39s be increased to 500 aircraft per month. The US president chose to pay heed to this request; he promised to increase P-39 production at the expense of other types and send some of the 'Cobras to the USSR. He was as good as his word: in 1943, Soviet air force units alone (not counting naval aviation units) received 2,627 Airacobras.

The heyday of the Airacobras came in the spring of 1943. In the period from late April to early June 1943, a part of southern Russia adjoining the North Caucasus and the Sea of Azov and known as the Kuban' area (after the Kuban' River) became a scene of fierce air battles. The Soviet command's plan envisaged gaining local air superiority above the bridgehead of German troops in the Kuban' area in order to render effective assistance to Soviet ground troops on the offensive. Both sides amassed large numbers of aircraft; in all, more than 2,000 machines. The Red Army Air Force units were equipped mostly with the latest Soviet types, supplemented by Lend-Lease aircraft accounting for 11 percent of the total number. Several units equipped with P-39s were committed to action in the course of the Kuban' battle. These units, belonging to the 4th and 5th Air Armies, were opposed by a Luftwaffe task force formed on the basis of the 4th *Luftflotte*. The German air units were staffed with aces and equipped with

ABOVE LEFT: 69th GvIAP squadron commander with the Guards, Capt. Fyodor I. Shikunov poses for a publicity photo with his P-39N-1-BE, adorned with twenty-one 'kill' stars and the Order of Aleksandr Nevskiy on the cockpit door.

LEFT: Fyodor Shikunov exchanges a few words with his mechanic as he puts on his parachute before a sortie.

RIGHT: Another view of Shikunov in the cockpit of his Airacobra. The 69th GvIAP was then waging war at the 1st Ukrainian Front.

'103 White,' a P-39Q of the 213th GvIAP.

LEFT: A mechanic sitting astride the nose of this P-39 points out something in the sky to his pilot—perhaps another of the unit's aircraft returning home. The P-39 belongs to a Guards unit and wears the appropriate emblem, together with the Order of Aleksandr Nevskiy, on the port door. The pilot is an ace with nine individual 'kills' and one shared 'kill.'

RIGHT: North Fleet air arm P-39s at Vayenga AB, with a GAZ-61-73 staff car in the background. The serials are unfortunately deleted, but the large nosewheels indicate this is a fairly late version of the Airacobra.

LEFT: 213th GvIAP P-39Qs on the flight line of a tactical airfield. All aircraft wear three-digit codes and sport the Order of Aleksandr Nevskiy on the port door.

RIGHT: A different view of the same flight line. The fighters wear the Guards emblem on the starboard door; the white noses and diagonal tail stripes are unit markings. As can be seen here, the 213th GvIAP operated a mix of P-39Q variants with three- and four-blade props.

the latest models of the Bf 109—the G-2 and G-4. Their Soviet opponents were flying Yak-1s, Yak-7s, La-5s, Spitfire Vs, and—notably—Airacobras. The latter type was operated by the 16th GvIAP and 45th IAP, both units reporting to the 216th IAD (*istrebitel'naya aviadiveeziya*; Fighter Division), and by the 298th IAP of the 219th BAD (*bombardirovochnaya aviadiveeziya*; Bomber Division). Each day, thirty to forty clashes with German aircraft would take place over the Myskhako Peninsula and later over the Cossack villages of Krymskaya, Kiyevskaya, and Moldovanskoye. It was during these air battles that the 45th IAP under Lt.-Col. Ibragim M. Dzoosov demonstrated to advantage both the skill and bravery of its pilots and the capabilities of the Airacobras they were flying. April 1943 was the most successful period for the unit. Within a month, Lt. Ivan I. Babak shot down fourteen enemy aircraft, and Lt. (SG) Dmitriy B. Glinka and Sgt Nikolay D. Koodrya scored six 'kills' each. True, there were also losses among the pilots of the 45th Regiment. Yet, the skill and courage displayed by its pilots in combat came as a rude shock to the Germans.

As soon as the fighting in the Kuban' area subsided, four 45th IAP pilots (Boris B. Glinka, Pavel M. Berestenev, Nikolay D. Koodrya, and Dmitriy I. Koval', who had fiftten, ten, eleven, and ten 'kills,' respectively) became HSUs. The unit's CO was promoted to colonel and given command of the 9th GvIAD (*Gvardeyskaya istrebitel'naya aviadiveeziya*; Guards Fighter Division), formerly the 216th IAD, which was given Guards status and renumbered on 17 July 1943. The division was included into the Reserve of the Supreme Command as one of the best air units and was intended to be despatched to the most-critical sectors of the front. In August–September 1943, during the operation for the

13

LEFT: Four 100th GvIAP P-39s run up their engines before a sortie over the Kuban' area on 8 February 1944. '13 White,' the mount of ace Dmitriy B. Glinka, appears to be P-39L-1-BE 42-4480, but this was not supplied to the USSR. In fact, it is P-39K-1-BE 42-4451 with a replacement rudder sourced from the wreck of P-39N-1-BE 42-9480 after the original rudder had been damaged in a collision on 22 October 1943.

RIGHT: 101st GvIAP pilots pose with one of the unit's Airacobras.

BELOW LEFT: North Fleet / 255th IAP Sqn 3 deputy commander capt. Pyotr A. Rassadkin (*second from right*) has a discussion with the pilots of his squadron, who are wearing life vests. Rassadkin earned the HSU title and ended the war as an ace with 13 'kills.'

liberation of the Donbass coal-mining area, the 9th GvIAD provided top cover for the mechanised corps and the cavalry corps that conducted offensive actions on the ground. As for the 45th IAP, it was also promoted to Guards status, becoming the 100th GvIAP on 17 June 1943. Together with other units of the 9th GvIAD, it saw action on all the fronts in the course of offensive operations of the Red Army in 1943–45. Among these, one may mention the Belgorod-Khar'kov operation (the Ukraine), the L'vov-Sandomir operation (Poland), the Berlin operation (Germany), and the Prague operation (Czechoslovakia). Five of the regiment's pilots were awarded the HSU title. These were Pyotr I. Guchok, Grigoriy U. Dol'nikov, Ivan I. Babak, Vasiliy D. Sharenko, and Mikhail G. Petrov.

The P-39s Remained in the Regiment's Inventory until 1952

Special mention must be made of the 16th GvIAP, which can arguably be regarded as the most famous of the wartime units in the Soviet air force. Originally known as the 55th IAP, initially it fought on Polikarpov I-153s, I-16s, and Yakovlev Yak-1s. In late 1942 it was rearmed with the P-39 and operated various models of Airacobras until the end of the war. This regiment, commanded by Aleksandr I. Pokryshkin, had attained the prestigious Guards status even before converting to the P-39; on 7 March 1942 its name was changed to the 16th GvIAP.

In the course of the air combat over the Kuban' area, between 9 and 30 April the unit flew 289 sorties on the Airacobra, claiming the destruction of eighty-one enemy aircraft, including seventy-five fighters. Within the same time frame, eighteen P-39s were shot down or went missing, two more were written off in accidents, and eleven pilots were killed. However, nineteen replacement aircraft were delivered in the same month, and the unit retained operational capability. Even more impressive are the results for the period from 9 April to 20 July 1943—the regiment's pilots shot down 141 enemy aircraft (116 Bf 109s, two Fw 190s, eleven Ju 87s, eight Ju 88s, one Heinkel He 111, two Dornier Do 215s, and one Do 217).

The unit owed both its successes and its fame to the winning tactics worked out and employed over the Kuban'. This was the 'Kuban' ladder' (or 'Kuban bookshelf,' as translated by James Gebhardt)—a multilayer squadron formation where the top pair flew 200–300 m (650–980 ft.) above the bottom pair, and each pair was placed farther away from the sun than the one flying below.

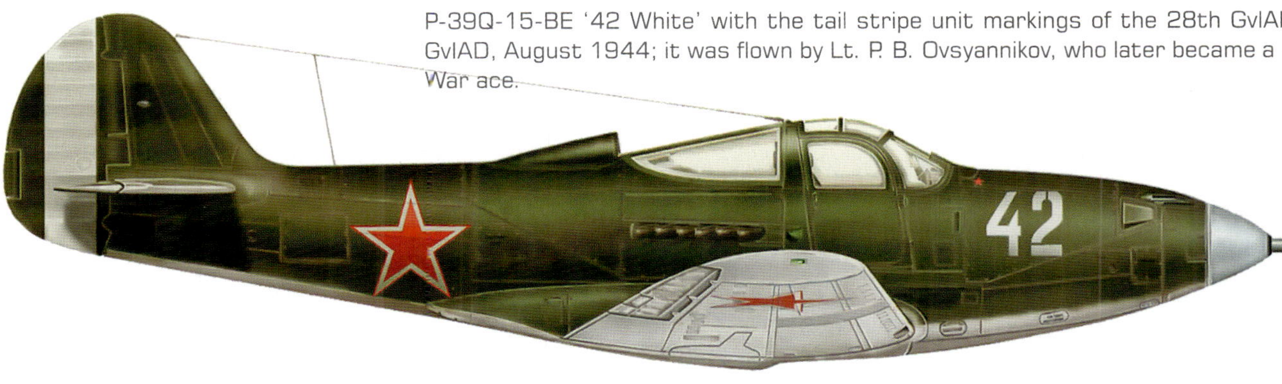

P-39Q-15-BE '42 White' with the tail stripe unit markings of the 28th GvIAP / 5th GvIAD, August 1944; it was flown by Lt. P. B. Ovsyannikov, who later became a Korean War ace.

LEFT: Technicians new to an Airacobra unit are given a lecture on the design and operation of the P-39's Browning M4 cannon (*visible in the foreground*). The lecturer is holding a 37 mm round for the cannon.

BELOW LEFT: A North Fleet air arm P-39Q receives maintenance in front of a makeshift shelter made of camouflage netting.

RIGHT: Taking advantage of a lull in the fighting, the officers of a P-39 unit stationed in the north while away the time playing checkers.

BELOW RIGHT: A similar scene at a tactical airfield in the summer, with two pilots engrossed in a game of chess.

The authorship of this tactical method is somewhat uncertain. In many publications it is directly ascribed to the famous ace Aleksandr I. Pokryshkin. He himself described the situation as follows. Even before the outbreak of the war, he had developed some new methods of air combat, but when the war began, he had to forget about them for a while because of pressure from his superiors, who insisted on strict adherence to established patterns. In 1943, when Pokryshkin was transferred to the Kuban' area, he decided to revive his ideas and introduce novel elements into the methods and tactics of air combat. He was a squadron commander at that time, but he succeeded in convincing his fellow pilots and commanders of the wisdom of his approach. *'I pressed the following point: one must seek the adversary, one must not merely wage defensive combat—on the contrary, one must attack, and attack from above; the combat must be conducted at high speed,'* he wrote.

It took some pains to overcome the resistance. Pokryshkin had a meeting with the 4th Air Army commander, Konstantin A. Vershinin, to which several other commanders of air units were invited. Pokryshkin presented to Vershinin his ideas on the methods of air combat; he was supported by General Yevgeniy Ya. Savitskiy who was also there. After this meeting, Pokryshkin notes, the situation improved considerably. Here he remarks that the pilots of his regiment made use of the method of stacked pairs (later known as the 'bookshelf,' or 'ladder').

It is interesting to compare this with the words of Yevgeniy Ya. Savitskiy, another famous Soviet ace, who commanded the 3rd Fighter Corps of the 4th Air Army and eventually became an air marshal. In his memoirs, titled *Half a Century in the Sky*, he wrote: *'The Kuban,' among other things, became a good school of combat proficiency for the pilots of our air corps. Together with the air warriors of the 4th Air Army, they perfected the methods of combat and the tactics of air battles. It was in those days that a new method came into being and then gained wide acceptance: it was the method of stacking groups of fighters and separating them in*

P-39Q-15-BE 44-2844 / '93 White'

the horizontal plane, which received the name "the Kuban' bookshelf." At present it is difficult to say who should be credited with the authorship of this tactical novelty, which afforded to our fighter aircraft a number of advantages in the assets' deployment and manoeuvring. I just want to mention in this connection Colonel A [Aleksandr] *A. Karyagin, the commander of the 265th Fighter Division, who, together with some other persons, pointed out the usefulness of that kind of combat formations and consistently put this idea into practise until it gained general recognition.'*

An interesting episode highlights the activities of the 9th GvIAD (which included the 16th GvIAP) and of Pokryshkin as

RIGHT: A 191st GvIAP/13th VA P-39 in action on the Leningrad Front undergoes routine maintenance in the summer of 1944. Note the white-painted rudder.

BELOW RIGHT: AOG, Red Army Air Force style. A repair team of the 7th VA has arrived at the scene of a forced landing to recover this damaged Airacobra and return it to flight status.

BELOW: Even when war is on, there are more-pleasurable pastimes than just chess! A 100th GvIAP pilot takes the welcome opportunity to dance with a Soviet Army servicewoman to the tune of an accordion.

LEFT: Lt.-Col. Nikolay G. Sobolev, 21st GvIAP pilot, Guards, with a P-39N bought for him by collective farmworker Klavdiya S. Shumkova. The aircraft was one of three named 'Krasnoyarskiy Komsomolets' (Young Communist League Member of Krasnoyarsk).

BELOW: Nikolay Sobolev thanks Klavdiya Shumkova for his new mount.

RIGHT: 21st GvIAP pilots during P-39 conversion training; Lt. (SG) Viktor N. Yakimov, unit CO, Guards, is second from left. P-39N 42-5023 was one of three named 'Krasnoyarskiy rabochiy' (Worker of Krasnoyarsk).

BELOW RIGHT: All ten P-39Ns bought by raising funds in the Krasnoyarsk Region for the 21st GvIAP.

the division's CO in 1944–45. In February 1945, when the 9th GvIAD was redeployed to Germany as a result of the Red Army's successful offensive operations, a problem arose with finding suitable airfields. Pokryshkin solved the problem in a very unconventional way: he used a stretch of the Berlin-Breslau highway adjoining the Aslau airfield as an airstrip for the division's Airacobras. For quite some time the improvised 'airfield' remained undetected by the Germans, who were trying hard to discover the Soviet fighters' base.

The 9th GvIAD included, among others, the 104th GvIAP, which was one of the units operating Aircobras. The 104th GvIAP was formed on 24 August 1943 on the basis of the 298th IAP. On the eve of this reorganisation, it had converted to the P-39 and was committed to action on the Southern Front, becoming a part of

the 9th GvIAD. The Airacobras remained in its inventory until 1949 and saw action in a series of major offensive operations, including the Belgorod-Khar'kov Offensive, Vistula-Oder Offensive, L'viv-Sandomierz Offensive, and Berlin and Prague Offensives. Nine of its pilots were awarded the title of Hero of the Soviet Union. To name but a few, Vladimir G. Semenishin, Vasiliy M. Drygin, and Vladimir I. Bobrov were known for their impressive score of aerial victories.

Yet another unit among those committed to action on the Southern Front was the 9th GvIAP, whose pilots flew P-39L-1-BEs. This unit, originally known as the 69th IAP, was equipped with LaGG-3s and Yak-1s until mid-1943, achieving impressive

ABOVE: The pilots of the 30th GvIAP / Sqn 3, including ace Lt. (SG) Aleksandr P. Filatov (*leftmost in the first row*), whose mount, P-39Q-5-BE 42-20414 / '93 Yellow,' is in the background. The 'three cards' nose art is an allusion to Aleksandr S. Pushkin's novel *The Queen of Spades*.

ABOVE RIGHT: The unit's entire personnel pose with the same aircraft in Poland in the autumn of 1944.

BELOW RIGHT: 42-08 / '73 Yellow,' another 30th GvIAP P-39Q-5-BE, with the unit's pilots and technicians.

combat results at the South-Western Front and the Stalingrad Front in 1942. From 1 August 1943 it underwent conversion training on P-39s and was committed to action on this type on 17 August.

In August 1943 the unit participated in the offensive that resulted in the breaking-up of the German defences near Molochnaya River and in the liberation of Taganrog. One of the aces who earned distinction in these battles was Capt. Sultan Amet-Khan, later twice HSU and a famous test pilot. In the course of two successive days, on 20–21 August, while intercepting large groups of Ju 88 and He 111 bombers together with his comrades, Amet-Khan shot down three enemy aircraft. It so happened that the air combat in which the ace downed two bombers was watched by Gen. Fyodor I. Tolbookhin, commander of the Southern Front. He immediately awarded Amet-Khan the Order of the Combat Red Banner. (Of the thirty-three personal 'kills' scored by Sultan Amet-Khan during the war, ten aircraft were shot down by him while flying the P-39.) During the nine most action-packed days the 9th GvIAP's pilots flying the 'Cobras destroyed thirty-five enemy aircraft. However, the war luck was not always on their side. In May 1944, during the fierce fighting that preceded the liberation of Sevastopol' and the whole of the Crimea, the 9th GvIAP suffered heavy losses. Of the thirty-nine Airacobras it had at the start of the campaign (including three in nonairworthy condition), five were shot down by enemy aircraft, two more by flak, and two went missing; another two were lost in accidents.

In late May 1944 the 9th GvIAP was withdrawn from the front and started conversion training on a new type—the Lavochkin La-7.

One of the air units that fought on the Airacobras was the 101st GvIAP (the former 84th 'A' IAP, which was renamed in June 1943). The regiment converted to the P-39 in October 1943; from 22 October the 101st GvIAP, with thirty-two machines in its inventory, was incorporated into the 329th IAD, taking part in the Kuban' air battle and in the liberation of Kerch, Feodosiya, and Sevastopol' (the Crimean operation). Opposed by highly experienced pilots from JG 3 'Udet,' this regiment initially suffered some losses but eventually succeeded in achieving air superiority. According to official records, the 101st GvIAP shot down eighty-two enemy aircraft in the Crimean operation. Later, the regiment's Airacobras flew combat missions ensuring air protection for the Poltava hub of shuttle bomber operations conducted by the USAAF

in cooperation with the Red Army Air Force; they took part in offensive operations on the territories of East Prussia, Poland, and Germany (the Berlin operation).

One of the facets of combat experience of the Airacobras on the Soviet-German front was the deplorable fact that that they were not infrequently subjected to 'friendly fire.' Pilots flying the Soviet fighter types (Yaks, LaGG-3s, and La-5s) often mistook the P-39s for German machines and attacked them—sometimes, alas, all too successfully.

Mention must be made of the 21st GvIAP, formed on 3 May 1942 by reorganising the 38th IAP. Starting its combat activities on I-16s and I-153s, superseded by LaGG-3s and Yak-1s, the regiment began conversion training on the P-39 from 1 March 1943. The conversion was started in Krasnoyarsk, Siberia, at the 45th ZAP and was completed in Ivanovo at the 22nd ZAP in June 1943. From August 1943 the regiment was committed to action on the Steppe Front and then fought in the ranks of the 1st Ukrainian Front in the period between October 1943 and May 1945, taking part in several major offensive operations of the Red Army involving the territories of the Soviet Ukraine, Poland (the Vistula-Oder Offensive), Germany (the Berlin operation), and Czechoslovakia (the Prague operation). Among the regiment's pilots who were awarded the HSU title, one may single out Nikolay I. Glotov, who shot down at least thirteen German aircraft while flying the Airacobra (that includes also the period of his subsequent service in the 129th GvIAP).

P-39Q '11 White,' North Fleet / 225th IAP.

P-39N 42-19*93 / '37 White,' 508th IAP; note the fourteen 'kill' markings.

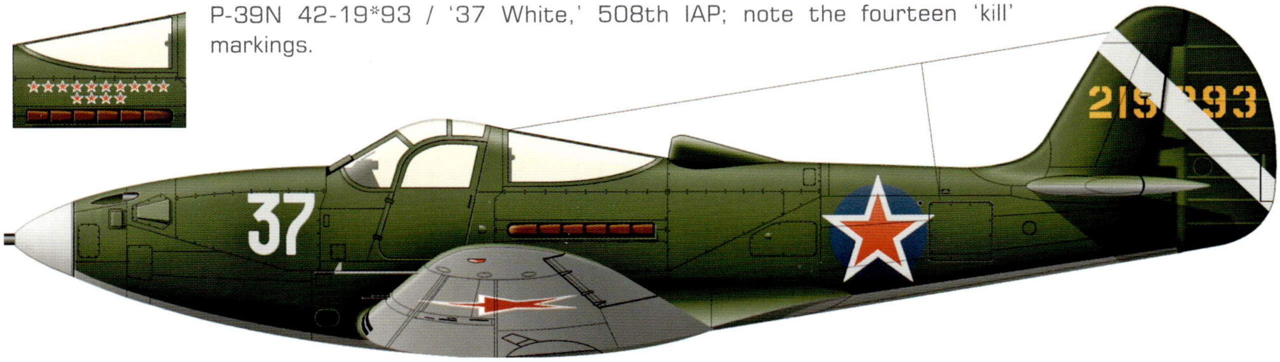

P-39Q '12 White' from the same unit, with seventeen 'kill' stars.

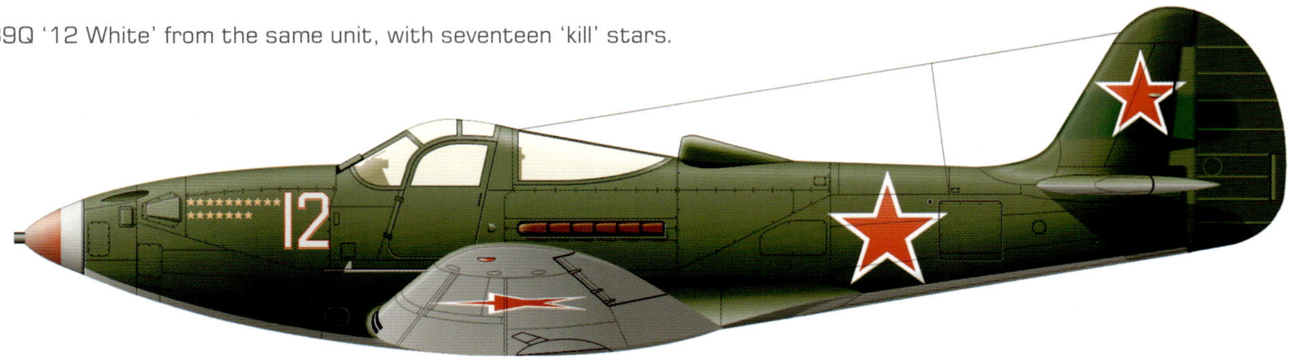

P-39N 42-8787 / '04 White' was one of several flown by Aleksey S. Zakalyuk, 104th GvIAP (see pages 148–49); the nose art depicts an eagle pecking a swastika.

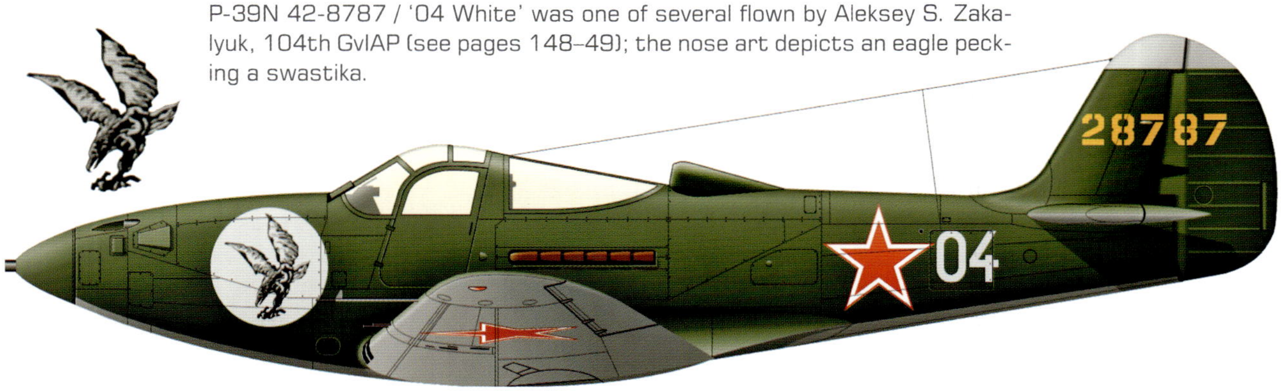

An interesting episode highlights the measure of success achieved by the Airacobra at the hands of Soviet pilots. In October 1943, US ambassador William Averell Harriman remarked in a conversation with Vyacheslav M. Molotov that *'there is one aircraft type, namely the Airacobra, which the Soviet Air Force employs with considerable success. The Russians seem to know how to use it even better than the Americans. It would make sense for Soviet pilots to share their experience with General Vandenberg* [Brig. Gen. Hoyt Sanford Vandenberg, the USAAF's deputy chief of air staff]. . . . *This is why Vandenberg would like to visit the Soviet air force squadrons flying the Airacobra.'* The Bell Aircraft Company expressed a similar request, and the Soviet leaders went

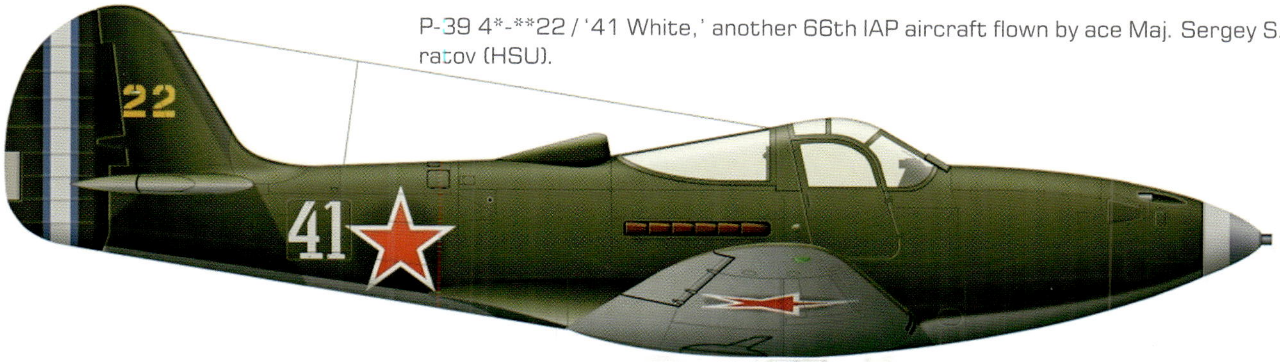

P-39 4*-**22 / '41 White,' another 66th IAP aircraft flown by ace Maj. Sergey S. Pankratov (HSU).

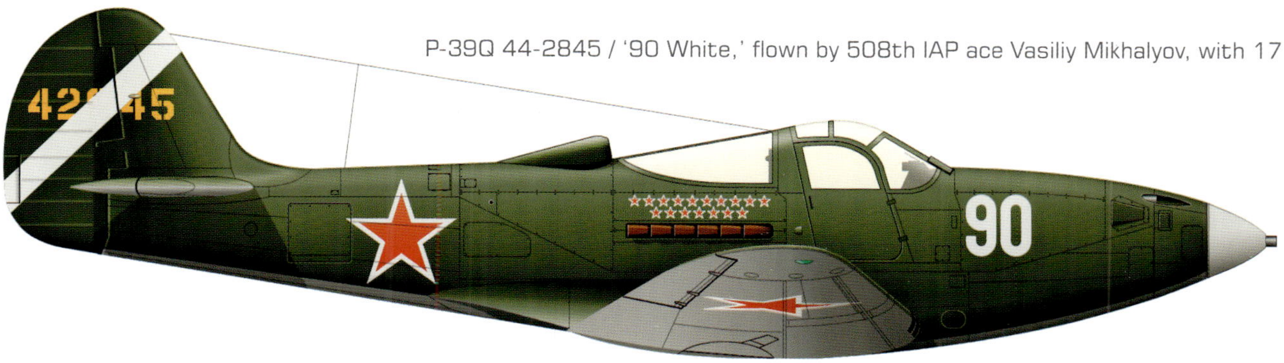

P-39Q 44-2845 / '90 White,' flown by 508th IAP ace Vasiliy Mikhalyov, with 17 'kills.'

along. Gen. Vandenberg and Bell representatives visited the 6th ZAB in Ivanovo, where conversion training was taking place, and two operational units (the 67th and 30th GvIAPs), where they had a chance to hear the Soviet pilots' comments, assessments, and requests concerning the improvements to be introduced.

Among the numerous Red Army Air Force units equipped with the P-39 Airacobra, one can mention several other regiments for the sake of an example. These are the 54th, 55th, and 57th GvIAPs; the 66th IAP; the 494th IAP; and the 67th, 69th, 72nd, and 129th GvIAPs. Here are some facts about them.

The 57th GvIAP was formed on 8 February 1943 on the basis of the 36th IAP, deployed at the North Caucasus Front. Until June 1943 it operated British-supplied Spitfire Vs. On 30 June 1943 the regiment started conversion training on Airacobras and was committed to action on these fighters from 11 September 1943 as part of the 329th IAD. It took part in air battles associated with operations for the liberation of the Crimea Peninsula, as well as in operations in East Prussia and Germany, the final episode being the Berlin operation.

The 66th IAP was formed in 1941and operated Yak-1 and Yak-7B fighters until March 1943, when it was withdrawn from the front for replenishment and conversion training at Adzhikabul in the 25th ZAP. Throughout the rest of the war the regiment flew P-39 Airacobras, being assigned to the 329th IAD of the 4th Air Army. It flew combat missions on the North Caucasus Front and later on the 2nd Belorussian Front, retaining its P-39s until January 1946. Major offensive operations in which it took part include the North Caucasus Offensive, the Krasnodar Offensive, the offensive in the Crimea, the operations in East Prussia and East Pomerania, and finally the Berlin operation. From May to November 1944 it took part in providing air defence for the Poltava air hub at Mirgorod, which was used by the USAAF Boeing B-17s for shuttle bombing raids. The regiment's pilots scored 179 'kills' in the combat over the Crimea; a further sixty-six enemy aircraft were shot down during the period from December 1944 to the end of the war.

The 494th IAP was formed on 10 December 1941 on the basis of the 10th IAP and went into action in January 1942 at the Southern Front. Until early 1943 it operated MiG-3 and Yak-1 fighters. In January 1943 it was withdrawn from the front for reorganisation and reequipment. In March 1943 the regiment underwent conversion training at the 25th ZAP in Adzhikabul and was equipped with P-39s; from May 1943 it was committed to action at the Western Front. Six months later, in November–December 1943, it underwent a new reorganisation in the 22nd ZAP at Ivanovo and was assigned to the Supreme Command's Reserve for some six months. From early June 1944 the regiment took part in military operations on the territories of Belorussia and the Baltic Sea area, retaining Airacobras in its inventory until they were supplanted by Kingcobras in August 1945. Between October 1943 and late April 1945 it took part in several major offensive operations, notably Operation *Bagration* and operations for the liberation of Orsha, Vitebsk, and Polotsk in Belorussia. Next came the Riga and Memel operations, followed by the East Prussian Offensive, including the siege and storming of Königsberg and, finally, the Zemland (Samland) Offensive.

The 67th GvIAP was formed on 18 March 1943 by renaming the 436th IAP. In April 1943 it was withdrawn from the North-Western Front to the Siberian Military District, where it underwent conversion training at the 45th ZAP in Krasnoyarsk and took delivery of thirty Airacobras. From the end of April 1943 the regiment was committed to action reporting at first to the 6th Air

LEFT: A P-39Q coded '31 White' is refuelled by a BZ-35 fuel bowser at a forward airfield.

BELOW RIGHT: P-39Q-25-BE 44-71050, a 212th GvIAP aircraft, is inscribed 'Otomstim za Nikolaya Zhivova!' (We shall avenge Nikolay Zhivov!), in a reference to Lt. (JG) Nikolay A. Zhivov, who was shot down by flak and killed over Germany on 19 April 1945.

Army and from 1 June 1943 to the 16th Air Army. Notable military operations in which the regiment took part include the Battle of Kursk in July 1943; the Oryol operation in July–August 1943; the Chernigov-Pripyat' operation in the Ukraine in August–September 1943; Operation *Bagration* in Belorussia from June to August 1944; several major operations in the territories of Belorussia, Poland, and Germany; and finally the Berlin operation in April–May 1945. Its P-39s soldiered on until March 1947, when the regiment was disbanded. Six pilots of the 67th GvIAP were awarded the HSU title: Vladimir F. Latyshev, Stepan M. Novichkov, Aleksey B. Panov, Igor' A. Fedorchuk, Pavel F. Shevelyov, and Vladimir S. Yeliseyev.

The 68th GvIAP was formed on 18 March 1943 by renaming the 46th IAP. At that time the regiment was operating P-40E Kittyhawks, which had just superseded obsolete I-153s and I-16s in its inventory. In June 1943, in field conditions, the regiment started converting to Airacobras. Between 20 September 1943 and 12 January 1944 the regiment was temporarily withdrawn from active service, but a group of its pilots who had mastered the new Bell machines were sent to the Kalinin Front and flew combat missions there, being seconded to the 28th GvIAP of the 5th GvIAD, which was part of the 3rd Air Army. In the meantime the 68th GvIAP, now reporting to the 5th GvIAD, completed the conversion training and reequipment with Airacobras. From 3 June 1944 the regiment was committed to action again, putting the newly mastered machines to combat test. It took part in offensive operations on the Baltic area. In October 1944 the regiment was awarded the Order of Kutuzov, 3rd Class, for its contribution to the breakup of the German defences southwest of Riga. In April 1945 the Supreme Command bestowed upon the 68th GvIAP the honorary name *Klaipedskiy* ('Klaipeda regiment') to mark its distinguished service in the battles for the capture of the city of Klaipeda (Memel).

The 69th GvIAP was formed on 18 March 1943 by renaming the 10th IAP (a different one from the unit mentioned earlier). At that moment the regiment was conducting conversion training on the P-39 at the premises of the 27th ZAP in Ivanovo. From 30 June 1943 the regiment's Airacobras went into action at the Steppe Front within the framework of the 304th IAD (later renamed as the 23rd GvIAD). The regiment's P-39s flew combat missions until the last days of the war and remained in the inventory until the regiment was disbanded in 1947. Among the numerous operations in which the regiment took part, one can single out the battles that ended in the capture of Krakow by the Red Army. The honorary title *Krakovskiy* ('Krakow regiment') was conferred on the 69th GvIAP to mark its role in that operation. Three pilots of the 67th GvIAP were awarded the HSU title: Pyotr I. Yefimov, Nikolay I. Proshenkov, and Fyodor I. Shikunov (the latter received the title posthumously in 1996).

The 72nd GvIAP was formed on 18 March 1943 by renaming the 485th IAP. This regiment had operated Yak-1 and Yak-7B fighters in the period preceding the renaming and for some time thereafter. In November 1943 the regiment converted to Bell P-39s; from 21 January 1944 its Airacobras took part in combat operations in the Baltic area and in the territory of Belorussia, notably in the Operation *Bagration* offensive (June–August 1944) and in the offensive operations bearing the names of Vitebsk-Orsha, Polotsk, Riga, Memel, East Prussia, Königsberg, and Zemland. Four of the regiment's pilots were awarded the HSU title; two of them deserve special mention because they flew Airacobras. Vasiliy M. Ziborov scored fifteen out of his twenty 'kills' while flying the Bell fighter; Ivan D. Likhobabin shot down fourteen enemy aircraft in a P-39, out of his total score of thirty-two individual aerial victories.

The 129th GvIAP was formed on 9 October 1943 by reorganising the 27th IAP, which had operated a variety of types since the beginning of the war (the I-15*bis*, I-153, I-16, MiG-3, La-5, and Yak-1). In July 1943 it ceded its Yak-1s to the 737th IAP and was withdrawn from the front for replenishment and conversion to Airacobras, which was conducted at the 22nd ZAP in Ivanovo. From 4 October 1943 the 27th IAP was in action again at the Steppe Front as part of the 205th IAD. On 9 October 1943 it received the Guards status and was officially renamed as the 129th GvIAP. Like the 104th GvIAP, it fought on the P-39s throughout the rest of the war and took part in the same offensive operations (see above), ending with the Berlin and Prague Offensives. Special mention may be made of the L'viv-Sandomierz Offensive. The regiment displayed valour and skill in combat; in particular, its excellent results in the battles for the capture of Sandomir (Sandomierz), Poland, earned it the honorary title *Sandomirskiy* ('Sandomir regiment'). From April 1943 the regiment was commanded by Vladimir I. Bobrov, who had started his combat career during the Spanish Civil War. He put this experience to good use at the Soviet-German front, building up an impressive score of 'kills.' At the end of the war he was nominated for the title of Hero of the Soviet Union, but the award was 'blocked' owing to Bobrov's strained relations with his superiors; he was awarded the HSU title posthumously in 1991. Another highly successful pilot of this regiment was Nikolay D. Gulayev, who eventually was awarded the HSU title two times.

The 211th GvIAP was formed on 27 October 1944 on the basis of the 9th IAP, from which it inherited the P-39s. The 9th IAP had operated I-16, I-153, and Hurricane fighters until June 1943, when it started conversion training on the Airacobras. In August 1943 the new machines were committed to action on the front and took part in several major offensive operations. On 27 October 1944 the regiment received Guards status and was accordingly renamed as the 211th GvIAP. Further operations in which the regiment was engaged included the Vistula-Oder Offensive, offensives in Lower and Upper Silesia, the Berlin Offensive, and the Prague Offensive. The Airacobras remained in the regiment's inventory until 1946, when it was stationed in Austria; the P-39s were superseded by P-63 Kingcobras.

The 212th GvIAP was formed on 27 October 1944 on the basis of the 438th IAP, which had consecutively operated LaGG-3, Hurricane, and Yak-7B fighters in 1941–43. From July to September 1943, prior to its renaming, the regiment was reequipped with Bell P-39s, which it retained until 1946. Conversion training took place at the 22nd ZAP. From October 1943 the Airacobras of the 438th IAP took part in several major offensive operations (the Kirovograd Offensive, Korsun'-Shevchenkovsky Offensive, Uman'-Botoshany Offensive, and L'viv-Sandomierz Offensive). From October 1944 until 11 May 1945, already under the Guards title, the P-39s of the 212th GvIAP took part in the following operations: the Carpatho-Dukla Offensive, Vistula-Oder Offensive, Sandomierz-Silesian Offensive, Lower Silesian Offensive, Aerial Blockade of Breslau, Upper Silesian Offensive, Berlin Offensive, and Prague Offensive. Many pilots of the regiment distinguished themselves in combat; six pilots were awarded the HSU title (Aleksandr V. Oborin, Anatoliy A. Grachov, Aleksey A. Yegorov, Nikolay A. Zinchenko, Anatoliy L. Kozhevnikov, and Pyotr A. Rassadkin). After the end of the war the regiment was redeployed to Austria, where its Airacobras were based first at Tulln an der Donau and then at Stockerau and were superseded by Kingcobras in 1946.

The 213th GvIAP was formed on the basis of the 508th IAP on 27 October 1944. In 1941–43 the 508th IAP consecutively operated MiG-3, LaGG-3, and Yak-7B fighters. In July–August 1943 it underwent conversion to the Bell P-39 and was committed to action on these fighters in October 1943, taking part in the Kirovograd Offensive, Korsun'-Shevchenkovsky Offensive, Uman'-Botoshany Offensive, and L'viv-Sandomierz Offensive. After gaining the Guards status the 213th GvIAP took part in the same offensive operations as listed above for the 212th GvIAP, which was natural because the two regiments reported to the same 205th IAD (later renamed as the 22nd GvIAD).

Two Soviet fighter pilots from a unit equipped with P-39s pose together with an American bomber crewman at Poltava, a base used by USAAF bombers making shuttle raids against Germany, in the summer of 1944. The P-39 sports nine 'kill' stars.

BELOW: A 213th GvIAP Airacobra in Germany has an engine change shortly after the end of the hostilities. An ATK-1 Yanvarets cable-controlled mobile crane on a ZiS-6 chassis is used to lift the V-1710 out of the airframe.

Seven pilots of the regiment were awarded the HSU tile. These were Fyodor F. Arkhipenko, Nikolay K. Delegey, Anatoliy I. Svistunov, Aleksey I. Sergov, Nikolay V. Stroikov, Vasiliy P. Mikhalyov, and Pavel I. Chepinoga. Like the 212th GvIAP, the 213th GvIAP was redeployed to Austria after the end of hostilities in Europe, sharing the bases at Tulln an der Donau and then at Stockerau and, last, at Parndorf, where its Airacobras were superseded by P-63s.

The 30th GvIAP also merits a brief mention. It was formed on the basis of the 180th IAP, which had operated I-16, LaGG-3, MiG-3, and Hurricane fighters in 1941–42, taking part in the Battle of Smolensk, the Battle of Moscow, and the action on the Stalingrad Front. On 13 July 1942 it transferred its Hurricanes to the 436th IAP and moved to Ivanovo, where it underwent reorganisation and started conversion training on Airacobras. On 22 November 1942 the regiment received Guards status and was

RIGHT: The crew chief paints another 'kill' star on the P-39 of Lt. (SG) Viktor D. Golushkov (129th GvIAP) after a successful sortie over Germany in the spring of 1945.

BELOW RIGHT: 'Rauchen verboten!' Soviet technicians use the hangar at a captured German airbase to perform heavy maintenance on a P-39Q. The aircraft has a white-painted nose.

renamed as the 30th GvIAP. In March 1943 it was assigned to the 1st GvIAD and was committed to active service, which lasted until 18 July 1943. On that date the regiment transferred seven of its aircraft to the 67th GvIAP and was withdrawn from combat, remaining in the reserve of the 1st GvIAD. In September–October 1943 the 30th GvIAP was engaged in the training of young pilots required for replenishing the frontline units. Starting in November 1943 the regiment was assigned to the Belorussian Front, and from June 1944 until May 1945 it was in action at the 1st Belorussian Front. It participated in several major offensive operations, notably in the territory of Belorussia and in the Berlin Offensive. After the end of the war the regiment retained its P-39s until 1949, being based in the Baltic Military District

The 821st IAP, formed in October 1941, operated Yak-1, LaGG-3, and Spitfire V fighters until the end of September 1943. In October 1943 it started converting to the Bell P-39. This process was completed in June 1944, whereupon the Aircobras remained in the regiment's inventory until the summer of 1945, to be superseded by Kingcobras. Between June 1944 and May 1945 the regiment took part in a number of major offensive operations, including the offensives associated with Vitebsk and Orsha, Riga, Memel, East Prussia, Königsberg, and Zemland (part of Latvia).

The 17th IAP was formed in 1938 and operated I-16, I-153, and LaGG-3 fighters until December 1942. In that month it was withdrawn from the front for replenishment and reequipment and started conversion to the P-39. Available information contains references to several pilots who scored a number of 'kills' flying this type. One of them was Vyacheslav F. Sirotin, who shot down twelve German aircraft in his P-39, his overall score being twenty-one aerial victories. He was awarded the Hero of the Soviet Union title.

The 352nd IAP, formed in September 1941, operated obsolete I-16 fighters until October 1943, when it started conversion to P-39 Airacobras. The regiment's pilots flew these machines until the

A 9th GvIAD P-39 uses a straight section of the Berlin-Breslau highway as a runway in the spring of 1945.

BELOW: The pilots of the 30th GvIAP, with Mikhail P. Rentz leftmost, pose with P-39N-1-BE 42-9553 / '84 White' at Finow AB in May 1945. The aircraft is inscribed Za pogibshikh brat'yev (Revenge for the fallen brothers). Finow later became a base of the Group of Soviet Forces in Germany.

end of the war, taking part in major offensive operations of the Red Army on the territories of Belorussia, Poland, and Germany, including the Berlin Offensive. After the war the P-39 remained in the inventory of the regiment until 1947, when the regiment was stationed in Austria.

The P-39s were used by the naval aviation (AVMF: *Aviahtsiya Voyenno-morskovo flota*) too. In the spring of 1943 they entered service with the 11th GvIAP of the Black Sea Fleet. This regiment received its Guards title on 31 May 1943 (previously it had been known as the 32nd IAP). The unit started mastering the Airacobras in late April 1943. Training of the technical personnel was conducted in Moscow and other bases in the rear, and a group of the regiment's pilots went to Krasnoyarsk, where they received brief conversion training and ferried the new P-39s to Abasha airfield at the Black Sea. By early June 1943 the 11th GvIAP's reequipment with new aircraft was completed. In July of the same year it was committed to action, ensuring top cover for the Gelendzhik naval base and the neighbouring airfields. The regiment was part of the 2nd GvMTAD (*Gvardeyskaya minno-torpednaya aviadiveeziya*; Guards Minelayer and Torpedo-Bomber Division), so it was natural that some of its P-39s were often tasked with escorting torpedo bombers. The regiment's fighters also flew 'free chase' missions, seeking out and destroying aerial targets over enemy-held territory. In the second part of 1943 the regiment scored ninety-two downed German aircraft (a large proportion of them were Junkers Ju 52/3m transports) for the loss of ten P-39s.

In March 1944 the regiment ensured top cover for the attack aircraft of the Black Sea Fleet air arm supporting the offensive of Soviet ground troops at Nikolayev. In recognition of the valour and courage displayed by its pilots, the 11th GvIAP received the honorary title *Nikolayevskiy* ('Nikolayev regiment'). By early April 1944 the regiment was assigned to the 8th Air Army; on 12 April it was redeployed to Odessa and was tasked with ensuring top cover for the city of Odessa and the ground troops in the adjoining area. The Airacobras provided top cover in many large-scale operations of the Black Sea Fleet air arm. Together with the P-39s of the 43rd IAP they took part in the massive air raid against the Romanian port of Constanţa, providing escort for Douglas A-20, Ilyushin Il-4, and Petlyakov Pe-2 bombers. In September 1944 the 11th GvIAP was temporarily deployed to Romania and then to Bulgaria; at that time it had 43 P-39s in its inventory. In October 1944 it returned to a base in the Crimea; between 4 and 11 February 1945, one of the regiment's squadrons flew top cover for Yalta, which hosted the conference of the leaders of three anti-Hitler coalition powers. That became the regiment's last combat mission in the war against Germany.

Several 11th GvIAP pilots were awarded the title of Hero of the Soviet Union. The first to receive this distinction was Dmitriy A. Starikov (January 1944). He was followed by Boris M. Litvinchuk, Vladimir S. Snesarev, Dmitriy V. Zyuzin, Nikolay A. Kislyak, Vladimir A. Narzhimskiy, Viktor I. Shcherbakov, and Yakov M. Ivanov (the latter posthumously).

In November 1944, when hostilities on the Black Sea had come to an end, the Black Sea Fleet air arm had 125 P-39s in its inventory.

In the North Fleet the first unit to receive Airacobras was the 2nd GvIAP, named after Boris F. Safonov—an ace with thirty claimed victories who had been killed in action on 30 May 1942. This regiment was formed on 14 October 1942 by reorganising the 2nd GvSAP (*Gvar**deyskiy smeshannyy aviapolk***; Guards Composite Air Regiment), which had Hawker Hurricane, Curtiss P-40E, and MiG-3 fighters in addition to Pe-2, Tupolev SB, and Ilyushin DB-3 bombers. The bomber squadrons were withdrawn to form a separate air unit, and the 2nd Regiment became a fighter unit. From 15 October 1942 the 2nd GvIAP began to receive P-39 Airacobras, retaining the previous fighter types for some time. By 1 January 1943 the regiment had sixteen P-40s, nine P-39s, and nineteen Hurricanes. The number of Airacobras increased to twenty-four as of 1 April 1943. From 1 June 1943 the P-40Es were gradually transferred to another fighter regiment; instead, the 2nd GvIAP started receiving P-39Ns, which entered the regiment's inventory in the second half of 1943.

In early March 1944, upon completion of the reorganisation and reequipment, the regiment was transferred to the Uzh-Guba airfield, located in the North just 17 km (11 miles) from the front line. Somewhat later, in October 1944, the regiment took part in the Petsamo-Kirkenes Offensive, operating from Ura-Guba airfield. The Soviet Supreme Command took special note of the bravery and heroism displayed by the regiment's pilots in this operation; an order issued by the Supreme Command on 31 October 1944 bestowed upon the 2nd GvIAP the honorary title *Pechengskiy* (a derivative of Pechenga—the Russian name of the town that was known by the Finnish name of Petsamo from 1920 to 1944).

As of 9 May 1945, the regiment stationed at Ura-Guba airfield had forty-three P-39s (all but one of them airworthy) and one airworthy Hurricane in its inventory.

Many of the regiment's pilots were decorated with orders and medals. Special mention must be made of Nikolay M. Didenko, Pavel D. Klimov, and Zakhar A. Sorokin, who were awarded the title of Hero of the Soviet Union.

The 255th IAP, belonging to the North Fleet air arm, also deserves mention. The regiment was formed in May 1941 within the Red Army Air Force as part of the 36th Air Division and was equipped with LaGG-3 fighters; it was based consecutively at several places, including the outskirts of Leningrad in May 1942, and fulfilled primarily air defence duties. In July 1942 the 255th IAP was transferred to the North Fleet and redeployed to Vayenga airbase near the eponymous township in the Murmansk Region (the base and the town are now called Severomorsk). The unit's LaGG-3s were supplemented by Yak-1s in October 1942. In February 1943 the regiment started reequipping with early models of the P-39s, while retaining the Yaks and LaGGs. After additional deliveries, its inventory, as of 1 July 1943, came to include twenty Airacobras of different versions (Mk.1, P-39D-1, P-39D-2, P-39M, and P-39N). Typical missions flown by the regiment included escorting bombers and torpedo bombers. To increase the Airacobras' range, the Soviet pilots started using PLGB-350 drop tanks of Soviet manufacture; this doubled the endurance to 2.5 hours. In the course of 1943 the pilots of the 255th IAP shot down ninety-seven enemy aircraft for the loss of sixteen Airacobras and six fighters of other types in combat. From July 1942 until 26 August 1943 the regiment was commanded by Major Pavel A. Panin, who was killed in action on that day, posthumously receiving the title of Hero of the Soviet Union. In 1944 the 255th IAP became the first unit of the North Fleet air arm to be equipped with Republic P-47 Thunderbolt fighters supplied under the Lend-Lease agreement.

The P-39s flew air cover missions for bombers, warships, and land-based facilities. They also escorted P-40E fighters when the latter flew ground attack missions.

The Airacobra did not serve with the Pacific Fleet's units during the war with Germany. Not before July 1945 were two naval fighter regiments equipped with P-39s transferred to the Far East. These were the 27th IAP from the North Fleet and the 43rd IAP from the Black Sea Fleet. Having a total of one hundred Airacobras on strength, these two regiments were tasked with providing air cover for the Pacific Fleet's bases during the hostilities with Japan. However, Japanese aviation activity was minimal, so the P-39s did not get a chance to add a new page to their war record.

Introduction of the P-39 into the air defence force (PVO: ***Pro**tivovoz**dooshnaya** obo**rona***) units was started on a limited scale. By the end of 1943, there were only sixty-five Airacobras in that service. However, the year of 1944 saw a dramatic increase in the number of P-39s in the PVO system; by early 1945 their number rose to 597. By the end of the war there were eight P-39-equipped regiments in the PVO. As an example, one can mention the 102nd GvIAP PVO (formed in July 1943 on the basis of the

124th IAP PVO). In the summer of 1943 it was equipped with P-39s, which remained in its inventory for several years; in July 1945 they were supplemented by Spitfire IXs and were fully supplanted by the latter type in 1949. Airacobras served in the 713th IAP PVO after the war (in 1949–51). Some PVO regiments had P-39s in limited numbers; this was the case with the 26th GvIAP PVO, which operated a whole series of types consecutively between November 1942 and February 1945, including Hurricanes, MiG-3s, Spitfire Vs, Yak-1s, and Yak-9s. In January 1944 it took delivery of four Airacobras.

Airacobras also served with the following PVO units: the 102nd GvIAP PVO, the 103rd GvIAP PVO, the 266th IAP PVO, the 403rd IAP PVO, and the 908th IAP PVO.

In all, more than fifty regiments of the air force (VVS), PVO, and AVMF operated Airacobras during the Great Patriotic War. The P-39 saw active service on the Soviet-German front until the end of the war. According to Vladimir R. Kotel'nikov, in May 1945 the joint inventory of P-39s in the air force and PVO comprised 3,078 machines (of these, some 700 were in the air defence units). The navy had received 691 P-39s by the end of the war.

The Soviet Pilots' Appraisal of the Airacobra

The P-39 was well liked by VVS pilots, quickly earning a reputation as a sturdy, reliable, and agile machine (especially after part of the heavy armament had been removed). Soviet pilots also liked the guns and the radio system very much (many Soviet fighters of the day lacked radios). The maintenance-friendly design of the Airacobra also made it very popular among the ground personnel. To illustrate the point, here are the opinions of two Soviet aces about the aircraft.

Gheorgiy G. Golubev, who went on to become Hero of the Soviet Union, recalls how the Soviet pilots reacted to the P-39: *'The first impression was rather negative. The aircraft seemed too heavy and sluggish when compared to the nimble Polikarpov I-16. But when we retracted the undercarriage and entered the aerobatics area we quickly found out that the first impression had been wrong. One thing we particularly liked was the radio. For the first time we could maneuver using ground control commands and not the flight leader's signals. The ground controller's voice directing us to the targets sounded like sweet music to us. Now we would give those "messers" the old what-for!'*

The famous Soviet ace Aleksandr I. Pokryshkin, then in the rank of captain and serving with the 16th GvIAP, said: *'It was a shapely aircraft. One thing I particularly liked about the Airacobra was the armament. That was really something to shoot the enemy down with—a hard-hitting 37 mm cannon, two fast-firing heavy machine guns, and four normal-calibre machine guns. . . . I wasn't put off when other pilots warned me that the 'Cobra was dangerously prone to spinning because of a CG located well aft.'*

Fyodor F. Arkhipenko, HSU, wrote thus in his memoirs, *Notes of a Fighter Pilot*: *'By the standards of that time, the Airacobra was a pilot's dream. Its main advantages were the excellent reliable armament and stable radio communication with an insignificant level of static. The armament comprised a 37 mm cannon, two heavy machine guns, and four normal-calibre machine guns. We usually removed the latter because the three-weapon complement was quite sufficient. This machine, however, had a serious drawback: if a connecting rod of the engine located behind the pilot broke off, the rod's fragments severed the control linkages, which frequently resulted in a crash.'*

One of the P-39 pilots, Nikolay G. Golodnikov, who fought in the ranks of the 72nd Composite Air Regiment of the North Fleet (later renamed the 2nd GvIAP), recalls that he flew the Airacobra from November 1942 and that these were initially machines from 'the British order' (apparently Airacobra Is). Later his unit received P-39s delivered from the US via the ALSIB route; these were P-39Qs of various production blocks (he mentions the Q-5, Q-10, Q-25, Q-30, and Q-35—the latter version obviously in error). He goes on to recall: *'I liked the 'Cobra. Particularly the Q-5. This was the best fighter of all those that I had a chance to fly in combat. It was the most lightweight one of the Cobras. . . . After the P-40 the cockpit seemed a bit cramped, but it was comfortable. The field of view from the cockpit was excellent. The instrument panel was very ergonomic, with a complete set of instruments, including a gyro horizon and a radio direction finder. . . . The bulletproof glass plates were mighty thick; the back armour plate was thick too. . . . The oxygen equipment was reliable, and the oxygen mask was quite tiny, covering only the mouth and the nose. The radio was powerful and reliable, a short-wave set. The sound quality was very high both for reception and transmission.'*

Drawing a comparison between the P-39 and German fighters (the Bf 109G and the Fw 190), Golodnikov bluntly stated: *'The 'Cobra, especially the Q-5, was quite a match for all German fighters and was even superior to them. I flew more than 100 combat sorties in the 'Cobra, thirty of them as reconnaissance missions, and conducted seventeen aerial engagements. The 'Cobra was not inferior, whether it be in speed, acceleration rate, or vertical and horizontal manoeuvrability. It was a very well-balanced fighter. It acquitted itself very well in our service.'*

Interestingly, Grigoriy A. Rechkalov, an ace renowned for having scored the biggest number of air victories on the Airacobra, singled out the excellent radio equipment as possibly the most important asset of the P-39. During a mission, he said, the pilots could communicate between themselves as though they were using a telephone; everybody instantly informed other members of the group about any changes, thus avoiding nasty surprises.

The comfortable cockpit of the Airacobra was also duly appreciated by Soviet pilots. In comparison with the cramped cockpits of Soviet fighters, it was more spacious; this was of no small importance for air units stationed in the northern areas, where pilots had to fly in heavy warm clothing during the winter.

Inevitably, Soviet pilots made a comparison between the Airacobra and the indigenous fighters that were in service with the Red Army Air Force. Judging by comments that can be found in memoirs and interviews given by Soviet airmen, they generally agreed that while the P-39 was a good machine, Soviet fighters, especially the Yak-1, were quite on a par with it. Moreover, some pilots were of the opinion that the Yak-1 was actually superior to the American machine in terms of performance and overall combat qualities. In the memoirs of one of the Airacobra aces, Fyodor Arkhipenko, one comes across the description of an episode when the commander of the 3rd Fighter Corps, General Yevgeniy Ya. Savitskiy, staged a mock combat session between

Soviet Air Regiments That Have Operated the P-39 Airacobra

In the following table the first-line regiments are subdivided into three groups: Red Army Air Force, naval air arm, and air defence force. In each group they are arranged in numerical order, with cross-references in the cases of renaming. The table is not exhaustive.

1. Regiments of the Red Army Air Force

Unit identification	Established	Disbanded	Period of operating the P-39 Airacobra	Larger formations incorporating the regiment during that period	Notes
9th IAP *(See also 211 GvIAP)*	10.10.1939	27.10.1944 (reorganised)	June 1943 – October 1944	304th IAD; 23rd GvIAD	Engaged in offensive operations in the Ukraine and Poland
9th GvIAP (ex-69th IAP)	07.03.1942	01.05.1992 (reorganised)	August 1943 – May 1944	6th GvIAD 8th Air Army	Saw action on P-39s in Operation Bagration offensive in Belorussia
10th IAP – *see 69th GvIAP*					
16th GvIAP (ex-55th IAP)	07.03.1942	1949 (reorganised)	December 1942 – the summer of 1945	216th IAD; 9th GvIAD	In action in the Kuban' air battles, the Crimea Offensive, L'vov-Sandomir and Berlin offensives
17th IAP	04.1938	01.06.1959 (reorganised)	Early 1943 – ?	190th IAD	Engaged in operations in Belorussia, the Baltic area and East Prussia
19th GvIAP (ex-145th IAP)	04.04.1942	10.07.1960	May 1942 – 1945	258th IAD; 258th SAD; 1st GvIAD 16th GvIAD	Engaged in operations in Karelia and Murmansk area, in Petsamo-Kirkenes Offensive
20th GvIAP (ex-147th IAP)	04.04.1942	1960?	August 1943 – the summer of 1945	258th IAD; 258th SAD; 1st GvIAD; 16th GvIAD	Engaged in operations in Karelia and the Murmansk area, in the Petsamo-Kirkenes Offensive
21st GvIAP (ex-38th IAP)	03.05.1942	01.03.1947 (reorganised)	March 1943 – March 1947	34th IAD 23rd GvIAD In the framework of the 7th IAK, 6th GvIAK, 5th, 8th, 2nd Air Armies	Engaged in offensive operations in the Ukraine, Belorussia, Poland and Germany. Service in Austria after the war
25th IAP	15.04.1938	08.12.60	December 1943 – 1946	236th IAD	No information is available
27th IAP *(See also 129th GvIAP)*			August-October 1943; converted to the P-39 prior to renaming		
28th GvIAP (ex-153rd IAP)	22.11.1942	09.2009 (reorganised)	March 1942 – 1950?		Engaged in offensive operations in Belorussia, the Baltic area and East Prussia
30th GvIAP (ex-180th IAP)	22.11.1942	06.08.1959 (reorganised)	November 1942 – 1949	1st GvIAD; 273rd GvIAD; 1st GvIAD In the framework of the 16th, 15th, 30th Air Armies	Engaged in the Kursk Battle and offensive operations in Belorussia, Poland and Germany
38th IAP – *see 21st GvIAP*					
45th IAP – *see 100th GvIAP*					
46th IAP – *see 68th GvIAP*					
53rd GvIAP	03.02.1943	?	September 1943 – the summer of 1945?	1st GvIAD (ex-512th IAP) in the framework of the 16th Air Army, 6th Air Army	Engaged in action at the Belorussian Front in June 1944 and in Germany from January 1945
54th GvIAP (ex-273rd IAP)	03.02.1943 (15.05.1941)	10.09.2002 (reorganised)	July 1943 – 1949	1st GvIAD in the framework of the 16th Air Army, 3rd Air Army	Engaged in offensive operations in Belorussia, Poland and Germany
55th IAP – *see 16th GvIAP*					
55th GvIAP (ex-581st IAP)	03.02.1943	?	July1943 – the summer of 1945?	1st GvIAD in the framework of the 16th Air Army, 6th Air Army	Engaged in action in Belorussia in the summer of 1944
57th GvIAP (ex-36th IAP)	08.02.1943	01.06.1978 (reorganised)	June 1943 – August 1946	329th IAD of the 4th Air Army	Engaged in providing top cover for the Poltava hub used by USAAF B-17 and B-24 bombers for shuttle air raids against Germany
66th IAP	16.10.1941	0.6.04.1965 (reorganised)	March 1943 – January 1946	329th IAD of the 4th Air Army	Engaged in the Kursk Battle and in offensive operations in Belorussia, Poland and Germany

69th IAP *(See also 9th GvIAP)*	18.03.1943	March 1947	June 1943 – March 1947	273rd IAD of the 16th Air Army, 2nd Air Army 239th IAD, 315th IAD, 5th GvIAD of the 11th IAK, 5th Air Army	Engaged in action in the Baltic area
69th GvIAP (ex-10th IAP No.2)	18.03.1943 (20.09.1941)	12.03.1947 (reorganised)	March 1943 – March 1947	304th IAD of the 5th Air Army, 23rd GvIAD of the 8th Air Army	Engaged in offensive operations in the Ukraine, Poland, Slovakia and Germany
72nd GvIAP (ex-485th IAP)	18.03.1943	01.12.2009. (reorganised)	November 1943 – September 1948	5th IAD of the 6th Air Army, 3rd, 15th, 64th Air Armies	Engaged in offensive operations in Belorussia, the Baltic area and East Prussia
84th 'A' IAP – see 101st GvIAP					
100th GvIAP (ex-45th IAP)	17.06.1943	06.1960 (reorganised)	June 1943 – January 1949	9th GvIAD reporting consecutively to several Air Armies	Engaged in offensive operations in the Ukraine, Slovakia, Poland and Germany
101st GvIAP (ex-84th 'A' IAP)	17.06.1943	18.04.1947 (reorganised)	July 1943 – April 1947	329th GvIAD reporting consecutively to the 8th and 4th Air Armies	Engaged in action in the Kuban' area, the Crimea, East Prussia, Poland and Germany
104th GvIAP (ex-298th IAP)	24.08.1943	30.06.1976 (reorganised)	July 1943 – April 1947	329th GvIAD reporting consecutively to the 8th and 4th Air Armies	Engaged in action in the Kuban' area, the Crimea, East Prussia, Poland and Germany
129th GvIAP (ex-27th IAP)	09.10.1943	1998 (reorganised)	July 1943 – 1946	205th IAD 22nd GvIAD In the framework of the 5th, 8th, 2nd Air Armies	Engaged in offensive operations in the Ukraine, Belorussia, and Germany. Service in Austria after the war
153rd IAP – *see 28th GvIAP*					
180th IAP – *see 30th GvIAP*					
185th IAP	1941	03.08.1942 (reorganised)	June-August 1942		Saw brief action in air defence of Lipetsk; used for forming a ferrying air regiment for ALSIB
196th IAP	June 1941	March 1960	April-June 1943 Conversion to the P-39	324th IAD	Engaged in action against Finland and in the Petsamo-Kirkenes Offensive 1943-44
211th GvIAP (ex-9th IAP)	27.10.1944	16.03.1947 (reorganised)	October 1944 – March 1947	23rd GvIAD 8th, 2nd Air Armies	Engaged in operations in Slovakia, Poland and Germany
212th GvIAP (ex-438th IAP)	27.10.1944	14.03.1947 (reorganised)	October 1944 – March 1947	22nd GvIAD, 2nd Air Army	Engaged in operations in Slovakia, Poland and Germany
213th GvIAP (ex-508th IAP)	27.10.1944	12.03.1947 (reorganised)	July 1944 – March 1947	22nd GvIAD, 2nd Air Army	Engaged in operations in Slovakia, Poland and Germany Post-war service in Austria
246th IAP (ex-295th IAP)	27.10.1941	06.10.1944 (reorganised)	Conversion to the P-39 in April 1943	215th IAD	In action on other types, P-39s were not operated
273rd IAP – *see 54th GvIAP*					
295th IAP – *see 246th IAP*					
298th IAP – *see 104th GvIAP*					
352nd IAP	12.09.1941	14.03.1947 (reorganised)	Nov. 1943 – March 1947	273 rd IAD 23 rd GvIAD In the framework of 16th Air Army, 2nd Air Army	Engaged in offensive operations in Belorussia, Poland and Germany. Service in Austria after the war
438th IAP *(See also 212nd GvIAP)*	21.09.1941	27.10.1944 (reorganised)	July 1943 – October 1944	205th IAD, In the framework of the 5th, 8th and 2nd Air Armies	Engaged in several offensive operations in the Ukraine and Poland
485th IAP – *see 72nd GvIAP*					
494th IAP (ex-10th IAP No.1)	10.12.1941 (May 1938)	01.09.1960 (reorganised)	1943-1945	11th IAK, 3rd Air Army, 15th Air Army	Saw action on the western front and in the Baltic area in 1944-1945.
508th IAP *(See also 213th GvIAP)*	14.09.1941	27.10.1944 (reorganised)	August 1943 – October 1944	205th IAD; 22nd GvIAD In the framework of the 5th, 8th and 2nd Air Armies	Engaged in several offensive operations in the Ukraine and Poland
512th IAP – *see 53rd GvIAP*					
821st IAP (ex-IAP 'V')	16.10.1941 (reorganised)	1994	October 1943 – July 1945, converted to the P-63	190th IAD 3rd, 15th Air Armies	Saw action in the Baltic area in 1944-1945, transferred to the Far East in July 1945, engaged in the war with Japan

67th GvIAP (ex-436th IAP)	18.03.1943	12.03.1947 (reorganised)	April 1943 – March 1947	239th IAD of the 6th Air Army, 1st GvIAD, 273rd IAD of the 16th Air Army, 2nd Air Army	Engaged in offensive operations in Belorussia, Poland and Germany
68th GvIAP (ex-46th IAP)	18.03.1943	12.03.1947 (reorganised)	April 1943 – March 1947	239th IAD of the 6th Air Army, 1st GvIAD,	Engaged in offensive operations in Belorussia, Poland and Germany

2. Regiments of the Naval Aviation

Unit identification	Established	Disbanded	Period of operating the P-39 Airacobra	Larger formations incorporating the regiment during that period	Notes
2nd GvIAP/North Fleet (ex-72th SAP)	14.10.1942 (18.01.1942)	29.04.1948 (reorganised)	October 1942 – May 1945?	?	Based in the Murmansk area. Engaged in the Petsamo-Kirkenes Offensive in October 1944
11th GvIAP/Black Sea Fleet (ex-32nd IAP/Black Sea Fleet)	31.05.1943	April 1948 (reorganised)	April 1948 – ??.1948	63rd Bomber Brigade/Black Sea Fleet 1st Torpedo-Bomber Div/Blk Sea Fleet	Engaged in action in the North Caucasus and the Crimea, Romania and Bulgaria
32nd IAP/Black Sea Fleet – *see 11th GvIAP*					
255th IAP/North Fleet	05.1941	?	February 1943 – May 1945?	5th Torpedo-Bomber Brigade ??th Torpedo-BomberDiv/North Fleet	Engaged in escorting torpedo bombers in the Murmansk area

3. Regiments of the Air Defence Force (PVO)

Unit identification	Established	Disbanded	Period of operating the P-39 Airacobra	Larger formations incorporating the regiment during that period	Notes
26th GvIAP PVO (ex-26th IAP)	22.11.1942	?	4 P-39s received in January 1944 (in addition to other types)	7th IAK PVO, 2nd GvIAK PVO	
102nd GvIAP PVO (ex-124 IAP PVO)	07.03.1943.	08.07.1960	July 1943 –1951	2nd GvIAK PVO	In action between 07.03.1943 and 15.10.1944
103rd GvIAP PVO (ex-158th IAP PVO)	07.07.1943	04.03.1961 (reorganised)	January 1944 – January 1949	2nd GvIAK PVO	In action in the area adjoining Leningrad and Novgorod in 1944-45
124th IAP PVO – *see 102nd GvIAP PVO*					
266th IAP PVO	08.07.1941		Summer of 1943 – ?	105th IAD PVO 10th IAK PVO	Engaged in providing top cover for troops during operations in the Ukraine in 1943-45
403rd IAP PVO	25.04.1944	17.06.1946	1944-1946	2nd GvIAK PVO	Ensured air defence of Leningrad
212th GvIAP (ex-438th IAP)	27.10.1944	14.03.1947 (reorganised)	October 1944 – March 1947	22nd GvIAD, 2nd Air Army	Engaged in operations in Slovakia, Poland and Germany
738th IAP PVO	19.11.1941	1992	1943 – ?	105th IAD 129th IAD PVO	Ensured air defence of Rostov, Taganrog and Zaporozhye
743rd IAP PVO (ex-348th IAP)	10.01.1942	15.08.1959	January 1949 – October 1951	123rd IAD in 1949-51	The regiment was part of the South-Western Military District's Air Defence
908th IAP PVO	05.04.1943	13.02.1946	Since July 1944	88th IAD PVO 310th IAD PVO 141th IAD PVO The Southern Front, later South-Western PVO Front	Engaged in air defence during the war. Transferred to Hungary after the war

4. Reserve Air Regiments responsible for conversion training of other regiments on Airacobras

Unit identification	Established	Disbanded	Period of operating the P-39 Airacobra	Larger formations incorporating the regiment during that period	Notes
22nd ZAP	26.09.1941	30.01.1946	1942-1946	6th ZAB	At least 10 regiments converted to P-39s
25th ZAP	13.09.1941	01.02.1946	November 1942 – February 1946	4th ZAB	At least 8 regiments converted to P-39s
26th ZAP	January 1942	July 1946	November 1943 – June 1945	4th ZAB	Several regiments converted to P-39s
45th ZAP	1942	1946	Early 1943		One or two regiments converted; in July 1943 reorganised into the 9th PAP for ferrying Lend-Lease aircraft

P-39Q '9 Yellow' seen at an exhibition shortly after the war.

an Airacobra and a Yak-1 with the intention of demonstrating the advantages of the Yak-1 to the pilots of one of the regiments. Savitskiy flew the Yak-1; his 'adversary' was Sergey I. Mironov, the CO of the 153rd IAP, who flew the Airacobra. The combat, which took place above the regiment's airfield, ended in a victory for the Yak-1: Savitskiy managed to get on the Airacobra's tail and stayed glued to it, thwarting all of Mironov's attempts to shake him off. But, of course, in such cases it was the pilot's skill that mattered most in the final count.

Later types of Soviet fighters, such as the Yak-9, La-5, La-7, and Yak-3, were considered to be equivalent and in some respects superior to the Airacobra, but this aircraft retained some special features throughout that endeared it to those who flew the Bell fighter. In February 1944, the then commander in chief of the Soviet air force, Air Chief Marshal Aleksandr A. Novikov, suggested to 16th GvIAP CO Aleksandr I. Pokryshkin that the latter should visit the Yakovlev design bureau and evaluate the Yak-3 fighter that might eventually supersede the Airacobra in the 16th GvIAP. Pokryshkin was impressed by the Yak-3's excellent performance, but its armament (one 20 mm cannon and two 12.7 mm machine guns) appeared to be insufficient for destroying armour-protected bomber aircraft—a task for which the P-39 with its 37 mm cannon was eminently suited. Pokryshkin bluntly stated this fact in a conversation with Aleksandr S. Yakovlev, unabashed by the latter's high standing (in addition to his post of chief designer, Yakovlev was then deputy people's commissar of aircraft industry).

An alternative was the La-7, which was superior to the Airacobra in most respects. Two 20 mm cannons with 130 rpg, coupled with the speed of up to 670 km/h (416 mph) at 6,000 m (19,680 ft.), made it a potent weapon. Pokryshkin, who in the meantime had become the commander of the 9th IAD, agreed to accept the La-7, which he considered to be a good machine. The unit began training flights in preparation for converting to the La-7. It was during one of these flights that Pokryshkin's most highly valued fellow pilot, Aleksandr F. Kloobov, was killed in a landing accident caused partly by the aircraft's malfunction (failure of the wing flaps). Pokryshkin was shaken by the tragic event, which possibly was one of the reasons behind his decision to cancel the reequipment. The proven Airacobras soldiered on in the 9th IAD to the end of the war.

It might be added that the tricycle undercarriage of the P-39, despite all its advantages, imposed some restrictions on the aircraft under the conditions of the Soviet-German front. Some pilots noted that in spring the sodden, unprepared airfields became impassable for the Airacobras for some time, while the La-5 and La-7 fighters retained their ability to fly from the most-primitive mud-covered airstrips.

In general, the Airacobra was a reliable aircraft that met the requirements of contemporaneous warfare and was remembered with affection by Soviet pilots. In fact, it was the most popular of all the Lend-Lease aircraft. Undeniably, the Bell P-39 made a valuable contribution to the activities of the Red Army Air Force on the Soviet-German front.

Several of the Soviet top aces flew the Airacobra during the major part of the Second World War. These included triple HSU Aleksandr I. Pokryshkin and double HSUs Aleksey V. Alelyukhin, Sultan Amet-Khan, the brothers Dmitriy B. Glinka and Boris B. Glinka, Nikolay D. Gulayev, Aleksandr F. Kloobov, Pavel S. Kutakhov, Vladimir D. Lavrinenkov, Grigoriy A. Rechkalov, Nikolay M. Skomorokhov, and Arseniy V. Vorozheykin.

The top-scoring Soviet Airacobra pilot was Grigoriy A. Rechkalov. Of the fifty-seven 'kills' marked on the nose of his P-39Q, fifty were scored when flying the Airacobra. (More on the aces can be found in chapter 5.)

CHAPTER 5

Soviet Aces Who Flew the Airacobra

According to Western publications, the highest number of aerial victories scored in the P-39 Airacobra by an American ace was achieved by William F. Fiedler, a pilot of the USAAF's 68th Fighter Squadron who fought against the Japanese in the Pacific Ocean (the Guadalcanal zone) in 1943. He racked up five victories in the Airacobra before his premature death in an accident.

Soviet aces flying the Airacobra are credited with considerably more impressive results. The highest score achieved by a Soviet pilot on the P-39 is forty-four 'kills' (Grigoriy Rechkalov). The overall number of pilots who were awarded the Gold Star medal and Order of Lenin that went with the prestigious Hero of the Soviet Union (HSU) title for air victories scored while flying the Airacobra approached one hundred. Six of these pilots were awarded the HSU title twice; one Airacobra pilot (Aleksandr Pokryshkin) earned this title three times.

In this chapter we present to the reader in some detail the individual stories of the most-prominent Soviet aces who flew the P-39 Airacobra. We have decided to include about a dozen names of the top-scoring aces according to the overall number of 'kills,' irrespective of the type of aircraft flown (the number of 'kills' related to the P-39 in each case may differ widely).

Soviet aces from the 16th GvIAP at Chernigovka in May 1944. *Left to right:* Lt. (SG) Nikolay L. Trofimov, Lt. Konstantin B. Sookhov, Lt. Aleksandr R. Ivashko, Capt. Aleksandr F. Kloobov, Lt. Grigoriy A Rechkalov, Maj. Boris B. Glinka, and 9th GvIAD CO Aleksandr I. Pokryshkin.

Aleksandr I. Pokryshkin (1913–1985)

Aleksandr Ivanovich Pokryshkin is one of the most famous Soviet fighter aces of the Second World War. He was officially credited with fifty-nine personal 'kills' and six shared victories, ranking second only to Ivan N. Kozhedoob, whose score was sixty-two air victories. Some researchers even traced Pokryshkin's score to seventy-two personal 'kills'—which would make him the top-scoring Soviet ace of all time. He is the only Soviet ace who was awarded the title of Hero of the Soviet Union three times. Importantly, Kozhedoob fought on the La-7, while Pokryshkin flew the P-39 Airacobra and was a staunch adherent of this type. Forty-four of the enemy aircraft he shot down were destroyed while flying the P-39.

A remark must be made at this point. In recent years, several Russian researchers of aerial warfare undertook a revision of the 'kill' statistics achieved by the leading Soviet aces of the Second World War. Ostensibly motivated by the wish to 'establish the historical truth,' they called into question some victories, with a particular bias in the case of Pokryshkin, whom they obviously sought to discredit for some reason. These 'findings' were met

LEFT: Aleksandr Pokryshkin dons his parachute before a sortie early in the war.

BELOW: Aces of the 6th Fighter Corps (Supreme Command Reserve). *Left to right:* Konstantin G. Vishnevetskiy, Nikolay Ye. Lavitskiy, Aleksandr I. Pokryshkin, Dmitriy B. Glinka, 6th IAK CO Maj.-Gen. Ibragim M. Dzoosov, Grigoriy A. Rechkalov, and Ivan I. Babak.

with criticism, notably on the part of the Russian researcher Andrey V. Marchukov. He dismissed as unfounded the 'calculations' of Mikhail Yu. Bykov reducing the number of Pokryshkin's individual victories to forty-six (plus six shared 'kills'), but his own research has led him to put the score at fifty-three individual and six shared 'kills.' At the same time, verification of results achieved by other top-scoring Soviet aces has led to the figures of fifty-six + six for Grigoriy A. Rechkalov and fifty-seven + three (or, according to some sources, fifty-five + five) for Nikolay D. Gulayev, thus placing them ahead of Pokryshkin in the personal ranking. However, as stressed by Marchukov, this does not in any way reduce the magnitude of Pokryshkin's achievements and his very special role as a brilliant fighter pilot, leader, and tactician.

To begin with, here are some basic points of Pokryshkin's biography.

Aleksandr Pokryshkin was born on 19 March 1913 in what was then the town of Novonikolayevsk in the Tomsk Governorate of the Russian Empire (which later became the city of Novosibirsk and a regional centre in its own right). He started his military career in 1932 when he enrolled in the Red Army, taking training as an aircraft technician. Between 1934 and 1938 he served in this capacity in the aviation liaison detachment of an infantry division stationed at Krasnodar. He managed to combine this service with studies in the local aero club in 1936–38. This helped him obtain the consent of his superiors to his transfer to the famous military flying school in Kacha near Simferopol', from which he graduated with excellent results in 1939. Thereupon Lt. Pokryshkin was enrolled as a junior pilot in the 55th IAP (the future 16th GvIAP), assigned to the Odessa Military District. When the war broke out, the regiment was stationed near the border in Moldavia, and Pokryshkin joined battle from the very first day. His first air victory took place on 26 June 1941, when he shot down a Messerschmitt Bf 109 flying a reconnaissance mission. By mid-November 1941 he had flown 190 combat sorties (144 of them were ground attack missions), scoring two individual 'kills' and one shared victory.

From 1942 Pokryshkin's air unit operated on the Southern Front and the North Caucasus Front. At that time Pokryshkin flew the MiG-3 and Yak-1 fighters. From the first days of the war Pokryshkin analysed the tactical methods of air combat then current in the Soviet air force and took a critical view of them, developing his own ideas on the subject. His attempts to put them into practice led to strained relations with his superiors, who resorted to groundless persecution, accusing Pokryshkin of various misdemeanours. In the end, he was acquitted and reinstated in his rights.

In January 1943 the 16th GvIAP underwent reequipment with the Lend-Lease P-39s; Pokryshkin's new mount was P-39D-2-BE 41-38520. In April 1943 he exchanged it for another Airacobra, P-39K-1-BE 42-4421, which, in defiance of superstition, received the Soviet tactical code '13.' On 9 April 1943, during his very first combat sortie in this Airacobra, Aleksandr Pokryshkin shot down a Bf 109. He flew 42-4421 without mishap until 20 June 1943, whereupon this aircraft became the mount of Lt. (SG) A. D. Samsonov, who amended the tactical code to '130'—just in case. Pokryshkin's new mount was a P-39N-0-BE (42-9004), which was coded '100 White.'

Aleksandr I. Pokryshkin before a winter sortie, suitably clad in a fur-lined flight suit and fur boots.

In the fierce air battles over the Kuban' River area in the spring of 1943, Pokryshkin showed excellent combat results. In April he shot down ten German aircraft and was awarded his first Hero of the Soviet Union title. In May 1943 he shot down a further twelve aircraft, supplemented by two in June. On 24 August 1943 Pokryshkin was awarded his second HSU Gold Star medal. By the end of 1943 he had flown 550 combat sorties, conducting 137 aerial engagements and scoring fifty-three 'kills.' It was on the basis of these results that Pokryshkin became the first Thrice Hero of the Soviet Union; the third HSU title was awarded to him on 19 August 1944. Five months earlier he had become CO of the 16th GvIAP.

In June 1944, Aleksandr Pokryshkin was promoted to the rank of colonel and appointed commander of the 9th GvIAD. Under his

command the division took part in several major offensive operations. He flew his last combat sortie on 30 April 1945.

Pokryshkin became a master of air combat thanks to his excellent piloting skills, determination, and courage, but no less important were his abilities as a leader and his gift for devising the most-efficient tactics of air combat. As commander of the 16th GvIAP he succeeded in guiding his fellow pilots in such a way that they, too, displayed their best qualities in combat. Under his command, thirty pilots gained the HSU title; some of them earned this title twice.

In his memoirs Pokryshkin gave vivid descriptions of episodes illustrating his manner and style of aerial combat and his approach to the tactics of aerial warfare. Here are a few examples. In 1943, during combat in the area of Novorossiysk on the Black Sea coast, a flight of four Airacobras commanded by Pokryshkin flew cover for a group of Il-2 ground attack aircraft. After the takeoff, Pokryshkin discovered that his radio receiver was unserviceable; still, he decided to continue the mission anyway. On the approaches to Novorossiysk Pokryshkin and his wingman were attacked by a pair of Bf 109s, but the warning sent over the radio by the wingman did not reach Pokryshkin. By sheer luck he spotted the attacking Messerschmitt at the last moment when the enemy's deadly salvo was imminent. The Bf 109 had latched on to the 'Cobra's tail and was within some 50 m (164 ft.) range. Pokryshkin violently sent his machine into an oblique roll and forestalled the adversary by a fraction of a second—the three-cannon burst of the 'messer' passed below the 'Cobra's wing. Obviously the German pilot was sure he had scored a hit, because he turned his attention to the *Shturmoviks*. Pokryshkin was enraged. He abruptly recovered his machine from the roll and chased the unsuspecting German pilot, catching him in the crosshairs of his gunsight. Before he had a chance to fire, the German, sensing the danger, made a quick roll and went into a vertical dive, with Pokryshkin close on his tail. When recovering from the dive, the enemy fighter was caught in Pokryshkin's gunsight again, and this time two healthy bursts sent the Bf 109 plummeting to the bottom of the sea.

Another episode in 1944 involved repelling a bomber attack on the *stanitsa* (Cossack village) of Krymskaya in the Kuban' River area. The 16th GvIAP's then-current CO Lt.-Col. Nikolay V. Isayev sent a group of eight Airacobras led by Vadim I. Fadeyev (some sources spell his last name as Faddeyev) on a combat air patrol (CAP) sortie over Krymskaya; forty minutes later they were to be relieved by a group of six P-39s led by Pokryshkin. The order they received was very explicit: not a single German bomb should fall on the Soviet troops there.

Pokryshkin had told Fadeyev that he would be ready to come to Krymskaya ahead of schedule if the situation required so. Soon Fadeyev reported over the radio that eight German fighters had

ABOVE LEFT: Aleksandr I. Pokryshkin fills out a flight plan on the wing of his P-39, displaying his impressive score on the gun bay cowl.

LEFT: Here Pokryshkin is seen with his first Airacobra, P-39D-2-BE 41-38520, on 28 May 1943. He is wearing the Guards badge and the Order of Lenin on his flight suit.

arrived on the scene; this meant that the bombers would make their appearance shortly. Pokryshkin immediately ordered his group to scramble. When his Airacobras reached Krymskaya he saw three groups of Junkers Ju 87 Stuka dive bombers approaching the front line, escorted by four fighters. Ordering Grigoriy Rechkalov and the latter's wingman to ensure cover, Pokryshkin led his group of four machines into an attack against the bombers. We shall continue the description in Pokryshkin's own words; the original style is retained:

'We are making a diving attack against the first group of nine machines. Now I have the leader in my gun sight. The Balkenkreuz *insignia are clearly visible. A devastating burst of my weapons—and the Ju 87 is torn to pieces. A second Ju 87 on the right-hand side of the group caught fire after being hit by a burst from* [Vladimir Ye.] *Berezhnoy. We see that the Junkers pilots are dropping their bombs. That's fine; they will fall on the German defensive lines. In the meantime, the bombers, scattering in all directions, made a turn to the West in a diving manoeuvre.*

During a repeat attack against the second group of nine, I downed one more Ju 87. The events followed the same pattern. The panic-stricken enemy pilots dropped their bombs and made off in a westerly direction. The third group of nine [Ju 87s], *having witnessed the fate that had befallen the forward-placed groups, decided not to wait for our attack—they dumped their bombs and headed for the home base. I succeeded in catching up with one more Ju 87 and shot it down with a long burst. Rechkalov's pair, having downed a Bf 109, was continuing a dogfight with three "messers." Under these conditions we could not pursue the fleeing bombers—it was necessary to help Rechkalov. Having noticed our presence, the Messerschmitts disengaged.*

I assembled the group into a battle formation and headed for Faddeyev. Here the situation was repeated. Our arrival made the Bf 109s enter a dive and disengage. . . .

In this action our two groups racked up a total of eleven "kills" without own losses. That appears to be the right way to build up the forces in the course of combat. However, after the landing I got it hot from the regiment CO for starting the mission ahead of time.

—Comrade Commander, if I had delayed the takeoff, we would not have fulfilled your order. The bombs would have fallen on the heads of our troops was my answer.

—This is your only justification. No more unwarranted actions!'

Pokryshkin was an innovator in the tactics of aerial combat; he displayed great perseverance in his efforts to introduce new methods into the combat activities of Soviet fighter aviation. His name is inseparably connected with such formulas as the 'Kuban' bookshelf,' the 'pendulum,' the 'falcon strike,' and many other new features of air combat. Let us give him the word and cite here (in abbreviated form) some of his comments on the subject, taken from his writings.

'Pendulum.' Pokryshkin was strongly dissatisfied with the officially prescribed method of CAP duty, when fighters orbited in large circles over the protected area at a low 'economical' speed. This turned them into easy prey for enemy fighters attacking at high speed. Instead, Pokryshkin introduced a 'roller coaster' manoeuvre in which the patrolling fighters gained altitude and then entered a shallow dive, accelerating to high speed. *'This was*

A still from a wartime documentary showing Aleksandr Pokryshkin immediately after a sortie, his buddies congratulating him with yet another 'kill.'

BELOW: A painted portrait of Aleksandr Pokryshkin in a leather overcoat that was typical of Soviet airmen at the time.

P-39D-2-BE 41-38520 / '100 White,' flown by Aleksandr I. Pokryshkin, 16th GvIAP, 1943.

P-39N 42-9004, which was Pokryshkin's next mount, inherited the tactical code '100 White' from his previous aircraft.

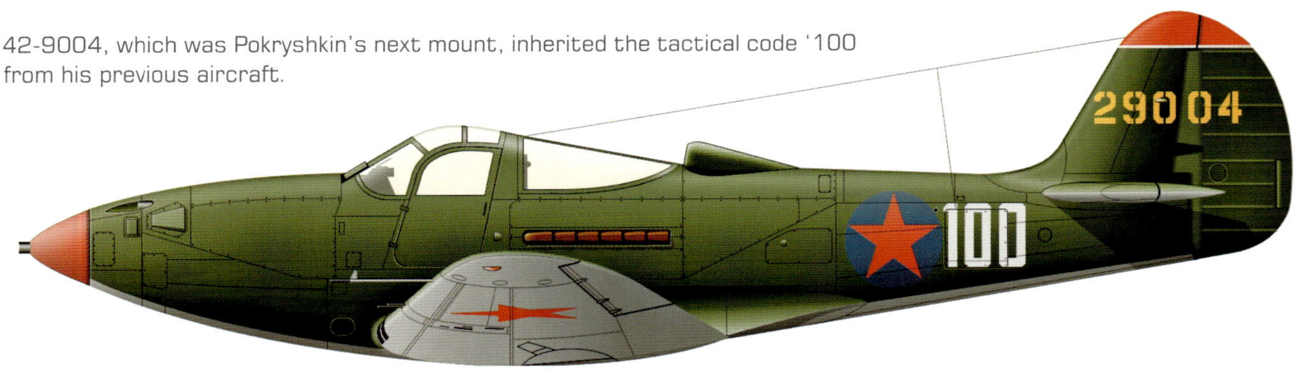

LEFT: Capt. Aleksandr I. Pokryshkin (already Twice HSU at the time) poses for a photo on the wing of his P-39, which has thirty 'kill' stars on the nose.

RIGHT: Aleksandr I. Pokryshkin, now in the rank of lieutenant-colonel and as CO of the 9th GvIAD, is shown with his P-39N in 1944. He was by then Thrice Hero of the Soviet Union; in addition to the three Gold Star medals, he is wearing two Orders of Lenin, three Orders of the Red Banner of Combat, and a foreign award.

BELOW RIGHT: An image of the three Gold Star medals awarded to Pokryshkin.

the essence of the manoeuvre. We achieved a surprise arrival at the protected area and dealt a swift blow against the aerial adversary, should he make an appearance. If need be, we could also quickly gain an advantage in altitude, making use of the speed attained during the descent. If you are flying higher then your adversary you are the master in the air. This was our new method of patrolling based on the principle of a pendulum's movement. It was tactically advantageous and ensured economical fuel consumption in flight.'

'Falcon strike.' Sometimes fighters performed attacks against ground targets with two 100 kg (220 lb.) bombs; the accuracy of this bombing conducted in level flight or in a shallow descent, as prescribed, was very low. Pokryshkin resorted instead to an attack in a vertical dive from an altitude of more than 1,000 m (3,300 ft.). Catching the target in the crosshairs of his gunsight, he dropped the bombs at an altitude of 500 m (1,640 ft.) and hit the target with deadly accuracy. Then he recovered from the dive and left the 'kill' zone of the enemy's AA fire. This 'falcon strike,' as he termed it, was also used with good effect in air combat.

'Bookshelf.' This figurative description (*etazherka*; multilevel bookshelf) was used for the tactic of dispersing pairs of aircraft during a combat mission so that they were spaced both vertically and horizontally, loosely corresponding to what is called the ladder formation. Pokryshkin wrote: *'The battle formation with pairs spaced in the horizontal plane and in altitude resembled the steps of a ladder departing to the side and upwards from the leading pair. This type of group formation ensured greater space for seeking out the aerial target. At the same time it made it harder for the enemy to spot the group. Dispersing the pairs in the horizontal plane and in altitude did not restrict the pilots' freedom of manoeuvre, prevented midair collisions, and, at the same time, made it possible to devote more attention to an all-around search.*

Now there was no need for each pilot to keep a constant vigil over his rear hemisphere. The mutual search conducted by the pairs made it possible to detect the enemy at long range and prevent attacks from the rear hemisphere. The manoeuvrability of the pairs and of the group as a whole was as high as that of a single aircraft.'

Pokryshkin painstakingly perfected the practical use of these methods by the pilots under his command. He recalls how on one occasion he arranged a meeting of the regiment's pilots and presented to them a detailed analysis of the successfully accomplished mission of his six-strong group. *'I shared my thoughts on the patrolling and the battle formation pattern. I recommended to the pilots that they should change the direction of the "pendulum" patrolling from the one running parallel to the front line to the one perpendicular to it, depending on the position of the sun. The sun should always be to the side of the group. I also recommended that the "bookshelf" battle formation should be built up as a "ladder" directed from the leading pairs away from the sun, so that the sun would not interfere with the observation conducted by the lower pairs. The line-of-sight angle between the pairs should be from thirty to forty-five degrees. This allows the pilots to observe each other easily; there is no need to turn the head "to the extremes." The long and short of it was that the pilots should not get unduly fatigued during the search for the enemy and should always be in good shape. In this type of battle formation the horizontal separation between the pairs should exceed the vertical spacing. In today's combat the middle pair of our group kept an excessively big line-of-sight angle. That was a mistake. The consequence was*

that the pilots got overstrained even before entering combat and then acted without due agility during an attack by the Bf 109s.'

Pokryshkin urged novice pilots still lacking combat experience to refrain from defensive tactics. *'A fighter aircraft,'* said he, *'is an offensive weapon. You must conduct combat in a fighter actively, audaciously, imposing your will on the adversary. If you wish to achieve victory in combat, you must base your combat tactics on the formula: "Altitude, speed, manoeuvre, fire." He who has an advantage in altitude over the adversary is the master in the air. Altitude means speed, speed means altitude. In other words, a manoeuvre conducted from high altitude gives speed, and speed makes it possible to gain altitude swiftly. A swift manoeuvre in the vertical plane enables you to deal a surprise blow and creates high rotation rates. The most advantageous vertical manoeuvre is the "falcon strike"—surprising, swift, and precise. Modern combat is combat based on vertical manoeuvre.'*

One of Pokryshkin's principles in organising combat operations was his emphasis on the need to prevent raids of enemy bombers against frontline positions of the Soviet troops. To achieve this, he found it necessary to intercept the German bombers on their way to the front line. On several occasions a group of eight Airacobras led by Pokryshkin performed such interceptions of German bombers in the enemy's rear.

Pokryshkin enjoyed great authority and popularity among his fellow pilots, who duly appreciated his personal mastery in combat, his novel tactical ideas, and his competent and skilful leadership of the groups that flew combat missions under his command. His personal qualities—honesty, readiness to help, and camaraderie—were also highly valued and universally recognised. Many

top-scoring pilots of the 16th GvIAP and of other regiments of his 9th Guards Fighter Division called themselves Pokryshkin's disciples and regarded him as an authoritative teacher of combat tactics.

After the war Aleksandr I. Pokryshkin took up studies in the Mikhail V. Frunze military academy, in Moscow, from which he graduated in 1948. His subsequent service was connected with air defence aviation, where he rose in the ranks to air marshal and consecutively commanded several large units. In particular, from August 1959 he was CO of the Kiev air defence army, and in July 1968 he became deputy commander in chief of the Soviet air defence force. From 1972 to 1981 he headed the DOSAAF voluntary paramilitary technical sports organisation (*Dobrovol'noye obshchestvo sodeystviya armiï, aviahtsiï i flotu*; Voluntary Society for the Support of the Army, the Air Force and the Navy). Air Marshal (Retd.) Aleksandr I. Pokryshkin died on 13 November 1985 at the age of seventy-two.

ABOVE LEFT: Grigoriy A. Rechkalov poses with his P-39N-0-BE (42-8747), showing forty-eight 'kill' stars.

LEFT: 16th GvIAP pilots congratulate Aleksandr Pokryshkin (*centre*) on his freshly awarded third HSU title. The pilots in the foreground are (*left to right*) Leonid I. Goreglyad, Aleksandr F. Kloobov, Vyacheslav A. Beryozkin, Aleksandr I. Pokryshkin, Nikolay L. Trofimov, and S. A. Pyzhikov. However, the P-39 in the background is that of Grigoriy Rechkalov, now with fifty-five 'kill' stars.

TOP RIGHT: Grigoriy Rechkalov in the cockpit of his fighter.

ABOVE RIGHT: Rechkalov's last wartime mount was P-39Q-15-BE 44-2547. Curiously, it was painted identically to his previous P-39N, sporting his initials, 'R.G.A.' (ê.É.Ä.), in lieu of a tactical code and wearing the 'kill' stars in the same fashion. However, the person in the cockpit is Aleksandr I. Pokryshkin, not Rechkalov!

RIGHT: Close-up of the cockpit section, showing Pokryshkin in Rechkalov's fighter. The identification panel on the nose reading 'P-39N-0-BE serial No. AC 42-8747' is visible at the bottom.

LEFT: Grigoriy A. Rechkalov poses in front of his aircraft, showing the two Gold Star medals that went with his two HSU titles.

RIGHT: Another publicity photo of Grigoriy Rechkalov on the wing of his P-39N-0-BE 42-8747, adorned with fifty-five 'kill' stars.

BELOW RIGHT: 16th GvIAP pilots Aleksandr F. Kloobov, Grigoriy A. Rechkalov, and Andrey I. Trood and regiment CO Boris B. Glinka pose for a photo with Rechkalov's aircraft in the summer of 1944. At the time Rechkalov had forty-six individual 'kills' and six shared 'kills,' which may explain the differently coloured victory stars.

Grigoriy A. Rechkalov (1920–1990)

Grigoriy Andreyevich Rechkalov was born in Khudyakovo village (Perm' Governorate) on 9 February 1920. He enrolled in a flying school in Perm' at the age of seventeen and graduated from it in 1939, taking up his duties as a pilot in the units of the Red Army Air Force in the Odessa Military District. In 1941 he was transferred to a fighter regiment based in Bel'tsy (Bălţi), Moldavia. Rechkalov's squadron was still operating obsolescent Polikarpov I-153 Chaika (Seagull) biplane fighters.

Curiously, Rechkalov was colour blind from birth, yet somehow he persuaded the medics to allow him to fly. Eventually in 1941 the medical commission did discharge him as unfit for service. When the war broke out, however, he was drafted again and, much to his surprise, immediately assigned to a fighter unit. When he pointed out why he had been discharged from the air force, the draft man asked him: *'Can you tell an enemy aircraft from a "friendly" one?'* Rechkalov said yes, and the draft man said: *'That's good enough.'* This goes to show how badly fighter pilots were needed.

Within the first week as a wartime pilot Rechkalov flew some thirty ground attack sorties and conducted ten dogfights in his I-153. It was then, on 27 June 1941, that he scored his first 'kill,' downing a Bf 109 with a salvo of 82 mm (3.22 in.) RS-82 unguided rockets. Somewhat later Rechkalov received a Polikarpov I-16 monoplane fighter as his new mount; on this machine he added a Polish-built PZL P-24 fighter (flown by a Romanian pilot) and a Junkers Ju 88 bomber to his score. His subsequent service started with conversion training in a fighter regiment, where he mastered the Yakovlev Yak-1 fighter. Rechkalov managed to return to his unit—the 55th IAP, which by then had been bestowed the Guards title, becoming the 16th GvIAP. During the operations of this regiment on the Southern Front, Rechkalov further increased his combat score, which came to include four personal and two shared 'kills.'

In December 1942 the regiment was withdrawn from the front for the purpose of conversion to the Lend-Lease Bell P-39 Airacobras. In the spring of 1943, upon completion of the conversion, the regiment was deployed to the Kuban' River area. Grigoriy Rechkalov displayed exceptional qualities as an aerial fighter. Being a flight commander in an air squadron led by Aleksandr I. Pokryshkin, he usually commanded a pair in the group of six to eight aircraft led by Pokryshkin during a specific mission. During the battles of the Kuban' River, Rechkalov fought on a P-39D-1-BE and later a P-39D-2-BE (41-38547), sporting the tactical code '40.'

P-39Q-15-BE 44-2547, flown by Grigoriy A. Rechkalov and inscribed with his initials, R.G.A.

Between 15 and 21 April, Rechkalov shot down three Bf 109s and one Ju 88. His score continued to grow. Within the first two weeks of the battle of Kuban' River, Rechkalov personally shot down eight enemy aircraft (seven Bf 109s and one Ju 88) and was nominated for the HSU title. (According to another source, *'during the first two weeks of combat Grigoriy Rechkalov shot down nineteen enemy aircraft; there were three combat sorties, in each of which he shot down two aircraft, and on one occasion he shot down three aircraft in a single action.'*)

In April 1943, Lt. (SG) Rechkalov received a new mount—P-39L-1-BE 42-4603. By May 1943 he had performed 194 combat sorties; in fifty-four aerial engagements he shot down twelve aircraft personally and two as shared victories. On 24 May 1943 he was awarded the HSU title for bravery and valour displayed in combat.

He recalled in an interview: *'My most successful air combat, in my opinion, was the one that took place over the Molochnaya River* ['Milk River,' in the Donbass area of eastern Ukraine], *when I shot down three aircraft; for this I was awarded the Order of Aleksandr Nevskiy. On that occasion my group shot down six aircraft, including the three that were downed by me, without own losses. I was the leader of a group of eight aircraft. We were opposed by eight German fighters and fifty bombers. That was on 14 October 1943'* [in actual fact, on 1 October].

There were further episodes of this kind. In the autumn of 1943 Rechkalov took part in 'free chase' mission over the Black Sea. On that occasion he shot down three aircraft in a single action—two Junkers Ju 52/3m fuel transport aircraft and one Italian Savoia S.55 flying boat.

When Pokryshkin was appointed commander of an air division, Rechkalov became the commander of the 16th GvIAP. However, he was soon replaced in this capacity by Boris B. Glinka; when the latter was seriously wounded in combat, Rechkalov was temporarily reinstated as commander but soon was replaced by another ace—Ivan I. Babak.

By June 1944, Guards Captain Rechkalov, by then holding the post of deputy CO of the 16th GvIAP (which was part of the 9th Guards Fighter Division / 7th Fighter Corps/5th Air Army, waging war on the 2nd Ukrainian Front), had flown 415 combat sorties and taken part in 112 aerial engagements; his score amounted to forty-eight individual air victories and six shared 'kills.' On 1 July 1944, in recognition of his skill in air combats, he was awarded the second Gold Star medal as Twice HSU.

Grigoriy Rechkalov conducted his last aerial combat in the skies of Berlin in April 1945. By the end of the war he became a top-scoring pilot among those flying the Airacobra, with forty-four 'kills' to his credit. Most of them were scored when flying a P-39N-0-BE serialled 42-8747 and a P-39Q-15-BE serialled 44-2547 (sometimes erroneously reported as '42-747' and '42-547,' respectively; the latter aircraft is also reported as 44-2092). Both fighters sported the same distinctive colour scheme; the standard olive-green upper surfaces and light grey undersurfaces were augmented with a red spinner and a red fin cap, the entire port side of the nose was bedecked in 'kill' stars, and the rear fuselage sported the pilot's initials, R.G.A., in lieu of a tactical code. Plane 44-2547 was well known thanks to numerous photos of Rechkalov himself and his fellow pilots, including Pokryshkin, with this aircraft as a backdrop.

Rechkalov's final score was more than 450 combat sorties and 122 aerial engagements; he shot down fifty-six aircraft personally and six as shared 'kills.' This was the official score that was recorded in documents at the end of the war; that made Rechkalov second to Pokryshkin, who at that time was credited with fifty-nine individual victories (reduced to fifty-three as a result of later archive research). Much later, Rechkalov's results were revised by some Russian aviation historians on the basis of new archive studies. Researcher Mikhail Yu. Bykov increases Rechkalov's score to sixty-one + four. Another researcher, Andrey V. Marchukov, gives a slightly different result. He wrote in a publication: *'An outstanding fighter pilot, a great master of air combat, Grigoriy Rechkalov is the top-scoring ace of the 16th GvIAP. All his aerial victories were achieved during his service in this unit. His official combat score at the end of the war was fifty-six individual and five shared "kills." However, it should be borne in mind that it did not include three "kills" achieved by him in 1941* [because the documents of the 45th IAP were lost]. *Only much later it became possible to restore justice and include these victories into his score.'* Marchukov lists Rechkalov's combat score as follows: fifty-nine individual 'kills' plus seven shared 'kills' plus one aircraft shot up on the ground (or 60+6+1, or 60+7—variations reflect the uncertainty of some cases that can be classed differently). Of these, fifty-one victories were scored when flying the P-39.

Importantly, Marchukov stressed in his study devoted to Pokryshkin and his colleague pilots that Rechkalov had achieved his mastery in air combat thanks in no small part to the guidance and tutorship of Pokryshkin; he was universally regarded by fellow pilots as Pokryshkin's disciple (although his ambitions and pride would hardly let him admit this). Pokryshkin, while recognising Rechkalov's talent and combat skill, had a critical attitude to some traits of Rechkalov's behaviour in combat. He reproached him for excessive zeal for increasing his personal score, sometimes forgetting about discipline and mutual protection in the group. This led to strained relations between the two airmen. In an interview given in 1994 (and published much later), Pokryshkin, while calling Rechkalov *'one of the most outstanding pilots,'* said: *'But he has certain aspects that I don't like. He has such a peculiarity: he makes a point of shooting down personally as many aircraft as possible. I make a point of something different; namely, if you enter combat, don't be overly zealous in shooting down enemy planes yourself, but organise the combat in such a way that the group can score more "kills" and so as to prevent the bombing of our sites or troops in battle positions.'*

After the war Grigoriy Rechkalov continued his service in the Soviet air force, retiring in 1959 as Guards air major-general. He died on 22 December 1990.

Nikolay D. Gulayev (1918–1985)

Nikolay Dmitriyevich Gulayev was born on 26 February 1918 in *stanitsa* Aksaiskaya (now the city of Aksai, Rostov Region). He joined the Red Army in 1938, graduating from a flying school in 1940. From July 1942 Lt. Gulayev served in frontline air units as a fighter pilot, flying initially the Yak-1 and later the Yak-7 fighter.

The P-39 flown by Nikolay D. Gulayev, 129th GvIAP; note the white 'scoreboards' and the eagle nose art.

He fought on the Yaks until July 1943; during the Battle of Kursk he shot down seventeen enemy aircraft. In the middle of July 1943 his air regiment was withdrawn from the front to be rearmed with new aircraft—specifically, the P-39N Airacobra. On 9 August that year Gulayev made his first flight in the Airacobra. His very first combat sortie on the new type proved a success—he destroyed a Junkers Ju 87 dive bomber. Two days later he shot down a Ju 88; on the following day he added two Bf 109s to his score, and one more Bf 109 on 29 October 1943. Importantly, Gulayev did not achieve his victories in 'free chase' sorties—most of his combat sorties were classed as ground troops support, sometimes as strafing of airfields or bridges, interception, and reconnaissance.

On 28 September 1943 Nikolay Gulayev was awarded the title of Hero of the Soviet Union for his courage and valour in combat. By that time he was credited with twenty-seven air victories, but his combat score continued to grow. On 1 July 1944 Guards captain Nikolay Gulayev earned his second HSU title, with attendant Gold

Nikolay Gulayev (HSU, *second from left*) explains combat tactics to his wingman Semyon Bookchin (*leftmost*), Leonid Zadiraka, and Valentin Karlov.

BELOW: Maj. Nikolay Gulayev in his colourful P-39 in the winter of 1944. At that time he had a score of 33 'kills.'

Nikolay D. Gulayev's P-39 '2 White,' wearing fifty-three 'kill' stars and appropriate titles.

Star medal. This was the recognition of his combat achievements: 125 successful combat sorties and forty-two aerial engagements in which he had shot down forty-two aircraft personally and three as shared victories. At that time he commanded a squadron of the 129th GvIAP, which was part of the 205th IAD/7th IAK/5th VA (*vozdooshnaya armiya*; air army) waging war on the 2nd Ukrainian Front.

In early September 1944, obeying a strict order, Gulayev was withdrawn from the front lines and enrolled as a student into the air force academy. The outcome of the war was already quite evident, and the military leadership found it wise to protect the famous aces from unnecessary risk by ordering them to take up studies in military academies.

To sum up his wartime combat results: according to the official records, Guards major Nikolay D. Gulayev made 250 combat sorties, took part in forty-nine aerial engagements, and shot down fifty-seven enemy aircraft personally, supplemented by three shared 'kills' (one of the researchers, Mikhail Yu. Bykov, credits him with fifty-five personal and five shared 'kills'). With a mere four combat sorties per one aircraft shot down, Gulayev was among the aces with the highest 'rate of kills.'

Fyodor F. Arkhipenko, one of the aces who flew combat missions together with Gulayev, described in his memoirs one such mission in which they attacked Ju 87 dive bombers escorted by Bf 109s. He wrote: *'I attacked the bombers and shot down one of them. . . . Right after this attack I saw Nikolay Gulayev's fighter approach*

Nikolay D. Gulayev, now Twice HSU, climbs out of the P-39 coded '2 White' he flew at the end of the war. The legend '53 pobedy' (fifty-three victories) is chalked on the nose to mark his then-current score.

RIGHT: The famous brothers Dmitriy B. Glinka (*on the left*) and Boris B. Glinka pictured on 19 July 1944. Both served in the 16th GvIAP, Boris Glinka being the unit CO. Three days earlier Boris Glinka had been shot down, suffering injuries that forced him to give up flying.

a "messer"; Gulayev despatched it with a short burst. In this air combat Gulayev produced a favourable impression. He showed himself to be a true master of high-precision gunnery and of subtle and sophisticated tactics. . . . Gulayev has forever remained in my memory as a cheerful, impetuous fellow, prone to mischievous and often-witty inventions.

Once he took as his wingman a pilot who, putting it mildly, was not noted for determination in attacks. Having encountered a group of enemy bombers, Gulayev caused disarray in their battle formation by his resolute actions, then he radioed to his wingman and gave him an order to advance and attack the rearmost bomber. The wingman obeyed; he moved forward and opened fire at some 200 m [660 ft.] *range.*

"Come closer," Gulayev commented over the radio. To underscore his words, he fired a cannon burst in such a way that the shells traced their path just a few metres from the wingman's cockpit. The wingman got the message at once; encouraged by his commander's determination, he closed in to within 50 m [164 ft] *and shot down the enemy machine with a long burst. In this unusual manner Gulayev made his wingman shake off the fear induced by the tracer streams that the enemy bomber's guns sent in his direction.'*

Nikolay Gulayev took part in combat operations at the Stalingrad Front, Voronezh Front, and the 1st and 2nd Ukrainian Fronts. He fought in the Stalingrad area, near Belgorod, and at the Kursk salient (the famous Battle of Kursk) and participated in the battles for the liberation of western Ukraine, Belorussia, Poland, Romania, and Czechoslovakia. During the war years Gulayev rose in the ranks from a junior pilot to deputy CO of an air regiment. After the war he served in the air defence force, taking training first in the air force engineering academy named after Nikolay Ye. Zhukovskiy (VVIA: *Voyenno-vozdooshnaya inzhenernaya akademiya*) and then in the academy of the general staff. He commanded various PVO units until he retired in 1979 in the rank of colonel-general. Nikolay Gulayev died on 27 September 1985 at the age of sixty-seven.

The Glinka Brothers

The P-39 became the fighter type that enabled two brothers, Dmitriy and Boris Glinka, to show to advantage their excellent skills as fighter pilots. They both graduated from a flying school in 1940 and fought together in the ranks of the 45th IAP from the first days of the war. This air regiment took part in combat operations in the south, in the region of Krasnodar, from late 1942 to early 1943.

Boris B. Glinka (1914–1967)

When the war broke out, Boris Borisovich Glinka, the elder of the two brothers (born on 27 September 1914 in Krivoy Rog, the Ukraine), was a flight commander (instructor) in the Konotop military flying school. In this capacity he, together with other pilots of the school, flew a number of combat sorties without getting

involved in air combat. The school not only trained new pilots but was also committed to the fulfilment of various combat tasks. In the summer of 1942 two fighter regiments, each comprising twenty machines, were formed on the basis of the flying personnel of the Konotop school; one of the regiments was equipped with Yak-1s, the other with I-16s. Boris Glinka flew the Yak-1. According to some sources, Boris Glinka scored his first victory in 1942 while flying the Yak-1. However, no records of his combat work of that period have survived, and the relevant information has been lost.

In September 1942, Lieutenant Junior Grade Boris Glinka was enrolled in the 45th IAP as a flight commander, and on 30 November he was promoted to the rank of lieutenant.

Official documents attribute the beginning of Boris Glinka's wartime combat career to the date of 20 February 1943. Information on the number of his combat sorties (115 in all) that can be found in the archives covers the period between 10 March 1943 and 14 July 1944.

In 1943, Boris Glinka converted to the Airacobra. His mount was P-39K-1-BE 42-4415, with the tactical code '1 White'; piloting this machine he shot down his first two aircraft on 10 March 1943. By the end of April 1943 he increased the number of his air victories to ten. On two occasions he was lightly wounded but went on flying combat missions. Shortly thereafter, on 24 May 1943, he was awarded the HSU title.

On 22 March 1943 Boris Glinka shot down two Bf 109s in a single action. His combat career includes several days on which he shot down three aircraft or more. For example, on 15 April 1943 he flew three sorties and added three downed aircraft to his score: a Ju 88 and two Bf 109s.

In May 1943, the 45th IAP was withdrawn from the front for a month's duration. At the end of May 1943 it resumed combat activities, taking part in the third stage of the Kuban' air battle. In the course of these battles Boris Glinka shot down three Bf 109s. In July 1943 they were supplemented by a coveted spoil—a Focke-Wulf Fw 189 reconnaissance aircraft, a type that was not only the source of much annoyance for the Soviet troops but was also notoriously hard to shoot down.

In August 1943, Boris Glinka, by that time promoted to lieutenant senior grade and posted as deputy squadron commander, fought with spectacular success when Soviet forces were storming the 'Mius Front' (*Mius-Stellung*), a German line of fortifications along the Mius River in southeastern Ukraine. Between 18 August and 1 September, he shot down eleven enemy aircraft personally and a further two together with his wingmen.

The date 31 August 1943 became the most 'productive' day in Glinka's combat career. On that day he performed four combat sorties and conducted three dogfights in which he shot down four aircraft and damaged one more. All of them were Bf 109s.

On 1 September 1943 Boris Glinka was seriously wounded and spent some time in a hospital. He resumed combat flying as late as the end of May 1944, during the Iassi-Kishinyov defensive operation. By that time he had made 105 combat sorties, conducted

OPPOSITE PAGE: Two aces, Maj. Aleksandr I. Pokryshkin (*left*) and Maj. Dmitriy B. Glinka, both of the Guards. The 16th GvIAP was in action at the 4th Ukrainian Front when this picture was taken.

RIGHT: Dmitriy Glinka's P-39K-1-BE 42-4403 / '21 White' is refuelled and rearmed before a mission. The BZ-38 fuel bowser on a GAZ-AAA 6x4 truck chassis is registered P-8-45-35.

BELOW: Maj. Dmitriy Glinka supervises as his mechanic performs engine maintenance on his Airacobra.

forty-six aerial engagements, and shot down twenty-five aircraft personally and two as shared 'kills.'

From the summer of 1944 Boris Glinka became the CO of the 16th GvIAP. Pokryshkin, by that time the commander of an air division, valued Boris Glinka very much and considered him to be a person of great experience, endowed with the qualities of a real leader. In the 16th GvIAP Glinka achieved his last air victories. On 4 June 1944 he shot down an Fw 190, and a Bf 109 on 14 July.

The flying career of Boris Glinka came to an end two days later, on 16 July 1944, when he was forced to bail out and was struck by

Here, Boris and Dmitriy Glinka are seen flying together over the Ukrainian countryside in April 1943.

LEFT: P-39 pilot Gheorgiy Basenko poses on the wing of his fighter; he ended the war as an ace with ten individual 'kills' and one shared 'kill.' Note the unusual 'racing number' style of the tactical code (red on a white circle) on the P-39 in the background.

the stabiliser of his Airacobra, in so doing sustaining serious injuries. The slow convalescence prevented him from resuming his flying activities before the end of the hostilities. During the war he made 115 combat sorties in the P-39 (plus an unspecified number of sorties in the I-16 and the Yak-1), taking part in at least forty-eight aerial engagements, and scored twenty-seven individual victories plus two shared 'kills.'

The postwar career of Boris Glinka in the Soviet air force was connected with flight-training activities in the Borisoglebsk military pilot college and the air force's cosmonaut training centre. In addition to the Gold Star medal and Order of Lenin that went with his Hero of the Soviet Union title, he was decorated with numerous Soviet orders and medals. Boris Glinka died on 11 May 1967 at the age of only fifty-two.

Dmitry B. Glinka (1917–1979)
Dmitriy Borisovich Glinka, the younger brother of Boris Glinka (born on 10 December 1917 in Aleksandrov Dar village, now a borough of Krivoy Rog), graduated from the military flying school in Kacha in February 1939 and was enrolled as junior pilot in the 45th IAP (reorganised as the 100th GvIAP on 17 June 1943), in which he served throughout the war. Initially the regiment was tasked with ensuring air defence for Baku, the capital of Soviet Azerbaijan; its frontline service started on 20 January 1942. Flying

a Yak-1 fighter, Lt. (JG) Dmitriy Glinka opened his personal tally of air victories on 9 April 1942. He managed to score six 'kills' and become an ace before being shot down in the spring of 1942. Having spent two months in hospital, he returned to his unit. On 11 September 1942 the regiment was withdrawn from the front for reequipment and recreation of the personnel. By that time Dmitriy Glinka was the unit's top-scoring pilot, being credited with ten individual 'kills' and one shared victory.

In early 1943 the 45th IAP started to operate P-39 Airacobras. Flying these machines, Dmitriy Glinka went on increasing his score while taking part in the combat associated with the Kuban' air battle and the action at the 'Mius-Front.' In the skies of Kuban', Dmitriy Glinka shot down several aircraft but happened to suffer defeats too.

One of the most memorable air battles for Dmitriy Glinka took place on 15 April 1943. On that day the Luftwaffe inflicted heavy bomb strikes on Krasnodar and the positions of Soviet troops. The German formations were opposed by the pilots of the 45th IAP, who shot down twenty aircraft (ten Ju 88s and ten Bf 109s). Dmitriy Glinka downed three aircraft in one sortie (it was the second time in his career that he achieved such a result), but he did not return to base on that day. The next day he reached the base of his regiment and reported that after shooting down a Ju 88 and two Bf 109s, he had had to make an off-field forced landing because of damage to his machine (P-39K-1-BE 42-4403, coded '21 White'). The fighter was recovered and subsequently repaired.

By mid-April 1943 Dmitriy Glinka had performed 146 combat sorties and scored fifteen 'kills.' Shortly afterwards he was awarded the title of Hero of the Soviet Union. His combat score continued to grow, and on 24 August 1943 the HSU title was conferred on him for the second time. He was awarded this title for twenty-nine enemy aircraft shot down in 186 combat sorties. More air victories were added as he participated in new air battles. From March 1943 until the end of the war, he flew the P-39 Airacobra, and thirty-seven of his 'kills' were scored on this type.

In September 1943, Dmitriy Glinka had to make a temporary respite in his combat activities for health reasons. He resumed his combat flying in the skies of Romania in May 1944. A notable feature of his combat style was his predilection for 'free chase.' In general, he advocated greater freedom of action for aces when flying in a group. On two more occasions (on 3 June 1944 and 18 April 1945) Dmitriy Glinka repeated his feat of shooting down three German aircraft in a single sortie.

Dmitry Glinka took part in several major military operations at various fronts of the Great Patriotic War, including, finally, the battle for Berlin in April 1945. His last air victory is dated 30 April 1945, and his last combat sortie was flown on 9 May (combat air patrol over Prague).

In all, Dmitry Glinka was officially credited with fifty air victories in ninety aerial engagements, having flown 300 combat sorties. He won recognition as a brilliant aerial fighting man, one of the top-scoring fighter pilots who reached the coveted mark of fifty victories. Much later, closer scrutiny by researchers produced a slightly different score (forty-nine individual 'kills' and one shared 'kill'), but this in no way detracts from his brilliant results.

According to Andrey V. Marchukov, Dmitriy Glinka flew 272 combat sorties, took part in ninety-one aerial engagements, and personally shot down forty-nine aircraft (six Ju 88s, seven Ju 87s, twenty-four Bf 109s, eleven Fw 190s and one Henschel Hs 123) plus one He 111 as a shared 'kill' that, it appears, was credited to him as an individual victory. He also destroyed one He 111 on the ground. *'Thus, his combat score could be presented as 49+1+1, which is the most correct way. Or else 50+0+1, which is erroneous but corresponds to documents and official statistics and is therefore also correct'*, Marchukov writes.

Maj. Aleksey S. Smirnov (HSU) was the top-scoring pilot of the 28th GvIAP, with thirty-four individual 'kills' and one shared 'kill.'

After the war Dmitriy B. Glinka continued to serve in the air force, becoming a regiment CO; he retired from active duty in 1960. He died on 1 March 1979, aged sixty-one.

Aleksey S. Smirnov (1917–1987)

Aleksey Semyonovich Smirnov was born on 7 February 1917 in Pal'tsevo village (Tver' Governorate, Russian Empire). He gained his license of a military pilot in 1938 after graduating from the Odessa military flying school. From the very first day of the Soviet-German war he took part in the action at different sectors of the front. He started his wartime service as a flight commander in the 153rd IAP and finished the war as the regiment's deputy CO. In its ranks Smirnov fought initially on the I-153 biplane, transitioning to the P-39D-2 Airacobra on 30 June 1942. This aircraft, in turn, gave way to the P-39Q on 1 August 1943. Before converting to the Bell fighter, Smirnov had scored four (some sources say three) air victories. Yet, it was while flying the P-39 that he became a real ace in the course of the air battles on the Voronezh Front,

North-Western Front, Kalinin Front, and 3rd Belorussian Front. Here are some episodes from his combat record.

On 23 July 1942 Aleksey Smirnov flew a mission, leading a group of six Cobras tasked with intercepting a group of Ju 87 dive bombers escorted by fighters. In a surprise attack he destroyed one Stuka and damaged a Bf 109, but his own machine was damaged as well and he had to bail out. Somewhat later, Smirnov and his wingman, aided by another pair of P-39s, managed to outmanoeuvre a group of four Bf 109s and get on their tails. A simultaneous volley of the 'Cobras sent all four Messerschmitt fighters to the ground. On 15 March 1943 Smirnov shot down two Fw 190s (a new type on the Soviet-German front at that time) in a series of successful aerial engagements. The confident conduct displayed by Smirnov in encounters with these fighters, and the victories scored by him, helped his fellow pilots overcome the psychological stress caused by the as-yet-unfamiliar adversary. In the time frame between 1 December 1942 and 1 August 1943 the pilots of his regiment shot down twenty-three Fw 190s (a sizeable part of the unit's total score of sixty-three 'kills'). By that time the regiment already bore the name of 28th GvIAP, having gained Guards status and the new number on 22 November 1942.

On 23 September 1943 Aleksey Smirnov was awarded his first title of Hero of the Soviet Union for thirteen individual air victories scored in thirty-nine aerial engagements and 312 combat sorties.

The luckiest day for Smirnov was 9 October 1943, when he flew three combat sorties in the area of Nevel' (Pskov Region). In the course of these sorties he shot down four enemy aircraft (one He 111, one Hs 126, and two Fw 190s). For this feat he was awarded the Order of Aleksandr Nevskiy.

From January 1945 Guards major Aleksey Smirnov fought on the 3rd Belorussian Front in the capacity of deputy CO of the 28th GvIAP and took part in the final air battles over Berlin. On 23 February 1945 he was awarded his second Gold Star medal of Hero of the Soviet Union for having scored thirty-one air victories in 396 combat sorties (as per September 1944).

Smirnov's official final score was thirty-five individual 'kills' and fifteen shared 'kills' (revised as 35+0 by later research). He flew 457 combat sorties (100 of them were ground attack missions) and took part in seventy-two aerial engagements (one may also encounter revised figures of 306 and 71, respectively). Aleksey Smirnov was wounded three times in air combat. Among the aircraft he shot down were three twin-engined bombers (two He 111s and one Ju 88), four Fw 189 reconnaissance aircraft (of which one was a shared 'kill'), three Ju 87 dive bombers, and two Hs 126 reconnaissance aircraft, and even a Messerschmitt Me 210 twin-engined fighter—a machine rarely encountered by the pilots of Soviet fighter regiments.

After the war Aleksey Smirnov was promoted to Guards lieutenant-colonel and commander of the 28th GvIAP. He took an active part in the Soviet air force's transition to jet aircraft, of which he flew several types, including the Mikoyan/Gurevich MiG-15 and the MiG-17. He retired from active duty in 1954, pursuing a civilian career that was no longer associated with aviation. Aleksey Smirnov died on 7 August 1987 at the age of seventy.

Vladimir D. Lavrinenkov (1919–1988)

Born in Ptakhino village (Smolensk Governorate) on 17 May 1919, Vladimir Dmitriyevich Lavrinenkov was one of the top-scoring Soviet aces. He graduated from a military flying school in Chugooyev (Khar'kov Region, the Ukraine) in 1941, remaining in the school as a flying instructor, but after the outbreak of the war he was immediately sent to the front. Lavrinenkov scored his first 'kill' in the skies of Stalingrad on 5 August 1942. At the end of October 1942 he was transferred to the 9th GvIAP of the 268th IAD, 8th VA, waging war on the Southern Front. By February 1943 Lt. (JG) Lavrinenkov, of the Guards, had performed 322 combat sorties, participating in seventy-eight aerial engagements, and had scored sixtten personal and eleven shared 'kills.' On 1 May 1943 he was awarded the HSU title. During that period he had flown consecutively the Polikarpov I-15*bis* biplane, the Yak-7, and the Yak-1.

By the end of July 1943 Lavrinenkov had made 368 combat sorties, conducted eighty-three aerial engagements, and scored twenty-two air victories. On 29 July his regiment was withdrawn from the front for reequipment with new materiel. Now flying P-39 Airacobras, the regiment resumed combat activities on 17 August 1943. In the course of the following two days, Lavrinenkov added a further three air victories to his score. However, his next air combat, which took place on 24 August, might well have been his last. On that day an Fw 189 reconnaissance aircraft put in an appearance over the command post of the 8th VA. The air army's commander, Lt.-Gen. Timofey T. Khryukin, gave a strict order to destroy the intruder. Four pilots, including Lavrinenkov, were sent on the intercept mission, but their attacks against the agile machine gave no result. Determined to fulfil the order at all costs, Lavrinenkov came as close as possible to the German aircraft in the hope of making a sure salvo, but he inadvertently rammed the tail of the Fw 189 with his Airacobra. Both aircraft plunged earthwards out of control, disintegrating as they fell. Lavrinenkov managed to bail out but was immediately taken prisoner when he landed by parachute. The Germans identified him as one of the Soviet top aces and subjected him to a harsh treatment. Having failed in their attempts to make him commit treason, the Germans sent Lavrinenkov to Berlin for a personal meeting with Reichsminister of the Luftwaffe Hermann Göring; they hoped the latter would make him change his mind and agree to serve in the Luftwaffe. Guarded by a special team, Lavrinenkov and another captured Soviet pilot were transported on a train. The valiant officers managed to dull their guards' vigilance and jumped off the train in the night. After this successful escape Lavrinenkov joined a partisan detachment and fought in its ranks before being transported across the front lines and returning to his unit on 30 September 1943. After passing the obligatory security check, soon he began to fly combat missions again. On 24 October 1943 he shot down an He 111 bomber.

In 1943 Vladimir Lavrinenkov and Aleksandr Pokryshkin met at a conference of fighter pilots sharing their experience in the 'free chase.' The two aces became close friends; Pokryshkin highly valued Lavrinenkov as a skilful pilot and a very able organiser of air combat in a group.

In February 1944 the 9th GvIAP took part in the operation aimed at liberating the Crimea Peninsula. The regiment widely practiced 'free chase.' On 25 February, while flying a 'free chase' mission in the vicinity of Nikolayev, Lavrinenkov received orders by radio to turn towards the city of Kherson, where a group of Fw 190 fighter-bombers escorted by Bf 109s had been observed. Lavrinenkov found this group and engaged it, shooting down one Bf 109. In April and May 1944, in the course of liberation of the Crimea. Lavrinenkov shot down three Fw 190s, increasing his score to thirty-three.

In July 1944 he was appointed commander of the 9th GvIAP. On 1 July 1944 Maj. Vladimir Lavrinenkov, of the Guards, was awarded his second HSU title.

Between 25 May and 25 October 1944 the 9th GvIAP was stationed near Moscow, where it reequipped with the new La-7 fighter. That was the end of Lavrinenkov's flying experience with the Airacobra.

In the course of the war Lavrinenkov made a total of 488 combat sorties, conducted 134 aerial engagements, and shot down thirty-five aircraft personally and eleven as shared victories (36+7 or 38+6, according to different assessments). Twelve of his 'kills' were scored while flying the Airacobra. These include two Bf 109s, four Fw 190s, two He 111s, one Ju 88, and one Fw 189.

After the war Vladimir Lavrinenkov commanded an air division, graduated from two military academies (in 1948 and 1954), and served in the air defence force. In 1971 he was promoted to the rank of air colonel-general. His subsequent service included the posts of deputy chief of civil defence of the Ukrainian Soviet Republic and, finally, military advisor in the Kiev PVO military school. Lavrinenkov died on 14 January 1988, aged sixty-eight.

26th GvIAP CO maj. Gheorgiy G. Petrov is depicted in the cockpit of his P-39 in 1943, with the unit's deputy CO, Capt. Vasiliy A. Matsiyevich, standing on the wing. Both pilots earned the HSU title (on 16 January 1942 and 14 February 1943, respectively).

Pavel M. Kamozin (1917–1983)

Pavel Mikhailovich Kamozin was born in the town of Bezhitsa (now a borough of the city of Bryansk) on 16 June 1917. He graduated from the Borisoglebsk military flying school in 1938. From June 1941 he served as a pilot with frontline air units and flew several types of Soviet fighter aircraft. By March 1943 deputy squadron commander of the 296th IAP (236th IAD, 5th VA, North Caucasus Front) Lt. (JG) Kamozin had made eighty-two combat sorties, conducting twenty-three aerial engagements and scoring twelve individual air victories. On 1 May 1943 he was awarded the title of Hero of the Soviet Union.

The period of his combat activities associated with Airacobras dates from the time when he was transferred to the 66th IAP. In March 1943 this regiment was withdrawn to the rear for replenishment and conversion training for the P-39 Airacobra, which took place at Adzhikabul (Soviet Azerbaijan). Kamozin was one of the pilots who were mastering the P-39 in the 25th ZAP based there. The 66th Fighter Regiment was committed to action on the new aircraft in October 1943. Kamozin's first 'kill' scored when flying the Airacobra is dated 21 November 1943, when he shot down a Bf 109 over the Crimea Peninsula. This was the beginning of an impressive series of air victories. By July 1944 squadron commander of the 66th IAP (329th IAD, 4th VA, Belorussian Front)

BELOW: Capt. Aleksandr D. Bilyukin, a squadron commander in the 196th IAP, is pictured in the cockpit of his P-39, coded '53 White' and named Aleksandr Nevskiy, in May 1944. He scored a total of 20 'kills,' earning the HSU title.

Pavel M. Kamozin (*leftmost*) explains his actions to the pilots of his flight after a sortie in 1943.

Capt. Pavel Kamozin had made 131 combat sorties and taken part in fifty-six aerial engagements in which he scored twenty-nine individual air victories and thirteen shared 'kills.' For this he was awarded his second Gold Star medal of Hero of the Soviet Union (the award is dated 1 July 1944). In all, during the war he flew at least 188 combat sorties and conducted sixty-three aerial engagements in which he shot down thirty-six enemy aircraft personally and thirteen as shared 'kills' (recent research puts his score at thirty-six individual and two shared victories).

Kamozin's combat career contains many dramatic episodes when his own life was at stake. In late 1943, in air combat over the city of Kerch, he had to fight against superior odds; he shot down two enemy fighters but his own machine was set ablaze. Kamozin bailed out and landed in the Black Sea; fortunately, he was rescued by the crew of a Soviet ship that happened to be nearby. One of his air victories was particularly memorable. On the last day of the year 1943, Pavel Kamozin and his wingman Vladimir Ladylin were on the way back to base after a reconnaissance mission when they spotted a German transport aircraft escorted by six Bf 109s. Kamozin reacted instantly, rushing to the attack. After an accurate salvo the enemy machine went down in a death dive, trailing smoke. Three months later, after the liberation of the Crimea, some facts behind this episode came to light. As it turned out, the aircraft shot down by Kamozin was a staff transport carrying no fewer than eighteen German generals (hence the strong fighter escort). Their mission was to confer Iron Cross decorations on 'Wehrmacht heroes' on New Year's Eve. Instead, the anticipated grand ceremony was replaced by mourning.

After the war Pavel Kamozin worked in the civil aviation system. He died on 24 November 1983.

Aleksandr F. Kloobov (1918–1944)

Aleksandr Fyodorovich Kloobov was born on 18 January 1918 in Yarunovo village in the Vologda Governorate. He started his flying career by attending an air club in Leningrad, where he was a factory worker; he became a military pilot after graduating from a military flying school in 1940. From August 1941 he joined action as a fighter pilot in the ranks of the 10th IAP and then, from 5 August 1942, of a unit with the unusual designation 84th 'A' IAP (it had been split off from the original 84th IAP in 1942). By the end of 1942 he had flown nearly 250 combat sorties in the I-153 biplane fighter (mostly on ground attack missions) and scored four individual aerial victories supplemented by eighteen shared 'kills.' In a dogfight that took place on 2 November 1942, Kloobov's aircraft was set on fire by a Bf 109; the Soviet pilot managed to cross the front line into own territory before bailing out, but his face was burnt and the recovery was long and painful. When he came back to his unit, the regiment started redeployment to the Kuban' River area, which was soon to become the scene of fierce air battles.

P-39N-1-BE 42-9434 / '45 White,' flown by Capt. Aleksandr F. Kloobov (16th GvIAP) in the summer of 1944; the score shows thirty individual 'kills' and nineteen shared 'kills.'

ABOVE: Capt. Aleksandr F. Kloobov (Twice HSU) poses on the wing of his P-39 on 22 September 1944.

ABOVE RIGHT: Aleksandr Kloobov beside the revetment housing his P-39Q-15-BE, 44-2589 / '125 White.'

In the 84th 'A' IAP, Aleksandr Kloobov started mastering a new machine—the P-39. By mid-May 1943, he, together with other pilots, passed exams after having studied the aircraft. However, his real acquaintance with the Bell fighter was in a different air unit. Kloobov and a group of other pilots were transferred to the 16th GvIAP of the 9th GvIAD, where they arrived on 31 May 1943. In the new regiment Kloobov was appointed deputy squadron commander. According to some sources, his original mount was P-39L-1-BE 42-4608.

On 16 August 1943 Aleksandr Kloobov scored his first victory at the Southern Front. This was followed by an astounding succession of nine 'kills' achieved in the course of just seven days, starting with 26 August.

By the beginning of September 1943 Kloobov had performed 310 combat sorties, conducting eighty-four aerial engagements and scoring fourteen individual 'kills' and nineteen shared victories. On 4 September 1943 he was nominated for the Hero of the Soviet Union title for courage and bravery in the battles against the enemy. Kloobov was awarded this title on 13 April 1944.

His subsequent combat activities are closely related with those of Aleksandr Pokryshkin, under whose command he served in the 16th GvIAP. Pokryshkin, Kloobov's commander and close personal friend, valued him very highly and characterised him thus: *'He was wholeheartedly devoted to his Motherland, to aviation, to friendship; he was a clever man, forthright in his judgments, passionate in disputes and subtle in the dangerous business of war. . . . He was a pure and mighty person.'* Pokryshkin emphasised that Kloobov *'fervently fulfilled his duties as a pilot and risked his life in order to prevent the bombing of our positions by enemy aircraft. No matter how huge the number of German aircraft was, he would be sure to rush into battle, disregarding the risk of being shot down.'*

Soon Pokryshkin singled out Kloobov as the best of his disciples, who surpassed others in the deep understanding and practical mastery of Pokryshkin's methods of air combat.

Kloobov's skill as a pilot was vividly demonstrated in an episode where he and his wingman Karpov flew a 'free chase' mission. They encountered a group of six Bf 109s above the front line and, despite being outnumbered by the Germans, engaged them. In a surprise attack from above (the 'falcon strike'), Kloobov downed the leader of the German group and, instead of zooming upwards, attempted to make another 'kill,' but his pair itself became a target

for the German machines. Karpov's aircraft was set ablaze, and he bailed out. Kloobov protected his wingman as he parachuted earthwards, thwarting all attempts of the Germans to shoot at him (as they were notoriously apt to), but he also had to pay a price for that. The violent manoeuvring warped his machine; it was riddled with bullets, which severed the elevator linkages. When Kloobov finally made it to base and was about to land, his friends on the ground watched in surprise as his aircraft pitched up and down instead of holding the glideslope. It was obvious that the elevators were inoperative and the pilot was using the trim tabs to control the machine. His safe landing looked like a miracle.

In 1944 Aleksandr Kloobov flew P-39N-1-BE 42-9434 (coded '45 White'). Later that year he received a new Airacobra—P-39Q-15-BE 44-2589 (coded '125 White'). On 25 August 1944 Kloobov

ABOVE: The pilots of the 9th GvIAP, including Aleksey V. Alelyukhin (*fourth from right*) and Sultan Amet-khan (*third from right*).

Aleksey Alelyukhin has a conversation with Sultan Amet-khan in the cockpit of his P-39. Both pilots eventually became Twice HSUs.

and his new wingman, Lt. (JG) Andrey Ivankov, flew a 'free chase' mission during which they encountered a Messerschmitt Bf 110 fighter. In a surprise attack Klubov shot down the German machine. This was Kloobov's last aerial victory. On 1 November 1944 he was killed in an accident while making a training flight in a new aircraft—a La-7 fighter, one of the machines intended for rearming Pokryshkin's 9th Fighter Division (the aircraft went off the runway into a ditch while landing in a crosswind and nosed over, crushing the cockpit). After this accident Pokryshkin withdrew his consent to convert to the La-7 from the P-39s and decided to stick to the well-proven Airacobra.

Guards captain Aleksandr Kloobov performed 457 combat sorties; he took part in ninety-five aerial engagements in which he destroyed thirty-one enemy aircraft personally and nineteen as shared victories. On 27 June 1945 he was posthumously awarded a second HSU title.

Sultan Amet-khan (1920–1971)

Sultan Amet-khan was born on 25 October 1920 in the town of Alupka (the Crimea) in a worker's family. His father had ancestors in Dagestan, and his mother ethnically belonged to Crimean Tatars. Amet-khan enlisted in the Red Army in 1939; prior to that, he had received some flying training at an aero club. He graduated from the flying school in Kacha in 1940 and served in an air unit in Belorussia for a while. Amet-khan joined combat from the first day of the war and fought in the ranks of the 4th IAP, flying the I-153, Hurricane, and Yak-7 fighters. From the outset he displayed outstanding qualities as a fighter pilot, skilful in handling his mounts, tactically clever and full of courage and determination. In May 1941, having run out of ammunition in an aerial engagement with a Junkers bomber, he resorted to a ramming attack and destroyed the enemy machine, severing its wing. His own machine was also disabled, and Amet-khan saved his life by bailing out.

In the subsequent months he conducted many successful aerial engagements and built up an impressive score of downed enemy aircraft, including several bombers. He was singled out for inclusion into a special independent group formed with the express purpose of waging combat against German aces. In this group he shot down two Bf 109s, was shot down himself, and had to bail out again. Shortly thereafter he was transferred to the 9th GvIAP, which was regarded as one of the top-notch fighter regiments. There he was appointed deputy squadron commander and soon promoted to squadron commander. In the new unit he initially flew the Yak-1. In August 1943 the regiment was reequipped with Airacobras; this type came to account for a sizeable part of Amet-khan's total score of air victories by the end of the war.

By August 1943 Sultan Amet-khan had made 359 combat sorties (110 of which had been flown in the skies of Stalingrad), conducted seventy-nine air engagements, and shot down eleven aircraft personally and nineteen as shared 'kills.' On 24 August 1943 he was awarded the title of Hero of the Soviet Union (the nomination had been made in April of that year).

In the 9th GvIAP, Sultan Amet-khan flew a P-39L-1-BE serialled 42-4582 and sporting the tactical code '28.' On this mount he shot down two Ju 88s and three Bf 109s between 19 and 23 August 1943. This machine was damaged beyond repair by another pilot making a check flight on 19 September 1943. Amet-khan's next Airacobra was a P-39N (serial unknown) that sported a yellow spinner and featured nose art—the picture of a snake on the fuselage side.

Until the spring of 1944 Amet-khan's unit fought in the South and took part in air battles in the Sevastopol' area. On 8 February 1944 he shot down his seventh twin-engined bomber (a Ju 88)—more than any of his fellow pilots in regard to such notoriously 'difficult' targets. Amet-khan also displayed much skill and efficiency in performing ground attack missions against enemy trains, road convoys, artillery batteries, and the like.

During the last months of the war Amet-khan flew the La-7 fighter, which superseded the P-39s in the inventory of the 9th GvIAP. He scored several air victories during combat operations in the Baltic area and East Prussia. His last Fw 190 was shot down over Tempelhof airfield in Berlin on 29 April 1945.

By the end of the war Sultan Amet-khan's combat record was as follows: 603 combat sorties, 150 air engagements, thirty personal 'kills,' and nineteen shared victories.

On 29 June 1945, Amet-khan, deputy commander of the 9th GvIAP Sultan, was awarded his second HSU Gold Star.

After the war, Sultan Amet-khan, in the rank of lieutenant-colonel, quit the army and found a new sphere of activity. He became a test pilot at the Flight Research Institute (LII: ***Lyot**no-**issled**ovatel'skiy insti**toot***), a branch of the Ministry of Aircraft Industry (MAP: *Minister**stvo** aviatsi**on**noy pro**mysh**lennosti*), and spent nearly a quarter of a century testing jet aircraft. On 23 September 1961 he was awarded the title 'Merited test pilot of the USSR.'

On 1 February 1971 Sultan Amet-khan took off for what proved to be his last flight. He was the captain of a Tupolev Tu-16LL flying test bed that was used for testing a new jet engine. The crew reported the start of the test (extension of the semirecessed test engine pod into the slipstream), whereupon radio contact was lost. The aircraft was found in a swamp where it had crashed, killing all the crew. One can only surmise that the tragedy was due to an explosion of the new engine.

Aleksey V. Alelyukhin (1920–1990)

Aleksey Vasil'yevich Alelyukhin was born on 30 March 1920 in the village of Kesova Gora (now a township) in the Tver' Region. In 1938 he enlisted in the Red Army and entered the Chkalov military flying school, from which he graduated in 1939. From the first days of the war, Alelyukhin served in the 69th IAP, renamed the 9th GvIAP in April 1942. He fought in the skies of Odessa on the Polikarpov I-16, taking part in numerous ground attack missions against the German troops. When German artillery began intensive shelling of Odessa, Alelyukhin in his I-16 succeeded in seeking out and destroying a large-calibre artillery piece.

In the autumn of 1941 the 69th IAP converted to LaGG-3s; at least two German aircraft were shot down by Alelyukhin while flying this type. In the autumn of 1942 the regiment was reequipped again; this time it received Yak-1 fighters. Those were the months of fierce fighting on the Stalingrad Front. Flying the Yak-1 until August 1943, Alelyukhin added at least fifteen 'kills' to his score. It was then that Alelyukhin painted the nose of his Yak red—he was not afraid to attract attention to himself in aerial engagements.

Aleksey V. Alelyukhin beside his Airacobra.

He had already built up a reputation as a skilful and courageous master of air combat.

On 24 August 1943 Aleksey Alelyukhin was awarded the title of Hero of the Soviet Union in recognition of his combat achievements: by that time he had made 265 combat sorties, taken part in sixty-five air engagements, and scored eleven individual 'kills,' supplemented by six shared victories.

From mid-August 1943 Alelyukhin flew the Lend-Lease Airacobra. By late October 1943 he had made 410 combat sorties, taking part in 114 aerial engagements, and personally shot down twenty-six enemy aircraft. This made him eligible for a second HSU title; the appropriate nomination met with an unusually quick response: on 1 November 1943 he was awarded his second Gold Star.

In late October 1944 Aleksey Alelyukhin was committed to action on a new fighter—the La-7, the 69th IAP having started conversion to the type in late May of that year. He flew the La-7 throughout the rest of the war. During the last months of the war Alelyukhin flew combat missions in the skies of the Baltic area and East Prussia; he also took part in the Berlin offensive operation. It was during that period that Alelyukhin achieved his final four air victories. He shot down two Fw 190s in a single action over the Baltic Sea west of Pillau on 27 March 1945.

In all, during the war Aleksey Alelyukhin made 601 combat sorties and conducted 123 air engagements; his score amounted to twenty-eight individual 'kills' and six shared victories. (These figures apparently reflect the results of recent research seeking documentary evidence for each 'kill'; some biographic materials credit Alelyukhin with a substantially higher score: forty individual and seventeen shared victories.) A list compiled by researcher Mikhail Bykov credits Alelyukhin with eight victories scored while flying the Airacobra. Notably, two 'kills' (Fw 190s) were made in the vicinity of Sevastopol' on a single day (29 April 1944). Alelyukhin's wartime service did not lack dramatic episodes. He was wounded several times; he had to save his life bailing out from a damaged machine or by making forced landings.

After the war Alelyukhin continued his service in the armed forces, graduating from the Mikhail V. Frunze military academy in 1948 and becoming deputy CO of the 151st GvIAD, where he flew the MiG-15 jet fighter. From October 1950 to February 1951 he took part in the Korean War, being appointed CO of the newly formed 28th IAD, but did not fly combat sorties himself. In 1954 he graduated from the general staff academy, occupying high command positions. Alelyukhin retired in 1985 in the rank of major-general; he died on 29 October 1990 at the age of seventy.

Ivan I. Babak (1919–2001)

Ivan Il'yich Babak was born on 26 July 1919 in Alekseyevka (Dnepropetrovsk Region, the Ukraine) in a peasant family. After graduating from a pedagogic college (institute), he worked as a teacher in a secondary school in the Zaporozhye Region of the Ukrainian Soviet Republic. He also received a pilot's training in an air club. In 1940 he was enrolled in the Red Army and became a cadet of the Stalingrad military flying school, from which he graduated in 1942. From May 1942 he joined battle in the ranks of the 45th IAP of the 216th SAD (***smesh**annaya **a**viadiv**eez**iya*; Composite Air Division). Later (in June 1943) these units were awarded the Guards title for their achievements in the air battles over the Kuban' area and were renamed as the 100th GvIAP and the 9th GvIAD, respectively.

In the summer of 1942, Ivan Babak, then fighting on a Yak-1, scored his first 'kill,' shooting down a Bf 109 in the skies of Mozdok (Ingushetia, the North Caucasus). His skills and bravery were duly noted, and soon he flew as a flight commander in the 45th IAP.

In September 1942 the regiment was withdrawn to the rear for rest, replenishment, and conversion to new machines. In December 1942 the pilots mastered P-40 Kittyhawks, but in early 1943 these were superseded by Airacobras. The regiment went into action on the P-39s on 9 March 1943. Babak received as his personal mount a P-39D-2-BE serialled 41-38416 and coded '40 White.' In March he downed two German aircraft—a Bf 109 and a Ju 87. In April he added to his personal score a further fourteen aerial victories! Together with Fadeyev, Pokryshkin, and Semenishin he was one of the top-scoring aces of the battles over the Kuban' River. Yet, things did not always go smoothly for him; Soviet archive records indicate that on 26 April 1943, SSgt Ivan Babak wrecked his aircraft in an accident. The pilot was unhurt but the aircraft was struck off charge two days later, together with another damaged Airacobra.

Ivan I. Babak displayed his best qualities as a fighter pilot during the operations that ended in the liberation of the East Ukrainian town of Mariupol' (Donetsk Region). One of his exploits of that period was particularly noted. The Germans had rounded up a large number of girls in Mariupol' and made arrangements for their transport by rail to Germany, where the girls would be used as a slave labour force. These plans were thwarted thanks to Babak. On 6 August 1943, flying an Airacobra, he attacked the locomotive of the last train in which the girls were being transported, destroying it with a well-aimed salvo of his weapons. The girls were saved. To show their gratitude, the residents of Mariupol' raised 20,000 rubles and bought a P-39N-BE fighter (42-9033) named 'From the schoolchildren of Mariupol,' which they presented to Babak. The aircraft gained the tactical code '01 White' and nose art—an image of Nike, the winged goddess of victory (which earned Babak the

ABOVE AND BELOW: P-39D-2-BE 41-38416 / '40 White,' the first Airacobra flown by Ivan I. Babak.

nickname *Letayushchiy demon*, 'Flying demon'). The very first sortie flown in the new machine ended in shooting down a Bf 109. Babak opened fire on this aircraft at point-blank range—some 20–30 m (66–98 ft.); the oil from the disintegrating Messerschmitt sprayed the windshield of his Airacobra, and Babak had to perform the landing looking through the side windows of the cockpit.

By September 1943 Ivan Babak had shot down eighteen enemy aircraft individually and four as shared 'kills.' On 1 November 1943 he was awarded the title of Hero of the Soviet Union for bravery and heroism in combat and for the excellent results of his combat activities.

In all, in the course of the war Ivan Babak shot down thirty-five enemy aircraft personally and five as shared 'kills' (according to the revised score established by Mikhail Yu. Bykov; previously Babak had been credited with thirty-seven individual and four shared 'kills'). In February 1945 Lt. (SG) Ivan Babak was appointed commander of the 16th GvIAP, which had previously been commanded by Aleksandr Pokryshkin (the latter had been promoted to division CO).

The war was drawing to a close. Up to then Ivan Babak had passed through the war without a scratch, but two months before the end of the hostilities, luck turned its back on him. On 15 March 1945 he received a highly important assignment from Pokryshkin—he was to locate and strafe a motorcade in which the Third Reich's minister of propaganda, Joseph Goebbels, with a movie crew was going to the town of Lauban (now called Lubań, Poland), which had just been recaptured in a counteroffensive by the German troops, for the purpose of shooting a fake propaganda film about 'the atrocities of the Bolsheviks.' Specifically, Babak's mission was to eliminate Goebbels. However, while he was en route to the target, ground reconnaissance reported that the motorcade had scattered around the town; finding Goebbels's staff car would now be impossible, and the mission was called off. By mischance Babak was flying someone else's aircraft that day instead of his regular mount, and one might be tempted to say his machine did not forgive him such infidelity. On the way back the Airacobra was shot down by enemy flak; he bailed out and was captured, becoming a prisoner of war. Despite the harsh treatment he was subjected to, Babak staunchly rejected all attempts to make him commit treason. He spent only two weeks in German captivity, but this dealt a blow to his further career. Babak was liberated soon after the victory and reinstated in the ranks of the Soviet air force thanks to the courageous protection of his friend Aleksandr I. Pokryshkin, but the well-deserved second HSU title was not awarded to him (the nomination had been submitted a few days before his last flight).

Ivan Babak served as CO of the 32nd GvIAP until 1947. In 1949 he was transferred to the reserve; soon thereafter he retired and resumed his activities as school teacher in Poltava (the Ukraine). Ivan Babak died on 24 June 2001 at the age of eighty-two. In addition to the HSU Gold Star and Order of Lenin, he was awarded two Orders of the Red Banner of Combat, the Order of the Patriotic War (1st class), and the Order of the Red Star.

Andrey I. Trood (1921–1999)

Andrey Ivanovich Trood (his last name is the Russian word for 'labour') was born on 20 August 1921 in Ingoolo-Kamenka village (Kirovograd Region, the Ukraine). He graduated from the Kacha flying school in June 1941 and went into battle on 20 July 1941, when he, together with a group of young pilots, was enrolled in the 55th IAP (later reorganised as the 16th GvIAP). Initially he flew the I-153, followed by the I-16, MiG-3, Yak-1, and, from 1943, the Airacobra; his aircraft was P-39L-1-BE 42-4894 (c/n 26D-191). By 30 August 1943 he held the post of deputy squadron commander in the 16th GvIAP, which was part of the 9th GvIAD/8th VA, Southern Front. By that time he made 198 combat sorties, conducted seventy-one aerial engagements, and shot down fifteen enemy aircraft personally and one more as a shared 'kill.' For this he was nominated for the title of Hero of the Soviet Union. Andrey Trood was actually awarded this title somewhat later—on 13 April 1944, in recognition of the fact that by 13 December 1943 he had made 314 combat sorties and shot down twenty-one enemy aircraft (the award nomination mentions eighteen personal victories).

Andrey Trood ranked fourth among the aces of the 16th GvIAP (after Rechkalov, Pokryshkin, and Kloobov). He achieved this standing in the course of fierce air battles in the Kuban' River area, during which he added several victories to his score. The first 'kill' scored by him during that period took place on 13 April 1943. Until 5 May, Trood flew combat missions as the wingman of Fadeyev; after the latter's death in action he became a leader of a pair and

P-39D-2-BE 41-38416 / '40 White,' flown by SSgt. Ivan I. Babak in the 45th IAP in the spring of 1943.

scored a further four victories, including his first bomber. On 26 May 1943 he shot down two enemy aircraft in a single action but was shot down himself and almost perished. He managed to crash-land his burning fighter, suffering burns to his face.

Here is a description of one of the aerial engagements in which Andrey Trood took part. In October 1943, he flew a mission with Captain Zherdev as his wingman, together with a further two pairs led by Major Yeryomin and Captain Olefirenko. They encountered a group of some fifty Ju 87s, with twelve Bf 109s flying top cover. Trood, being the leader of the group, chose the bombers as his target and attacked them together with Olefirenko's pair. In the meantime, acting on Trood's orders, Yeryomin's pair engaged the German fighters, attacking them in a dive. Trood and Olefirenko shot down two Ju 87s; the other bombers hastily dropped their bombs over the territory held by German troops and fled westward. The group of four led by Trood made a quick descent and went into a sort of 'hiding' below the German bombers, avoiding in this manner an attack from the German fighters, which Yeryomin and his wingman tried to attract away at the higher altitude. As a result, the group of six Airacobras led by Trood fulfilled the main task, preventing the Germans from bombing Soviet troops. Into the bargain, five German aircraft (two Ju 87s and three Bf 109s) were shot down in that action, of which two were credited to Trood and the other three to other members of the group. The group suffered a loss too—Olefirenko's wingman, a young pilot, was shot down.

OPPOSITE PAGE: Lt.-Col. Ivan Lyubimov, CO of the Black Sea Fleet air arm's 11th GvIAP; in October 1943 he was promoted to CO of the Black Sea Fleet's 4th IAD. He ended the war with ten 'kills'; four of these were scored in the P-39, despite the fact that he had lost a leg when he was shot down earlier in the war.

Ace Lt. Andrey I. Trood (16th GvIAP) receives a government award from Nikolay M. Shvernik, chairman of the Presidium of the Supreme Soviet of the Russian SFSR, at a ceremony in the Moscow Kremlin.

TOP: This view shows Yevgeniy P. Mariinskiy's score of eighteen 'kills' at the time when this picture was taken. The gun bay cowl is darker than the rest of the nose and may be a replacement item.

ABOVE: Front view of the P-39 '4 White' flown by Mariinskiy.

TOP: Here we see Yevgeniy Mariinskiy's P-39 'undressed' for maintenance in the spring of 1945, with crew chief Nikolay Volkov, engine mechanic Sergey Karpushkin, and armourer Protsyuk at work.

ABOVE: The same crew plus an unknown pilot; the job is done.

By 1 May 1945, Guards gaptain Andrey Trood had flown 415 combat sorties and shot down twenty-five enemy aircraft personally and one as a shared victory. Later research puts his score at twenty-six personal 'kills' and one shared 'kill.'

After the war Andrey Trood continued his service in the Soviet air force, rising to the rank of colonel in January 1962. In 1972 he was transferred to the reserve and devoted himself to literary activities. He died on 27 July 1999 at the age of seventy-seven.

Arkadiy V. Fyodorov (1917–1992)

Arkadiy Vasil'yevich Fyodorov was born in Ivanovo-Voznesensk (now simply Ivanovo, a regional centre in Russia) on 6 January

The P-39 flown by Yevgeniy P. Mariinskiy, Germany, 1945.

1917. He was drafted into the Red Army in 1938 and sent to the 1st Chkalov military flying school in the city of Chkalov (at present called Orenburg), from which he graduated in 1940. His service in the air force started in the ranks of the 131st IAP. When the war broke out on 22 June 1941, Fyodorov joined the battle from the first day as flight commander, making five combat sorties on that day. On 25 June 1941 he shot down his first German aircraft (a Ju 88D reconnaissance aircraft) with a salvo of rocket projectiles. In February 1942 Fyodorov's squadron was transferred to the 55th IAP, which was transformed into the 16th GvIAP on 7 March 1942. This regiment became famous thanks to its cohort of aces, with Aleksandr I. Pokryshkin as the recognised leader and master of air combat. Fyodorov flew many combat missions as Pokryshkin's wingman. By December 1942 he mastered the P-39 Airacobra and fought on this type until the end of the war; his aircraft was P-39L-1-BE 42-4612 coded '40 White.'

During the air battle over the Kuban' River area, Fyodorov displayed to advantage his qualities of a leader in air combat. In particular, this came to the fore in a fierce battle with a big group of German fighters that took place on 29 April 1943. A group of eight Airacobras led by Pokryshkin encountered some eighty Ju 87 dive bombers escorted by fighters. Fyodorov's flight engaged a number of enemy fighters and thus enabled the rest of Pokryshkin's group to fulfil the main task—thwarting the enemy bombers' attack against the Red Army positions. The enemy lost twelve aircraft.

In August 1943 Arkadiy Fyodorov took part in combat operations for the liberation of the Donbass area. Flying missions over the Mius River, he added several new air victories to his score.

By September 1943, Fyodorov, at that time a deputy squadron commander, had flown 498 combat sorties and taken part in sixty-two aerial engagements in which he scored sixteen individual air victories and four shared 'kills.' He was nominated for the title of Hero of the Soviet Union.

In November 1943 Fyodorov was appointed commander of the 16th GvIAP's 3rd Squadron. Under his command this squadron successfully fulfilled missions for ensuring top cover for the troops that were waging an offensive into the Crimea in the region of Sivash (the 'Rotten Sea,' a system of shallow, swampy lagoons separating the eastern side of the peninsula from the mainland).

Fyodorov's skill and bravery in air combat received due recognition. In early October 1944 he received his Gold Star medal that went with the HSU title at a ceremony in the Kremlin.

Together with his regiment, Arkadiy Fyodorov took part in the combat operations for the liberation of the Ukraine west of the Dnieper, of Belorussia, and of Poland. He was promoted to the post of deputy regiment CO but continued to fly combat missions.

On 16 March 1945 Fyodorov was appointed commander of the 16th GvIAP. In this capacity he witnessed Victory Day.

In all, during the war Fyodorov made 554 combat sorties, including 136 sorties on ground attack missions. He conducted 183 aerial engagements and was credited with twenty-four individual 'kills.' A further eighteen aircraft were destroyed by him and his fellow pilots in the air and on the ground in the course of group attacks. (Later some researchers stated differing figures: 22+4 or even 14+2, apparently applying more-stringent criteria to the documentation corroborating the 'kills.')

After the war Arkadiy Fyodorov continued his service in the Soviet air force, mastering the first generation of jet aircraft. In 1955 he retired with the rank of colonel from the post of air division commander, returning to Ivanovo to pursue a civilian career. He died on 9 March 1992, aged seventy-five.

Yevgeniy P. Mariinskiy (1923–1993)

Yevgeniy Pakhomovich Mariinskiy was born in Balta (Odessa Region, the Ukraine) on 27 January 1923. He enrolled into the Red Army in November 1941 and graduated from a flying school in Vyazniki (Vladimir Region, Russia) in 1942. In October 1943, after a period of service in a reserve air regiment, he joined battle in the ranks of the 27th IAP, which was renamed 129th GvIAP in the same month. The regiment was equipped with P-39 Airacobras. Yevgeniy Mariinskiy took part in the action over the Dnieper area and over the territories of Moldavia, Romania, Poland, and Germany. He impressed his fellow pilots as a brave and skilled air fighter, vigorous and enthusiastic.

One of the pilots who served together with him relates the following episode, which occurred on 21 March 1944 over Moldavia, in the Dnestr River area. The German aviation was conducting persistent bombing raids against Soviet ferrying sites on the river. The 129th GvIAP's command received orders to ensure protection from the air for an important river crossing. A group of four fighters led by the regiment's deputy CO, Fyodor F. Arkhipenko, was tasked with this mission; one of the P-39s was piloted by Mariinskiy. Uneventful patrolling did not last long—a large group of Ju 87 dive bombers put in an appearance. Observers on the ground counted some eighty machines capable of dealing a formidable strike. Arkhipenko did his best to intercept the bombers before they reached their target, and his group charged to the attack, making the Germans rearrange their battle formation into three defensive rings at some distance from the river crossing. As for Mariinskiy, he also displayed determination and skill: his first attack sent a Ju 87 plummeting to the ground. A further two attacks resulted in two more dive bombers shot down. But his own machine was also seriously damaged and caught fire. Mariinskiy promptly made a wheels-up emergency landing. Getting out of the burning machine was not easy, but he managed to save himself. The overall result of the aerial battle was excellent. Eight enemy machines were shot down; the remaining bombers dispersed and left the scene without making a strike against the river crossing. Mariinskiy's Airacobra was the only own loss, with no hands lost.

By 18 January 1945 the flight commander of the 129th GvIAP Guards, Lt. Yevgeniy Mariinskiy, had made 156 combat sorties, conducted forty-seven aerial engagements, and personally shot down seventeen enemy aircraft. For this achievement he was nominated for the nation's highest award—the title of Hero of the Soviet Union.

By the end of the war, Lt. (SG) Yevgeniy Mariinskiy of the Guards had made 238 combat sorties and conducted nearly sixty aerial engagements. His final score was eighteen individual 'kills.' Most of the aircraft shot down by Mariinskiy were fighters, twelve in all—six Bf 109s and six Fw 190s. He also shot down five Ju 87 dive bombers and one Fw 189 reconnaissance aircraft, as well as one German observation balloon, which is not included in the above score. On 27 June 1945 he was officially awarded the title of Hero of the Soviet Union.

After the war Yevgeniy Mariinskiy continued his service in the Soviet air force until 1954, when he retired in the rank of lieutenant-colonel and took up a career in journalism. He died on 22 March 1993, aged seventy.

Pyotr I. Guchok (1923–1945)

Pyotr Iosifovich Guchok was born in Lysovshchina village (Minsk Region, Belorussia) on 18 March 1923. He started his service in the Red Army in 1940, having previously received flight training in an aero club in Minsk. In 1942 he graduated from a military flying school in Bataisk (Rostov Region, Russia). His service in the frontline air units began in August 1943 in the 45th IAP (which was soon transformed into the 100th GvIAP). In the ranks of this unit he fought on the 1st, 2nd, and 4th Ukrainian Fronts.

By September 1943 Pyotr Guchok converted to a new type—the Airacobra, which he flew to his last day. For a long time Guchok was the wingman of one of the most prominent Soviet aces—Ivan Babak. Together with his regiment he took part in several major offensive operations of the Red Army and gave proof of bravery and skill in air combat. Between 1 August 1943 and 10 October 1943 he made eighty-one combat sorties and shot down six aircraft individually and three as shared 'kills.' In recognition of this he was awarded the Order of the Red Banner. Guchok added a further seven air victories to his score in the period between 11 October 1943 and 10 June 1944. This achievement earned him his second Order of the Red Banner. The remainder of his service career was marked by five air victories; the last aircraft shot down by him was an Fw 189 reconnaissance aircraft.

Guchok's last combat operations took place over the territory of Germany during the Spremberg-Torgau Offensive, which was part of the Battle of Berlin. On 18 April 1945, when he took part in a strafing attack against a German troop convoy near Spremberg, his Airacobra was hit by antiaircraft fire. Guchok did his best to bring his burning machine to Soviet-held territory, but the fighter stalled and crashed, killing the pilot.

In all, in the course of his combat activities Guchok made 209 combat sorties, took part in fifty-six aerial engagements, and scored eighteen individual air victories supplemented by three shared victories. The majority of the aircraft shot down by Guchok were Bf 109 and Fw 190 fighters, supplemented by two Ju 87s and one Fw 189 as individual 'kills.' A further three Fw 189s were shot down in attacks conducted by a pair of 'Cobras.

On 27 June 1945, Lt. (SG) Pyotr Guchok, Guards, was posthumously awarded the title of Hero of the Soviet Union.

Vasiliy M. Drygin (1921–2009)

Vasiliy Mikhaïlovich Drygin was born in Checheliyevka village in what is now the Kirovograd Region of the Ukraine on 8 March 1921. He started his pilot's training in an aero club. In 1941 he graduated from the prestigious military flying school in Kacha. He passed his exams on 20 June 1941, two days before the war. Drygin and his young colleagues were immediately enrolled into the 298th IAP, which was being formed in the Odessa Military District (later it was transformed into the 104th GvIAP). Drygin fought in the ranks of this air unit throughout the war. Initially he flew an I-16 fighter, scoring at least one air victory and flying ground attack missions. This combat work was not devoid of dramatic situations. In one dogfight his I-16 was opposed by four enemy fighters. Soon his machine went down in flames, and it was a miracle that he remained alive after being thrown out of the aircraft as it exploded. Seriously wounded, the pilot crawled through a snow-covered forest for four days before he was discovered by a Soviet reconnaissance group and taken to a hospital. It took much effort to recover and regain his strength for further combat work.

In late 1942 the 298th IAP was withdrawn to the rear for replenishment and conversion to the new Lend-Lease Airacobras; Drygin started his acquaintance with the type by flying P-39D-2-BE 41-38421. In February 1943 the regiment proceeded to the North-Caucasus Front and became part of the 4th VA. Right from the start the regiment became involved in heavy air battles over Novorossiysk. In those days Vasiliy Drygin got a chance to display his qualities as a fighter pilot, and he did that with distinction. On 20 April 1943 he managed to shoot down two enemy bombers in single action over the so-called Blue Line (a.k.a. *Gothenkopf*, a German defensive line near the Taman' Peninsula) before his own aircraft was also hit by a burst of enemy fire. Drygin parachuted to safety and was fortunate to land amid the positions of Soviet troops.

Captain Vasiliy Drygin's next mount Airacobra was P-39L-1-BE 42-4611, coded '23 White.' By May 1943 he had made 261 combat sorties and taken part in forty aerial engagements in which he

OPPOSITE PAGE: Lt. Feres Z. Lepelenko, the 9th IAP's chief of navigation, beside one of the unit's P-39s, coded '74 White.'

RIGHT: 298th IAP CO lt.-col. I. A. Taranenko (*left*) congratulates Vasiliy M. Drygin on his early promotion to captain and decoration with the Order of Aleksandr Nevskiy; by then Drygin had scored eight 'kills.' His squadron commander, Maj. Vladimir Semenishin, is on the right. Korenovskaya airfield, May 1943.

BELOW: Vasiliy Drygin's buddies cheer as he returns from a sortie in his P-39L-1-BE 42-4611 on 12 June 1943 in which he claimed two 'kills.'

scored twelve individual air victories and five shared 'kills.' In July 1943, P-39L-1-BE 42-4611 was transferred to another unit and Vasiliy Drygin received a new aircraft.

On 3 May 1943 Drygin became the hero of an episode that received wide acclaim. On that day, by virtue of circumstances, he and his wingman Aleksandrov were up against nine Ju 87 dive bombers. Despite being outnumbered, the Soviet pilots attacked. In two passes Drygin shot down two enemy bombers, while Aleksandrov nailed a third Stuka. At that moment Drygin's aircraft was attacked by two German fighters. Drygin was shot down for the third time, yet again his luck did not betray him. He managed to bail out from his burning machine and landed on a tree that happened to be near the command post of the famous Marshal Gheorgiy K. Zhookov. Drygin's torn uniform at first set Zhookov

LEFT AND FAR LEFT: Very few photos exist of ace Vadim I Fadeyev because of his brief combat career. Here he is seen discussing the plan of a sortie with fellow 16th GvIAP pilot Andrey I. Trood over an area map.

BELOW LEFT: Vadim Fadeyev poses with his P-39. This photo shows well his signature beard.

on his guard, but he quickly understood the situation. He gave an order to decorate the pilot with the Order of Aleksandr Nevskiy, to promote him to the next rank, and to lead him into the presence of Air Marshal Aleksandr A.Novikov, who had overall command of the air force.

On 24 May 1943 Vasiliy Drygin was awarded the title of Hero of the Soviet Union for his courage and valour in combat with the enemies. In the course of the war he flew 320 successful combat sorties, conducting fifty aerial engagements, and shot down seventeen aircraft personally and eight as shared victories.

After the war Vasiliy Drygin served on in the ranks of the Soviet air force until 1962, when he was transferred to the reserve in the rank of colonel. Later he received economic education and worked as an air traffic controller at Rostov-on-Don airport until his retirement. He died on 3 September 2009 at the age of eighty-eight.

Vadim I. Fadeyev (1917–1943)

Vadim Ivanovich Fadeyev is a very colourful figure among the Soviet aces who flew the P-39 Airacobra. Born on 25 December 1917 in Fed'kino village in the Simbirsk Governorate (now Ul'yanovsk Region), he became a military pilot in 1940 after graduating from the 1st Chkalov military flying school in the city of Chkalov (renamed Orenburg in 1957). From 19 August 1941 he served in frontline air units, flying initially an I-16 and then a Yak-1 fighter. From May (some sources say August) 1942 onwards, Fadeyev fought in the ranks of the 16th GvIAP under Aleksandr I. Pokryshkin's command. The regiment was equipped with P-39 fighters.

Vadim Fadeyev was extremely popular among his fellow airmen. His bravery, indomitable energy, optimism, and sincere spirit of comradeship earned him everybody's admiration. Being of giant stature and athletic build, he flew five or six missions a day without any sign of fatigue. He was officially granted double food rations and the right to have his uniform tailor-made for him because the standard sizes were all too small. Out of joyous mischief he grew a beard, which earned him the nickname *Boroda* (Beard), and he used the word as his call sign.

His brilliant talent as a fighter pilot came to the fore during the famous air battle over the Kuban' River area, which took place between April and June 1944. In the course of a mere three weeks Vadim Fadeyev succeeded in shooting down close to twenty enemy aircraft. He fearlessly engaged numerically superior groups of enemy aircraft, displaying complete mastery of his machine and accurate gunnery.

As an illustration, here is a brief account of the air combat that was conducted by Fadeyev (at that time in the rank of Guards lieutenant senior grade) on 17 April 1943. Fadeyev was leading a group of eight aircraft that acted as a strike group (that is, intended for making a strike against bombers). A second group of four fighters commanded by Grigoriy A. Rechkalov flew top cover. Both groups were to pass over the northern spurs of the Caucasus and make a turn over the Black Sea. When the 'Cobras were in the vicinity of the coastal town of Anapa, they noticed a formation of twelve Ju 87 dive bombers escorted by Bf 109 fighters. They were heading for Cape Myskhako near Novorossiysk, where Soviet assault troops had secured a bridgehead; it was this site that was to be protected from the enemy bombers. Fadeyev ordered

ABOVE: Maj. Vladimir G. Semenishin stands on the wing of his mount, P-39K-1-BE 42-4420. He fought at the North Caucasian Front and was an ace with at least eight 'kills.'

RIGHT: Here Maj. Vladimir Semenishin is seen after receiving the HSU title. He became CO of the 298th IAP in the summer of 1943.

Rechkalov to attack the Bf 109s; his own target was the bombers, which he immediately attacked. Rechkalov's group shot down two Bf 109s, but soon the enemy called in reinforcements in the form of some fifteen Fw 190s.

Unabashed by the enemy's greater numbers, Fadeyev made a stake on the precise and bold manoeuvre and close interaction of the fighter pairs. He shot down one fighter in a vertical pass and another one in a dogfight; in addition, a Ju 87 was downed. Four other pilots of his group also scored five 'kills' among them, including an Fw 190.

Sadly, some of Fadeyev's best qualities—his audacity and self-confidence, his fighting zeal—at times made him reckless and were ultimately his undoing. On 5 May 1943, while flying a ground troops protection sortie near Krymskaya village in P-39D-2-BE 41-38428 (coded '37 White'), he apparently decided to chase a prospective 'victim' and lost contact with the rest of the group led by Pokryshkin. Together with his wingman Andrey Trood (flying an Airacobra coded '39 White'), he encountered a group of twelve Bf 109s. In the ensuing free-for-all, Fadeyev shot down two aircraft, but his machine was also hit by enemy fire and he was wounded; Trood was unable to protect him because he, too, was having a hard time with several Messerschmitts. Disengaging, Fadeyev managed a belly landing on the bank of the River Adagum (a

P-39K-1-BE 42-4420 / '30 White,' flown by Maj. Vladimir G. Semenishin in the spring and summer of 1943.

tributary of the Kuban') but died of his wounds. His death in combat was a sore loss for all his friends, including Pokryshkin, who valued him very highly both as a person and as a combat pilot.

On 24 May 1943 Vadim I. Fadeyev was posthumously awarded the title of Hero of the Soviet Union for his courage and valour in combat. In fact, the nomination for the HSU title had been filed a few days before he was killed in action.

Vladimir G. Semenishin (1910–1943)

Vladimir Grigor'yevich Semenishin was born in St. Petersburg on 15 June 1910. He enrolled in the Red Army in 1932, graduating from the Kacha flying school in 1936. In June 1941 he joined combat in the ranks of the 67th IAP (21st Composite Air Division, Air Force of the Southern Front). During the initial period of his wartime service he flew the I-16 fighter. In May 1942, he was seriously wounded and spent several months in the hospital. After recovery he mastered a new fighter type—the P-39—in the 25th ZAP in Adzhikabul. From 25 December 1943 Vladimir Semenishin was a squadron commander in the 298th IAP (which, interestingly, reported to the 219th Bomber Division of the 4th VA, North Caucasian Front). There he flew the Airacobra—specifically, P-39K-1-BE 42-4420 (coded '30 White'). Flying this machine, he quickly achieved impressive results.

On 24 May 1943 Semenishin was awarded the title of Hero of the Soviet Union for his eight personal air victories and seven shared victories scored in twenty-nine aerial engagements. On 18 July 1943 he became commander of the 298th IAP and was promoted to lieutenant-colonel a few days later (the unit was reorganised as the 104th GvIAP on 14 August that year).

Lt.-Col. Semenishin, CO of the 104th GvIAP, lost his life on 29 September 1943, when his small group of fighters tangled in a fierce dogfight with a numerically superior Luftwaffe group. Semenishin managed to shoot down three German aircraft before his Airacobra was set on fire. He was heavily wounded and bailed out, but the damaged parachute did not open and he fell to his death. The pilot's body fell in no-man's land, and it was two days before the Soviet troops managed to recover it after a lengthy shootout with the German troops, which were also attempting to get it.

Information on the results of Vladimir Semenishin's combat activities is somewhat controversial. According to one source, the final score was twenty-three individual 'kills' plus thirteen shared 'kills,' another source speaks of twenty + thirteen, and yet another (Mikhail Bykov) puts it at fifteen personal victories and eleven shared victories in more than 300 combat sorties. Of the last-stated score (Bykov's version), thirteen individual and ten shared victories were achieved while flying the Airacobra. The fifteen individual 'kills' included twelve Bf 109s, one Ju 87, and two Bf 110s.

ABOVE LEFT: Aleksandr I. Pokryshkin (*left*) and his wingman Gheorgiy G. Golubev at Mokrzeszów, Poland, in the autumn of 1943.

LEFT: Lt. Georgiy Golubev grins cheerfully as he poses on the wing of his Airacobra.

OPPOSITE PAGE: 213th GvIAP pilots (*left to right*) Lt. (SG) Anatoliy I. Svistunov (Sqn 1 commander), Lt. (SG) Nikolay V. Stroykov (Sqn 2 commander), and Lt. Mikhail I. Orlov are pictured with Svistunov's P-39Q-25-BE 44-32286 / '77 White' at Rozwadów, Poland, in September 1944. The fighter bears thirteen 'kill' stars.

Nikolay L. Trofimov (1922–1995)

Nikolay Leont'yevich Trofimov was born in Ignat'yevskiye Vyselki village (Moscow Region) on 19 September 1922. In 1939, he enlisted in the Red Army; that same year he enrolled in the Kacha flying school, from which he graduated in 1940. During the Great Patriotic War he went into battle as a lieutenant junior grade of the 84th 'A' IAP. Rising in the ranks as the war progressed, by the end of hostilities in 1945 he had become a Guards captain, serving as a squadron commander of the famous 16th GvIAP. Until the end of May 1943 Trofimov fought on the I-153 biplane, flying mostly ground attack missions. On 30 May 1943 he was transferred to the 16th GvIAP and was immediately appointed flight commander. By that time he already had several personal and shared 'kills' to his credit.

In the new regiment Trofimov avidly learned new tactics of air combat from Pokryshkin. who had made a point of sharing his experience and ideas with his fellow pilots. On 22 August 1943 Trofimov achieved his first air victory on the Airacobra, when he shot down a Bf 109 (it was credited to him as a shared victory). Soon he added to his score several aircraft of other types—a Ju 87, an Hs 129, and an Fw 189. On 1 November 1943 Trofimov shot down two Bf 109s in a single action and damaged a further two. This was not the last time he scored two air victories in a single mission—a similar event took place in 1944 during the air battles over Romania. On 31 May 1944 he shot down two Ju 87s. Trofimov's skill, bravery, and fighting spirit were duly noted by his fellow pilots and commanders alike.

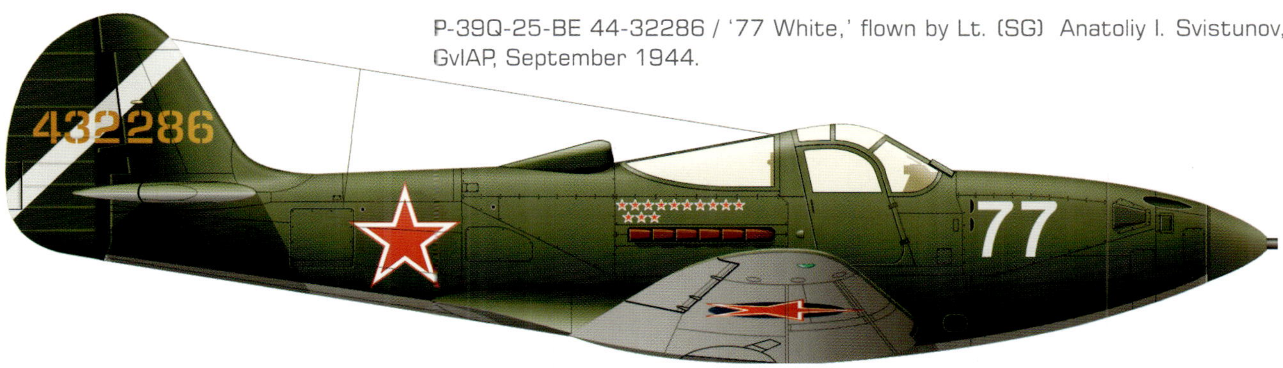

P-39Q-25-BE 44-32286 / '77 White,' flown by Lt. (SG) Anatoliy I. Svistunov, 213th GvIAP, September 1944.

12
BX 237

LEFT: 19th GvIAP CO Maj. Gheorgiy A. Kalugin, Sqn 1 commander Capt. Pavel S. Kutakhov, and the commanders of the unit's other two squadrons pose with Kutakhov's Airacobra I BX231, coded '12 White.' Note the unusual location of the 'kill' stars, of which there are at least thirty-one.

BELOW LEFT: Kutakhov is greeted by his fellow pilots as he returns from a sortie.

RIGHT: Pavel Kutakhov poses on the wing of his Airacobra; this is probably a different aircraft, judging by the location of the 'kill' markings.

BELOW RIGHT: Squadron commander Pavel Kutakhov in the cockpit of his fighter.

By the end of the war Trofimov had made 387 combat sorties and scored fifteen individual and eleven shared 'kills.' All of them are related to the period when he flew a P-39 in the ranks of the 16th GvIAP (the number of his earlier victories could not be established officially due to disorder and gaps in the files of his previous air unit). On 27 June 1945 Nikolay Trofimov was awarded the title of Hero of the Soviet Union and a Gold Star; prior to that, he had been awarded several other orders and medals.

After the war Trofimov continued his service in the 16th GvIAP. He was sent to the Korean War and flew combat sorties in the 72nd GvIAP of the 64th IAK (the Soviet task force in Korea) for a short time without scoring any 'kills.' After returning from Korea, at the end of 1952 he was appointed a fighter regiment CO. Subsequently he rose in the ranks to division CO and eventually air army commander in the air defence force. Nikolay Trofimov retired in 1982 in the rank of lieutenant-general. He died on 1 March 1998 at the age of seventy-five.

Gheorgiy G. Golubev (1919–2005)

Gheorgiy Gordeyevich Golubev (born on 7 April 1919 in the village of Zhgootovo in what is now the Krasnoyarsk Region of Russia) is one of the best-known pilots of the 16th GvIAP. He was transferred to this regiment in 1943, having previously served in the 40th IAP and the 84th 'A' IAP. There he had mostly flown ground attack and reconnaissance missions in the I-16; it was only in the 16th GvIAP that he got a chance to become a real fighter pilot and an ace. Having completed conversion training to the P-39 in the 84th 'A' IAP, Golubev and a group of pilots were sent to the 16th GvIAP. He arrived there on 31 May 1943 (or 29 April, according to his own recollections), when the famous battle over the Kuban' River area was drawing to a close. Regiment CO Aleksandr Pokryshkin took a liking to the new pilot. On 3 August 1943 Golubev made his first flight as Pokryshkin's wingman. He flew as wingman with Pokryshkin and later with Grigoriy A. Rechkalov, helping these aces to score many of their air victories by ensuring reliable protection for them in combat. In so doing he was shot down on 22 August 1943, managing to cross into Soviet-held territory before bailing out. Apart from that, he achieved a number of 'kills' to his own credit.

According to an official document of the regiment, by 24 December 1944, Guards flight commander Lt. Golubev had made 256 combat sorties (fifty on the I-16 and 206 on the P-39) and conducted fifty-six aerial engagements in which he shot down twelve enemy aircraft personally and one as a shared victory.

In the autumn of 1943 Golubev shot down several Ju 87 dive bombers and Ju 52/3m transports, some of the latter in the course of 'free chase' missions over the Black Sea. From June 1944 his aircraft was P-39Q-25-BE 44-32488 (coded '55 White').

In 1945 Golubev shot down three aircraft; of these, two Fw 190s were downed in the course of a single action on 18 April 1945. On that day a group led by Lt. Konstantin B. Sookhov clashed with eighteen Fw 190s and two Bf 109s. The end result was nine Fw 190s

shot down without own losses. The third machine destroyed by Golubev during that period was a Dornier Do 217, which he shot down near Prague on V-day, 9 May 1945. Golubev thus was the pilot who achieved the final Red Amy air force 'kill' in the Great Patriotic War—and possibly the final 'kill' on the European TO of the Second World War.

The final result of Golubev's combat activities during the whole period of the war was 308 combat sorties and seventy aerial engagements, in which he shot down fifteen enemy aircraft personally (fourteen, according to some sources) supplemented by one shared victory. On 27 June 1945 he was awarded the title of Hero of the Soviet Union (for which a nomination had been signed several months earlier).

After the war Gheorgiy Golubev continued his service in the Soviet air force. In 1956 he commanded an air regiment, and somewhat later, an air division. He retired in 1977 in the rank of colonel. Gheorgiy Golubev died on 12 April 2005, aged eighty-six.

Pavel S. Kutakhov (1914–1984)

Pavel Stepanovich Kutakhov was born in Malokirsanovka village (Rostov Region) on 16 August 1914, enlisting in the Red Army in 1935; he graduated from the Stalingrad military flying school in 1938. He gained his first combat experience during the Winter War with Finland. Immediately after the outbreak of the war with Germany he joined combat in the ranks of the 145th IAP (later renamed 19th GvIAP), in which he fought until May 1944. After that, until May 1945, he served in the 20th GvIAP. He rose in the ranks from squadron commander to Guards air regiment CO.

Kutakhov took part in the action on the Karelian Front in 1943. His unit was engaged in the defence of Murmansk, Kandalaksha (a town in the Murmansk Region on the White Sea coast), and the Kirov Railway, connecting Murmansk and Leningrad. Kutakhov also took part in ensuring air cover for the Allied northern convoys.

In 1941–42 he fought on the MiG-3 and LaGG-3. Starting in 1942 he successively flew several versions of the Airacobra, starting with the Airacobra I received from Great Britain (specifically, BX228, c/n 14-469) and ending with a P-39Q delivered from the US.

By February 1943 Guards major Pavel S. Kutakhov, commander of the 1st Squadron of the 19th GvIAP (258th IAD, 7th VA, Karelian Front), had made 362 combat sorties, conducted forty aerial engagements, and shot down seven enemy aircraft personally and twenty-four as shared victories. Things did not always work out well for him; on 27 March 1943 Kutakhov was shot down in his Airacobra during a dogfight, parachuting to safety.

On 1 May 1943 Pavel Kutakhov was awarded the title of Hero of the Soviet Union for courage and valour in combat. This was not the only major distinction that he earned. In 1944 King George VI of the United Kingdom awarded to Guards major Pavel Kutakhov the Order of British Empire, 4th Class, for his piloting skills and valour displayed in missions for the protection of the Allies' northern convoys.

During the combat activities of his unit, Kutakhov displayed the qualities of a good leader. On many occasions he commanded groups of fighters in combat and ensured successful accomplishment of the missions. For example, on 22 June 1942 a squadron led by Kutakhov repelled an air raid on Murmansk involving thirty German aircraft. In this episode the Soviet pilots shot down two Bf 110s and one Bf 109F without own losses. On 28 June 1942, nine fighters under the command of Kutakhov scrambled to intercept German aircraft that were heading towards the Tuloma hydroelectric power station (currently called the Lower Tuloma hydroelectric power station because another was built farther upstream on the Tuloma River after the war), with the intention of bombing it. The Soviet fighters were opposed by eight Bf 110s and three Bf 109Fs. Again, Kutakhov's group emerged victorious, scoring three 'kills' with no losses to themselves.

Pavel Kutakhov was known for his propensity for analysing his unit's combat experience and for planning the forthcoming combat missions carefully; he made a point of preparing in advance several possible scenarios of a battle. Fairly often he practiced 'free chase'; on such occasions he singled out enemy reconnaissance aircraft as his targets and had luck in chasing and shooting them down.

ABOVE LEFT: Here Pavel S. Kutakhov is seen as major and HSU after flying a sortie on 18 August 1943.

LEFT: Pavel Kutakhov among the pilots of the 19th GvIAP at the unit's base near Murmansk after a government award handing-out ceremony.

TOP RIGHT AND ABOVE RIGHT: 19th IAP deputy squadron commander, Capt. I. D. Gaidayenko. His P-39, which sported twenty-six 'kill' markings, was fancifully named Krasatoolechka ('Tootsie') as a tribute to the P-39's looks.

RIGHT: Lt. (SG) Konstantin B. Sookhov (16th GvIAP) takes off from a German highway in 1945; his P-39 is toting a bomb. Sookhov scored nineteen of his twenty-two 'kills' in the P-39 and became HSU.

Kutakhov's fellow pilots and subordinates highly valued his talent for teaching the essentials of combat tactics to young pilots. He devised new tactical methods of air combat, notably with a view to ensuring effective protection to the Il-2 *shturmoviks*.

On 8 September 1944, Guards major Pavel Kutakhov was appointed commander of the 20th GvIAP stationed nearby. Despite the load of new functions and responsibilities, he found time to fly combat missions.

By May 1945 Kutakhov had made 367 successful combat sorties and conducted seventy-nine aerial engagements. He was credited with fourteen aircraft shot down personally and twenty-eight as shared 'kills.' Some of these victories have not been documented; in the light of later research his score was revised to thirteen + twenty-four or even thirteen + fifteen.

After the war Kutakhov continued his service in the Soviet air force, where he rose in the ranks and in 1969 was appointed commander in chief of the Soviet air force and deputy minister of defence of the USSR. In 1972 he was promoted to the rank of air chief marshal. He remained an active pilot until the age of sixty, flying state-of-the-art jet fighters.

On 15 August 1984 Pavel Kutakhov was awarded the second Hero of the Soviet Union title for his outstanding contribution to introducing new weaponry into the air force and in connection with his seventieth birthday. He died on 3 December 1984.

Vasiliy D. Sharenko (1916–1944)

Vasiliy Denisovich Sharenko was born in Kuzemin village, in what is now the Soomy Region of the Ukraine, on 21 March 1916. He obtained his pilot's licence in 1939 after graduating from the prestigious military flying school in Kacha, where he enrolled in December 1937. His service in the frontline air units started in January 1942. He was enrolled in the 45th IAP, which was transformed into the 100th GvIAP on 18 June 1943. This regiment was equipped with Airacobras (before converting to this type, Sharenko had flown the Yak-1 and the Curtiss P-40 Kittyhawk).

Starting his flying career as a flight commander, Sharenko rose in the ranks and became a squadron commander in 1943; in 1944 he was appointed the regiment's chief of navigation. His personal courage and skill went hand in hand with a taste for devising new methods of air combat. For example, he suggested that the P-40s still remaining in the regiment be used as a lure for German fighters because Luftwaffe pilots considered them to be less dangerous than the P-39s. The idea behind the proposal was to thwart German attempts to 'clean the sky' for their bombers before the latter arrived at the target area. The proposal was approved and put into effect. In anticipation of a German air raid, the regiment's command sent on a mission a mixed group of aircraft. The Kittyhawks were at the forefront of the group, while the more potent Airacobras, flying at different flight levels, tried to hide their presence. The situation developed as follows. As expected, the German pilots immediately pounced on the Kittyhawks; at that moment the Airacobras jumped them in a diving attack out of the sun and shot down two or three Bf 109s, engaging the rest of them in combat. In the meantime, German bombers arrived on the scene, which their crews confidently expected to be free of Soviet fighters. They counted wrongly—and paid the price for this miscalculation.

Thus, the tactic proposed by Sharenko worked—he ran the risk but helped other pilots shoot down enemy aircraft. Of course, the Germans eventually grew wise to the trick and could no longer be fooled easily.

By November 1943 the squadron commander of the 100th GvIAP Guards, Captain Vasiliy Sharenko, had made 223 combat sorties, taking part in fifty-one aerial engagements in which he shot down twelve aircraft personally and four as shared victories. This became his final score. Of the twelve aircraft mentioned above, eight were bombers (four Ju 87s, two Ju 88s, and two He 111s); the rest were two Fw 189 reconnaissance aircraft and two Bf 109 fighters. Six of these twelve victories were scored while flying the Airacobra. On 13 April 1944 Sharenko was awarded the title of Hero of the Soviet Union for his courage and valour in combat.

Sadly, on 30 July 1944, Guards major Vasiliy Sharenko was killed in action. He was sent on a mission in a Polikarpov Po-2 biplane with the task of selecting sites for new airfields, which became necessary due to the rapid advancement of the Soviet troops towards the Wisła River. During that flight his aircraft was shot down by ground fire. He was buried in the city of L'vov (L'viv in Ukrainian spelling) at a war memorial.

Pavel P. Kryukov (1906–1974)

Pavel Pavlovich Krykov, born in Biryovo village (Moscow Governorate, Russian Empire) on 15 December 1906, was one of the oldest pilots in the 16th GvIAP, where he fought on Airacobras together with Aleksandr Pokryshkin and other renowned aces. When the Soviet-German war started in June 1941, he already had some combat experience. Krykov's military career began in 1932, when he graduated from the air force military theory school in Leningrad. Two years later he graduated from a military flying school and served as a pilot in air force units deployed east of Baikal in Siberia. During the fighting against Japanese forces on the Khalkhin-Gol River (a.k.a. the Nomonhan Incident) in 1939, he took part in air battles over Mongolian territory, flying an I-15 fighter. He was credited with three air victories and was decorated with the Order of the Red Banner.

From June 1941 Pavel Krykov served in frontline air units. Until May 1944 he served in the 55th IAP (renamed as the 16th GvIAP from March 1942). In 1941–42, he consecutively flew the I-16, the MiG-3, and the Yak-1. Kryukov became a close friend of Pokryshkin, who had a great respect for the experienced airman's skill, bravery, and wisdom. Kryukov, for his part, supported Pokryshkin wholeheartedly in the latter's search for new tactical methods of air combat. In late 1942 and early 1943, when the 16th GvIAP was converting to the P-39s, Kryukov put in much effort into teaching his fellow pilots new tactics of air combat.

From April 1943 all pilots of the 16th GvIAP flew Airacobras; Kryukov's aircraft was P-39L-1-BE 42-4596. Having completed conversion training at the 25th ZAP in Adzhikabul, Azerbaijan, the regiment was transferred to the Kuban' area, which became the scene of fierce air battles. In those battles Pavel Krykov displayed both skill and great fighting spirit, scoring a number of 'kills.' On one memorable occasion (12 April 1943?) he had to fight alone against four Bf 109s. Two of the German fighters were shot down by Kryukov, and one Bf 109 was driven into a dive from which it failed to recover. Three days later, on 15 April, Kryukov and his wingman flew a mission in a group of six that also included Pokryshkin and his wingman, and a third pair. The group engaged a large formation of Ju 88 and He 111 bombers, and Krykov shot down one Ju 88 but was jumped by several Bf 109s immediately afterwards. The situation was desperate. Luckily, in the ensuing mêlée one of the 'messers' inadvertently overshot, placing itself right in front of the Airacobra's nose, and was promptly set alight by a burst from Kryukov's cannon. However, his own machine was also hit and damaged. Krykov succeeded in throwing the pursuing German fighters off his tail and made a successful forced landing on a lawn with the undercarriage extended.

By May 1943, Guards major Pavel Krykov, navigator of the 16th GvIAP, had made 415 combat sorties, which included

ABOVE LEFT: 104th GvIAP pilot Capt. Aleksey S. Zakalyuk in his P-39, wearing tiger's-head nose art; the pilot and the tiger have the same grin. Zakalyuk scored nineteen individual 'kills' and four shared 'kills.'

LEFT: Flight leader Lt. (SG) Aleksey Zakalyuk with his P-39L at Korenovskaya AB.

ABOVE: Zakhar Sorokin, a North Fleet air arm / 2nd GvIAP P-39 pilot who continued to fly and fight after losing both feet when he was shot down in October 1941.

RIGHT: Zakhar Sorokin explains combat tactics to a fellow pilot in early 1944.

Aleksandr I. Pokryshkin, Thrice HSU, CO of the 16th GvIAP and later of the 9th GvIAD

Grigoriy A. Rechkalov, Twice HSU

Nikolay D. Gulayev, Twice HSU

Boris B. Glinka, HSU, 16th GvIAP CO

Dmitriy B. Glinka, Twice HSU

Aleksey S. Smirnov, here shown as Twice HSU

Vladimir D. Lavrinenkov, Twice HSU

Pavel M. Kamozin, Twice HSU

Aleksandr F. Kloobov, HSU

Sultan Amet-khan, HSU

Aleksey V. Alelyukhin, Twice HSU

Ivan P. Babak, HSU

Andrey I. Trood, HSU

Arkadiy V. Fycdorov (HSU), here shown in post-war-style everyday uniform

Yevgeniy P. Mariinskiy, HSU

Vasiliy M. Drygin, HSU

Vladimir G. Semenishin, HSU

Nikolay L. Trofimov (HSU), here shown in post-war-style parade dress

Gheorgiy G. Golubev, HSU

Pavel S. Kutakhov, here shown in 1944 as HSU (a second HSU title was conferred on him in 1984

Pyotr I. Guchok, HSU

Vasiliy D. Sharenko, HSU

Pavel P. Kryukov, HSU

Zakhar A. Sorokin (HSU) in postwar navy uniform parade dress

Combat achievements of the Soviet aces who flew the P-39 Airacobra					
Name and surname	Hero of the Soviet Union title	Number of air victories (individual+shared), early official data	Number of air victories (individual+shared), recent research data	Number of combat sorties and aerial engagements	Number of air victories scored on the P-39 (individual+shared)
Aleksandr I. Pokryshkin	HSU (three awards)	59+6	53+6 (46+6)	600/139	45+4
Grigoriy A. Rechkalov	HSU (two awards)	56+6	61+4 (59+7)	452/?	50
Nikolay D. Gulaev	HSU (two awards)	57+3	55+5	250/49	37+3
Dmitriy B. Glinka	HSU (two awards)	50+0	49+1	272/?	37
Aleksey S. Smirnov	HSU (two awards)	35+15	35+0	457/72 (306/71)	32
Vladimir D. Lavrinenkov	HSU (two awards)	35+11, 36+11	36+7	448/134	12
Pavel M. Kamozin	HSU (two awards)	36+13	36+2	188/63	24
Aleksandr F. Kloobov *	HSU (two awards) †	31+19	31+3	457/95	28
Sultan Amet-khan *	HSU (two awards)	30+19	30+19	603/150	11?
Aleksey V. Alelyukhin	HSU (two awards	40+17	28+6	601/123	8
Ivan I. Babak	HSU	35+5	35+5	330/103	35+5?
Boris B. Glinka	HSU	30+1	27+2	115/48	27
Andrey I. Trood	HSU	25+1	26+1	400+/?	24
Arkadiy V. Fyodorov	HSU	24+18	19+5 (22+4) (14+2)	600+/?	12+1
Yevgeniy P. Mariinskiy	HSU	20	18 +0	238/60 (210/60)	18
Pyotr I. Guchok ‡	HSU	?	18+3	209/56	18+3
Vasiliy M. Drygin	HSU	?	17+8	320/50+	13+7
Vadim I. Fadeyev ‡	HSU †	17+3	17+1	394/43	15+1
Vladimir G. Semenishin ‡	HSU	20+13	15 + 11	≈ 300	14
Nikolay L. Trofimov	HSU	15+11	15+11	387/75	15
Gheorgiy G. Golubev	HSU	15+1	14+1	308/70	15 (14)
Pavel S. Kutakhov	HSU + HSU 1984	14+28	13+15	367/79	?
Vasiliy D. Sharenko ‡	HSU	16+4	12+4	240/51 '(300?)	6
Pavel P. Kryukov	HSU	12+1	10+1	600+/?	8
Zakhar A. Sorokin	HSU	18	10+0	267	5+1

* Killed in flying accident; † (Second) HSU title awarded posthumously; ‡ Killed in action

(The list is not exhaustive. With some exceptions, the names are arranged in the descending order of the number of air victories; the corrected figures are based on research be Mikhail Bykov and Andrey Marchukov)

reconnaissance and ground attack missions as well as flying top cover for the ground troops and providing escort for bombers. In forty aerial engagements he shot down six aircraft personally and one as a shared victory. On 24 May 1943 Pavel Krykov was awarded the title of Hero of the Soviet Union.

In the course of subsequent intensive combat activities in the skies of the Crimea, Donbass, Moldavia and Poland Kryukov added several further air victories to his score.

From May 1944 Pavel Krykov served in the 104th GvIAP and was its CO before being appointed deputy commander of the 9th GvIAD in the autumn of 1944. By the end of the war he had made more than 600 combat sorties, in which he scored ten individual air victories and one shared victory. In addition to six Bf 109s, he shot down four bombers—two Ju 88s and two He 111s.

After the war Pavel Krykov continued his service in the Soviet air force as an air division commander, rising to the rank of major-general, in which he retired in July 1956. He died on 11 November 1974 at the age of sixty-seven.

Zakhar A. Sorokin (1917–1978)

Among Soviet pilots who fought on the P-39 Airacobra, Zakhar Artyomovich Sorokin does not lay claim to being a top-scoring ace, yet he deserves attention due to a special circumstance: he flew the Bell fighter after losing both feet, which were replaced by prosthetic limbs. Here is his story.

Zakhar Sorokin was born on 17 March 1917 at Glubokoye railway station settlement in the Novosibirsk Region. He graduated from the Yeisk naval aviation flying school in 1939 and served in Sevastopol' in an air unit of the Black Sea Fleet air arm. In July 1941 he was transferred to the North Fleet and served in the 78th IAP at Vayenga-1 AB, commanded by the famous pilot Boris F. Safonov. There he flew a MiG-3 fighter. In September 1941 he shot down four German aircraft and was awarded the Order of the Red Banner. In a dogfight that took place on 25 October 1941, Sorokin damaged a Bf 110 by ramming it, but his own machine was also damaged, crash-landing in the frozen tundra. Fortunately, he survived the impact, but he had to fight for his life immediately afterwards because the German aircraft had also made a forced landing nearby, and its two crew members, armed with pistols, opened fire on him. Sorokin returned fire with his pistol, killing them, and then headed in the direction of his home unit. It took him six days to crawl through the wilderness, covering a distance of 70 km (43.5 miles) before he reached the positions of Soviet troops. Unfortunately both of his feet were severely frostbitten and

Capt. Pavel I. Chepinoga (HSU) with his P-39, bearing an impressive score of twenty-four 'kills.'

had to be amputated; nevertheless, this did not prevent him from continuing his career as a pilot. As soon as he recovered and learned the use of his artificial limbs, he returned to his regiment and resumed flying activities—this time on an Airacobra. In February 1943 he shot down his seventh aircraft. Amazed by the courage and fortitude of the Russian pilot, the British military attaché came to Vayenga from Moscow and handed to the pilot a high award—the Order of the British Empire.

On 19 August 1944 Zakhar Sorokin was awarded the title of Hero of the Soviet Union. By that time he had performed 117 combat sorties (including four reconnaissance missions and ten missions for escorting bombers and torpedo bombers), conducted aerial engagements, and scored eleven individual 'kills' (presumably this is the official score listed in the nomination for the HSU title).

By the end of the war Zakhar Sorokin had shot down eighteen aircraft, twelve of them during the period when he was flying with artificial limbs. That was the score with which he was officially credited at that time. Later these figures were revised in the light of documentary research. One of the researchers, Mikhail Yu. Bykov, credits Sorokin with ten confirmed 'kills' and one 'probable.'

After the war Zakhar Sorokin returned to the Black Sea Fleet air arm, where he served until his retirement from active duty in 1955. After that, he took up writing and journalism. He died on 19 March 1978, aged sixty-one.

Pavel I. Chepinoga (1912–1963)

Pavel Iosifovich Chepinoga was born in the village of Ivanovka (Kherson Region, the Ukraine). He was drafted into the Red Army in 1933; in 1940 he graduated from the Khar'kov military flying school. Chepinoga's frontline service started in January 1942 in the rank of lieutenant; he fought on the Leningrad, Voronezh, and 2nd Ukrainian Fronts. In March 1943 he was assigned to the 27th IAP (renamed as the 129th GvIAP in October 1943) as squadron commander. There he flew combat missions in MiG-3, Hurricane, Yak-1 (the type on which he scored his first 'kills'), and Airacobra fighters. In October 1943 he was transferred to the 508th IAP (later renamed as the 213th GvIAP), where he continued to fly Airacobras; one of them was a P-39Q coded '100 White.'

By 20 May 1944 the squadron commander of the 508th IAP, Captain Pavel I. Chepinoga, had made one hundred combat sorties, conducted thirty-seven aerial engagements, and achieved twenty-two individual aerial victories and one shared 'kill.' On 26 October

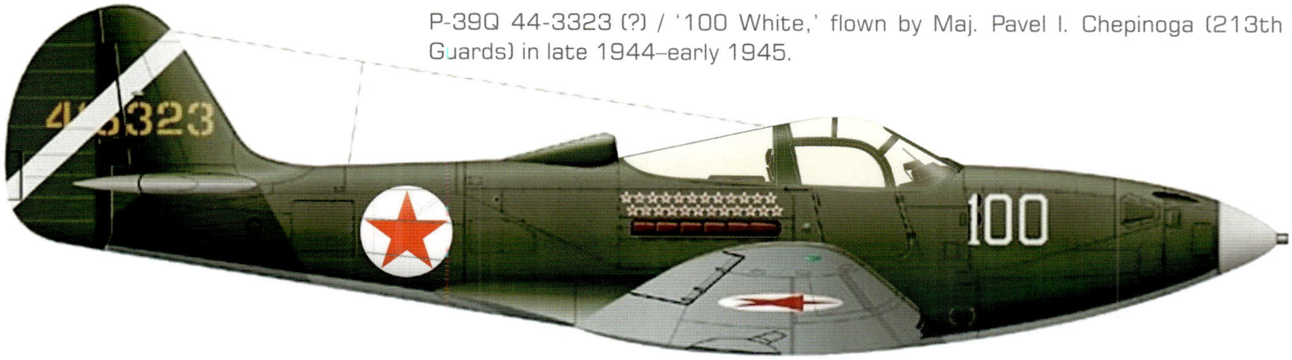

P-39Q 44-3323 (?) / '100 White,' flown by Maj. Pavel I. Chepinoga (213th GvIAP, Guards) in late 1944–early 1945.

Vyacheslav F. Sirotin (HSU) in the cockpit of his P-39 wearing famous nose art—an eagle swooping down on a German ship and a German aircraft.

BELOW LEFT: Sirotin poses with his aircraft in the spring of 1945, with his scoreboard of twenty personal 'kills' and one shared 'kill' on the cockpit door.

BELOW RIGHT: Capt. Nikolay I. Proshenkov (*left*) and Capt. V. N. Yakimov with the 21st GvIAP's P-39Ns, paid for by public subscription. The nearest aircraft is named Krasnoyarskiy kolkhoznik (Collective farm worker of Krasnoyarsk).

1944 he (by then a Guards major in the 213th GvIAP) was awarded the title of Hero of the Soviet Union.

In April 1945 Chepinoga was transferred to the 104th GvIAP. In all, during the war he flew 127 combat sorties, conducted some forty aerial engagements, and shot down twenty-five enemy aircraft personally (eleven Ju 87s, eight Bf 109s, one Ju 88, one Do 217, one He 111, one Hs 126, one Hs 129, and one Fw 190), complemented with one shared victory (another Hs 126). Of these, fourteen 'kills' were scored while flying the Airacobra.

After the war Pavel Chepinoga continued active service in the Soviet air force until 1947, when he was transferred to the reserve and took up activities in the DOSAAF paramilitary technical sports organisation. He died on 12 July 1963.

Vyacheslav F. Sirotin (1913–1948)

Vyacheslav Fyodorovich Sirotin was born on 22 September 1913 in St. Petersburg. In 1937 he graduated from the Khar'kov military flying school. During the first months of the war (June–October 1941) he fought in the 123rd IAP of the 10th Composite Air Division, flying the I-153 biplane in action on the Western Front; later he flew the Yak-1 in the ranks of air defence force units, first in the Moscow area (6th IAK PVO) and then near Leningrad (7th IAK PVO). In 1942–43 he fought at the North-Western Front in the ranks of the 238th IAP (239th IAD/7th VA), flying the LaGG-3.

From June 1944 Sirotin was assigned to the 17th IAP of the 190th IAD / 3rd VA, which flew P-39N Airacobras during military operations in Belorussia (the 3rd Belorussian Front) and the Baltic area (the 1st Baltic Front). On 15 August 1944 he was shot down in a dogfight with German fighters; despite being wounded, he managed to bail out and returned to action after recovering from his wounds. By October 1944 the deputy CO of the 17th IAP, Captain Sirotin had made twenty-three combat sorties and personally shot down fifteen enemy aircraft. On 23 February 1945 he was awarded the title of Hero of the Soviet Union.

By the end of the war, Sirotin (by then promoted to major) had made 326 combat sorties, conducted sixty-five aerial engagements,

The P-39 flown by Maj. Vyacheslav Sirotin (17th IAP) in the spring of 1945.

and scored twenty-one individual 'kills,' of which twelve were achieved while flying the P-39, plus a shared 'kill' against a tethered observation balloon. Interestingly, all twelve of these 'kills' are listed as Fw 190s.

In August–September 1945 Sirotin took part in military operations against Japan, flying the P-63 Kingcobra in the 17th IAP, which, along with the 190th IAD, had been transferred to the 12th VA waging war on the Transbaikalian Front. This included a single skirmish with Japanese fighters who attacked a Soviet transport aircraft carrying fuel for the advancing Soviet troops (the transport was escorted by Sirotin and his wingman, the latter managing to shoot down one of the attackers).

After the war, Maj. Vyacheslav F. Sirotin served on as CO of the 17th IAP. His postwar service in the Soviet air force tragically ended when he was killed in an air crash on 7 August 1948.

Nikolay I. Proshenkov (1918–1963)

Nikolay Ivanovich Proshenkov was born on 7 January 1918 in the village of Putyatino, in what is now the Vladimir Region. He joined the army in 1938, having previously received some flight training in an aero club. In 1939 he graduated from the 1st Chkalovsk military flying school.

Proshenkov's wartime service started in August 1941. In the period up to June 1942 he flew combat missions in the I-153 and

LEFT: Wearing a helmet liner, Capt. Nikolay I. Proshenkov, of the Guards, grins as he sits on the wing of his P-39N-1-BE '46 White.' Apart from the lightning bolt and the way how the sixteen 'kill' stars were arranged around the tactical code, the aircraft is notable for its nose art—the closest you could get to pinup pics in the Soviet air force. Such artwork was extremely rare—although the pictures are very restrained by Western standards!

BELOW: With Proshenkov's fighter as a backdrop, 69th GvIAP pilots read the much-awaited letters from home during a lull in the fighting on the 1st Ukrainian Front.

OPPOSITE PAGE: Lt. (SG) Ivan V. Bochkov's Airacobra I AH692 / '12 White' at the scene of its forced landing near Arkhangel'sk. The starboard cockpit door has been jettisoned.

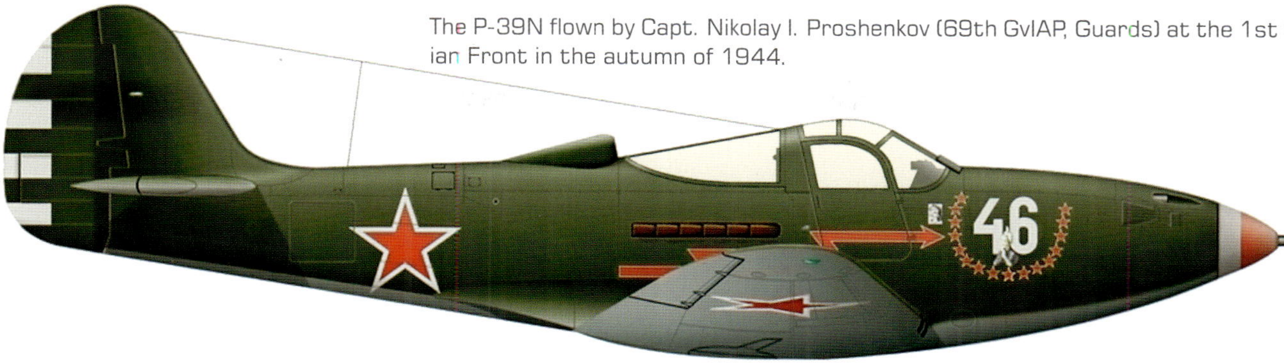

The P-39N flown by Capt. Nikolay I. Proshenkov (69th GvIAP, Guards) at the 1st Ukrainian Front in the autumn of 1944.

then in the Yak-1. From June 1942 Proshenkov was assigned to the 21st GvIAP, where his mount was first the Yak-1 and then the Airacobra. He continued to fly the P-39 after his transfer to the 69th GvIAP, waging war on the 1st Ukrainian Front in September 1944; in this unit his mount was a P-39N coded '46 White.'

By the end of the war, squadron commander of the 69th GvIAP Guards major Nikolay I. Proshenkov had made 380 combat sorties and conducted eighty-six aerial engagements in which he scored eighteen individual aerial victories and four shared 'kills' (an official document credits him with nineteen individual 'kills' and four shared 'kills'). For his bravery and gallantry in combat he was awarded the title of Hero of the Soviet Union on 27 June 1945.

Nikolay Proshenkov's postwar service in the Soviet air force lasted until 1960, when he was transferred to the reserve. He died on 27 April 1963 at the age of only forty-five.

Ivan V. Bochkov (1915–1943)

Ivan Vasil'yevich Bochkov was born on 17 September 1915 in the village of Fil'kino, of the present-day Kaluga Region, in a peasant family. Moving to Moscow, he got a chance to join an air club and receive primary flying training. In 1937 he was enlisted in the Red Army and sent to the Borisoglebsk flying school, from which he graduated in 1939. Bochkov served in the frontline air units from the first days of the Soviet-German war, flying initially I-16 and then LaGG-3 fighters. The 19th GvIAP of the Karelian Front, in which he served, completed its transition to Airacobra Is by 15 May 1942. Lt. (SG) Bochkov quickly mastered the new machine; in his very first aerial engagement in this fighter, on that same day, he downed a Bf 110. On that occasion he was flying as wingman to Capt. Pavel S. Kutakhov, who also shot down a Bf 110; these were the very first Airacobra 'kills' in Soviet service.

When his original aircraft (AH692 / '12 White,' c/n 14-123) was turned over to a repair shop after an off-field forced landing near Arkhangel'sk on 22 May 1942, Ivan Bochkov received another Airacobra I (AH726 / '36 White,' c/n 14-167). By February 1943 Guards captain Bochkov had made 308 combat sorties and conducted forty-five aerial engagements; he was credited with seven individual 'kills' and thirty-two shared victories (later research found confirmation for five and seventeen victories, respectively).

On 4 April 1943 Ivan Bochkov, flying Airacobra I BX168 / '15 White' (c/n 14-409), and his wingman were intercepted by a group of six Bf 109s near Yoorkino village (Murmansk Region). In the ensuing dogfight Bochkov scored his last 'kill' but was shot down as well, losing his life. This was his 350th combat sortie.

On 1 May 1943 Guards major Ivan Bochkov was posthumously awarded the title of Hero of the Soviet Union.

Pavel D. Klimov (1920–1992)

Pavel Dmitriyevich Klimov was born on 7 February 1920 in Baku, the capital of the Azerbaijan Soviet Socialist Republic, in a worker's family. Joining the Soviet navy in November 1938, he was sent to the Yeisk naval flying school, from which he graduated in June 1941. Initially he was a pilot of the Black Sea Fleet air arm's 3rd ZAP, but shortly after the outbreak of the war, in September 1941, he was transferred to an active unit—the 8th IAP.

In January 1942 Sergeant Pavel Klimov was transferred to the North Fleet, where he initially served in the 78th IAP equipped

LEFT: Here Capt. Ivan V. Bochkov is seen with another Airacobra I of the 19th GvIAP in East Karelia in 1942 (coded '16 White'). It is not certain whether he flew this particular fighter.

BELOW: Bochkov (*leftmost*) and other 19th GvIAP pilots pose with the same aircraft at Shongui airfield in East Karelia, 1942.

BELOW RIGHT: Lt. Pavel D. Klimov, North Fleet air arm / 2nd GvIAP pilot, poses with his P-39, which wears nose art in the form of a flying seagull.

with Hawker Hurricanes and then in the 2nd GvIAP (formerly 72nd IAP). There he consecutively flew the Hurricane, P-40E Kittyhawk, and P-39M-1-BE. It was on the Airacobra that Pavel Klimov gained the distinction of becoming the first Soviet pilot to score a night 'kill' in the High North, destroying a German bomber on 15 December 1942.

By May 1943 Klimov had become an officer (Guards lieutenant junior grade) and had flown 306 sorties (including twelve night sorties), participating in thirty-three aerial engagements and scoring eight 'kills' (one of which was listed as a 'probable'). For these achievements he was awarded the Hero of the Soviet Union title on 24 July 1943.

After studying at the higher officers' courses from December 1943 to July 1944, Pavel Klimov returned to his unit and was appointed deputy commander of the 2nd GvIAP's Squadron 3; in January 1945 he became squadron commander. By the end of the war his score had risen to eleven 'kills' (including one 'probable'); five of these were achieved on the P-39. Mikhail Bykov puts his score at nine plus one 'probable.'

After the war Pavel Klimov served on with the 2nd GvIAP until November 1946. Later, he took up studies in the air force academy, subsequently serving as CO of the North Fleet's 172nd IAP (1951–54) and the 458th IAP (1954–55); later he became chief of flight training in the North Fleet's 90th IAD. Subsequently the latter

19th GvIAP Airacobra I AH692 / '12 White,' in which Capt. Ivan V. Bochkov made a forced landing on 22 May 1942.

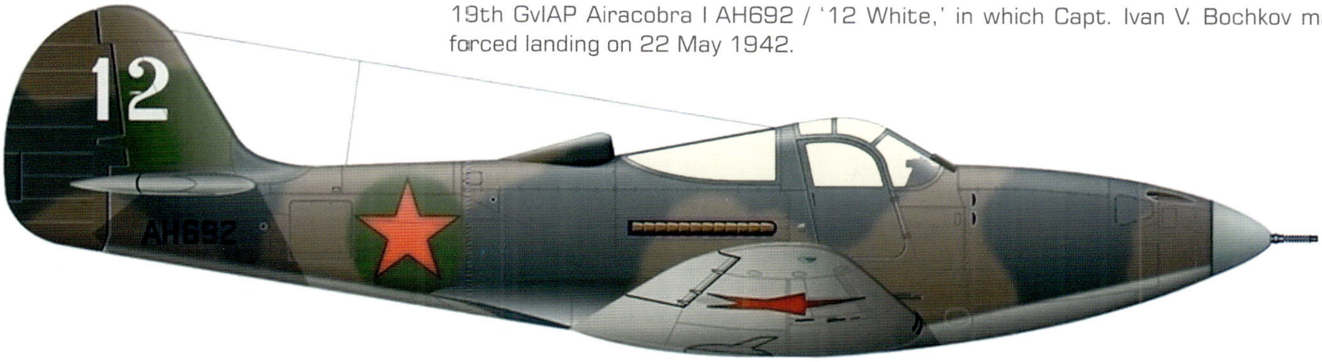

19th GvIAP Airacobra I BX168 / '15 White,' in which Bockhov was shot down and killed on 4 April 1943.

division (and Pavel Klimov with it) was transferred to the air defence force. Klimov held a number of other high-ranking positions in the PVO and the naval aviation until he retired in October 1970 in the rank of colonel. After this he worked in the Soviet Union's service for hydrometeorology and environmental monitoring. He died on 8 December 1992 at the age of seventy-two.

Pavel A. Panin (1908–1943)

Pavel Alekseyevich Panin was born on 23 March 1908 in the city of Tsaritsyn (later known as Stalingrad, now called Volgograd) in a worker's family. In 1932 he joined the Red Army and took theoretical aviation courses in Leningrad; two years later he graduated from a military flying school in Engels. In 1938 he took part in the action in the skies of China, fighting against Japanese invaders.

After the outbreak of the Great Patriotic War in June 1941, Panin was engaged in active frontline service from the outset, flying combat missions in the I-16, LaGG-3, and Yak-1 fighters in the 255th IAP (originally a Kiev special military district unit). In July May 1942 this regiment was assigned to the Supreme Command HQ's strike group defending Leningrad. Two months later the group was redesignated as the special naval aviation group (which was active until October) and redeployed to the North Fleet. In 1943 the regiment reequipped with Bell P-39 fighters and continued operating in the North Fleet air arm. By August 1943 Major Pavel A. Panin was promoted to the post of commander of the 255th IAP, which reported to the 5th MTAD (***min**no-**torped**naya **avia**di-**vee**ziya*; Minelayer & Torpedo-Bomber Division) and flew top cover missions for the protection of torpedo bombers.

On 26 August 1943 Pavel Panin headed a group of six fighters that scrambled to intercept thirty enemy aircraft (the latter were flying top cover for a German shipping convoy that was attacked by the 5th MTAD). In the ensuing aerial engagement the German

ABOVE LEFT: Pavel D. Klimov (here, in the rank of captain) is pictured climbing into his P-39. At least two 'kill' stars' are visible on the aircraft's nose (he scored a total of 11 'kills').

LEFT: Maj. Pavel A. Panin, CO of the North Fleet air arm's 255th IAP. He managed to score thirteen 'kills' before losing his life in action on 26 August 1943 and was posthumously awarded the HSU title.

P-39M-1-BE / '05 White,' flown by Lt. (JG) Pavel D. Klimov in the spring of 1943, North Fleet air arm / 2nd GvSAP.

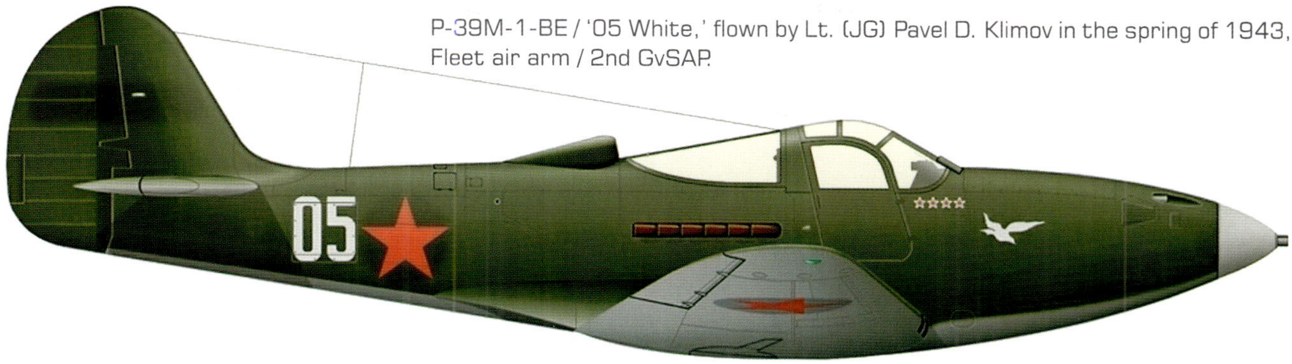

formation suffered tangible losses, but the regiment's Airacobras returned to base without their commander. Major Panin, doing his best to frustrate a German fighter's attack against a torpedo bomber, exposed his own machine to a deadly salvo. Panin's courage, skilful leadership in air combat, and self-sacrifice were duly recognised; on 22 January 1944 he was posthumously awarded the title of Hero of the Soviet Union. According to the nomination document, he had made 113 combat sorties and conducted eighteen aerial engagements in which he had shot down thirteen aircraft (later research by Mikhail Bykov established documentary confirmation for six individual 'kills').

Dmitriy V. Zyuzin (1921–1976)

Dmitriy Vasil'yevich Zyuzin was born on 1 November 1921 in the town of Maikop, in what was then the Maikop District of the Kuban' Region, North Caucasus (this later became the Cherkes Autonomous Region and is now the Republic of Adygea). He was drafted into the Red Army in 1938; in 1940 he graduated from the Yeisk naval flying school. From January 1941 he served as a pilot of the 8th IAP of the Black Sea Fleet air arm.

When the war broke out, Zyuzin fought in the ranks of the same regiment, flying I-16 and LaGG-3 fighters. In October 1941 he was slightly injured in a forced landing caused by battle damage. In January 1942 Zyuzin was transferred to the 32nd IAP of the Black Sea Fleet air arm, which was reorganised as the 11th GvIAP on 31 May 1943. In this regiment he rose to deputy squadron commander and took part in military operations associated with the defence of the Crimea, Sevastopol', and the Caucasus; with the liberation of the Kuban' area and the Crimea; and in the Iassy-Kishinyov offensive operation.

In the summer of 1943 the 11th GvIAP was reequipped with Bell P39 Airacobras, and Zyuzin flew this type in 1943–45. The serial of his aircraft appears on a photo as '42-1953,' but this was actually a Vultee BT-15 trainer; the bogus serial may have resulted from a damaged and replaced rudder, and the correct identity is unknown. By April 1944 Lt. (SG) Dmitriy Zyuzin had made 535 combat sorties, conducted fifty-one aerial engagements, and shot down ten enemy aircraft personally, augmented by eight shared 'kills' (some sources credit Zyuzin with '15 aerial victories' without specifying individual and shared ones). On 16 May 1944 he was awarded the title of Hero of the Soviet Union. The results achieved while flying the Airacobra included five personal 'kills' and four shared ones; the 'victims' were two Bf 109s, one Fw 190, four He 111s, and single examples of the Ju 87, Ju 88, and Arado Ar 196.

By December 1944, Guards captain Zyuzin had flown 496 combat sorties (one source states the number as 596) and conducted fifty-six aerial engagements. His combat score remained unchanged. Zyuzin's service in the 11th GvIAP lasted until February 1945.

In September 1945 Zyuzin served as squadron commander in the 17th IAP of the Pacific Fleet air arm, where he flew a Yak-9U. His service in the naval aviation was terminated in June 1948, when he opted for the career of a test pilot. In 1950 Zyuzin graduated from the test pilot school in Zhukovskiy and was assigned to the colocated LII test establishment, where he worked until 1954. During the following three years he was a test pilot of the Tupolev design bureau. Among the numerous tasks successfully fulfilled by him, we may note the testing of the Kuznetsov NK-12 turboprops (developed for the Tu-95 bomber) on the Tu-4LL flying test bed, the testing of the Yak-1000 experimental fighter, the Tu-91

P-39D-2-BE / '18 White,' flown by North Fleet / 255th IAP CO maj. Pavel A. Panin in the spring of 1943.

attack aircraft, and the Tu-110 airliner (a four-turbojet derivative of the production Tu-104 twin-turbojet medium-haul airliner).

Between 1957 and 1962 Dmitriy V. Zyuzin worked as leading engineer in the Tupolev design bureau. He died on 12 July 1976.

Nikolay M. Didenko (1921–1975)

Nikolay Matveyevich Didenko was born on 5 December 1921 in Prokhladnyy village, now a town in Kabardino-Balkaria (the North Caucasus). Having received primary flight training in an air club, he joined the army in 1938 and was sent to the Yeisk naval flying school, from which he graduated in 1941.

Didenko's frontline wartime service started in October 1941, when he was assigned to the 78th IAP of the North Fleet air arm. His mounts were I-16 and Hurricane fighters; these types were also flown by him after his transfer to the 27th IAP of the North Fleet air arm in March 1942. In May 1943, Didenko, by that time a flight commander, was transferred to the 2nd GvIAP of the North Fleet air arm. This unit was equipped with Bell P-39Q Airacobras.

In the new regiment, Didenko was promoted to the position of deputy squadron commander. By 10 July 1944 he had made 283 combat sorties, conducted thirty-four aerial engagements, and scored ten confirmed 'kills' plus three 'probables.' On 5 November 1944 he was awarded the title of Hero of the Soviet Union.

By the end of the war, Guards captain Nikolay M. Didenko had made 378 combat sorties and conducted forty aerial engagements. His final score was fourteen confirmed individual victories plus three 'probables'; all except one of them were achieved while flying

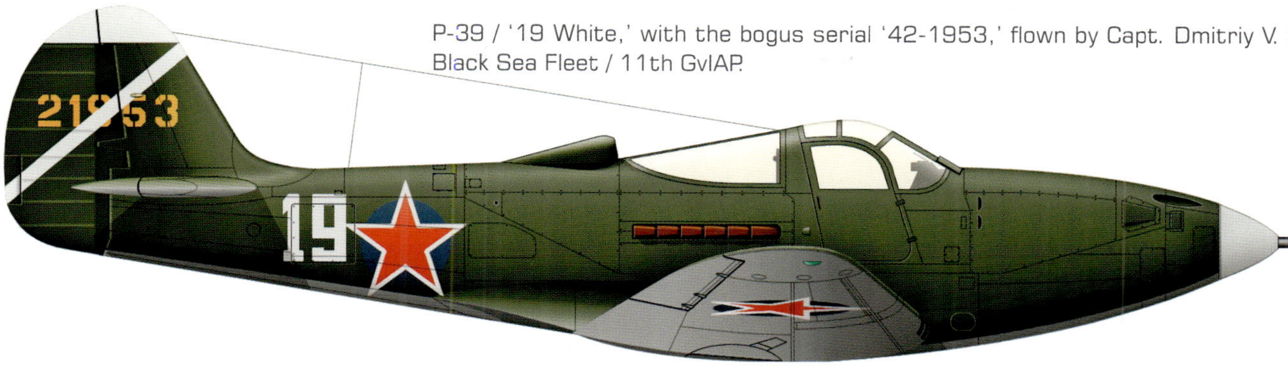

P-39 / '19 White,' with the bogus serial '42-1953,' flown by Capt. Dmitriy V. Zyuzin, Black Sea Fleet / 11th GvIAP.

LEFT: Capt. Dmitriy V. Zyuzin, Black Sea Fleet air arm / 11th GvIAP pilot, with parachute and headset, poses in front of his P-39 wearing the Guards emblem on the cockpit door.

BELOW LEFT: Here Dmitriy Zyuzin is seen in the cockpit of a different P-39, lacking the Guards emblem but sporting fifteen 'kill' stars and the unusual code 'W.'

Another Airacobra flown by Zyuzin was this P-39Q, '19 White,' which is seen being serviced at Odessa in April or May 1944. The serial 42-1953 is bogus and probably appeared as a result of the original rudder being damaged and replaced.

the Airacobra. In June 1944 his mount was a P-39Q coded '05 White' (regrettably, the USAAF serial is unknown because it was painted out). In October 1944 Didenko shot down three Ju 52/3m transports; the rest of his 'kills' were mostly Bf 109s supplemented by four Fw 190s.

After the war, Nikolay M. Didenko continued his service in the Soviet air force as commander of air regiments and large units. He finished his active service in 1971 in the rank of air major-general. Didenko was killed in a traffic accident on 2 February 1975.

Pyotr L. Kolomiyets (1917–1974)

Pyotr Leont'yevich Kolomiyets was born on 18 September 1917 in the village of Zhavinka, in the present-day Chernigov Region of the Ukraine, in a worker's family. In 1936 he was drafted into military service in the navy and successfully passed a course of training in the Yeisk naval flying school.

The frontline service of Lt. (JG) Pyotr Kolomiyets started in January 1942. As a pilot of the 78th IAP of the North Fleet air arm, he flew combat missions in the High North. His first mount was

P-39Q / '05 White,' flown by Lt. Nikolay M. Didenko, Guards, North Fleet air arm / 2nd GvIAP, Vayenga-2 AB, 1943.

ABOVE: Lt. (SG) Nikolay M. Didenko, Guards, poses with his P-39 during his service with the North Fleet's 2nd GvIAP.

ABOVE RIGHT: Here Nikolay Didenko (*second from left*) discusses a recent dogfight with his fellow pilots. Note the nose art on his P-39—an eagle carrying a Messerschmitt Bf 109 in its claws and the hapless German pilot in its beak.

BELOW: 2nd GvIAP pilots Ivan Grudakov (*left*) and Nikolay Didenko before a sortie. Note that the pilots are equipped with life vests for overwater sorties—an item that once saved Didenko's life.

the Hawker Hurricane II. In October 1942 he was transferred to the 2nd GvIAP of the North Fleet air arm, which operated Airacobras. Flying this machine, Kolomiyets displayed courage, determination, and the ability to make a quick and accurate appraisal of the situation in combat. He scored several 'kills,' but in one of the engagements he was shot down himself and had to bail out over the sea. Fortunately he was rescued by Soviet patrol boats whose crews had witnessed the shootdown. On 23 May 1943 Kolomiyets added to his score a German aircraft of a fairly rare type—a Heinkel He 115 floatplane.

By the middle of October 1944, squadron commander Guards captain Kolomiyets had made 118 combat sorties, conducted thirty-eight air engagements, and scored thirteen aerial victories. This was supplemented by his participation in bombing and strafing raids against German troops and warships. His valiant service received due recognition: on 5 November 1944 he was awarded the title of Hero of the Soviet Union.

In all, he made some 120 combat sorties and conducted some forty aerial engagements. He was credited with thirteen individual 'kills' (plus two 'probables') and two shared 'kills.' Later research by Mikhail Yu. Bykov provided confirmation for ten individual 'kills' plus three shared victories and one 'probable.'

After the war Pyotr Kolomiyets continued his service in the naval aviation. In 1949 he graduated from the air force academy, working as a tutor there, and later in the naval academy named after Kliment Ye. Voroshilov until his retirement in 1954 in the rank of colonel. He died on 24 December 1974.

ABOVE: North Fleet/2nd GvIAP pilot Pyotr L. Kolomiyets.

ABOVE RIGHT: 508th IAP pilot Vasiliy P. Mikhalyov.

BELOW: Here Pyotr L. Kolomiyets is seen as commander of the 2nd GvIAP's Sqn 1 in 1943.

Vasiliy P. Mikhalyov (1917–2006)

Vasiliy Pavlovich Mikhalyov was born on 2 March 1917 in the town of Verkhneudinsk (at present the city of Ulan-Ude) in Buryatia, eastern Siberia, in a worker's family. He enlisted in the army in 1940; in the same year he graduated from the Ul'yanovsk military flying school and remained in this school as an instructor pilot.

Vasiliy P. Mikhalyov poses with his P-39, '94 White.' The picture was taken after the 508th IAP had been reorganised as the 213th GvIAP, as the Guards emblem indicates.

It was not before 1943 that Mikhalyov was allowed to join a frontline air unit. He flew combat missions as a pilot of the 508th IAP (later renamed as the 213th GvIAP). Initially he flew the Yak-7 fighter. On this machine he made his first ramming attack, destroying a Ju 88 bomber; having run out of ammunition, he saw no other way to deal with the enemy. Mikhalyov managed to make a safe landing.

In July 1943 the 508th IAP underwent replenishment and conversion training to a new type—the P-39 Airacobra. Equipped with new machines, the regiment was committed to action at the front near Khar'kov. By the autumn of 1943 deputy squadron commander Mikhalyov had increased his combat score to ten 'kills.'

On 30 October 1943 Vasiliy Mikhalyov, by that time promoted to squadron commander, destroyed two Ju 87 dive bombers in a single action. One of them was downed in a ramming attack (although some sources ascribe this to an accidental collision of the two aircraft).

By February 1944 squadron commander Lt. (SG) Mikhalyov had made 104 combat sorties, conducted thirty-five aerial engagements, and scored seventeen individual 'kills' supplemented by two shared victories. On 1 July 1944 Vasiliy Mikhalyov was awarded the title of Hero of the Soviet Union.

By the end of the war Guards major Mikhalyov made some 160 combat sorties, took part in fifty aerial engagements, and increased his combat score to twenty-three individual kills plus sixteen shared victories.

After the war Mikhalyov continued his service in the air force. Flying jet aircraft, he became one of the first Soviet pilots to earn the 'military pilot 1st class' skill rating. In 1958 he retired from active duty. Vasiliy Mikhalyov died on 10 December 2006 at the age of eighty-nine.

Grigoriy U. Dol'nikov (1923–1996)

Grigoriy Ustinovich Dol'nikov was born on 8 May 1923 in Sakharovka village (in the Mogilyov Region of Belorussia) in a peasant family. After leaving school he moved to Minsk, where he worked as a fitter and a foreman at the local railway's rolling stock repair factory and took up studies in the Minsk air club in his time off. In 1940 Dol'nikov joined the Red Army; after the outbreak of the war he was sent to the military flying school in Bataisk (Rostov Region, Russia), from which he graduated in 1943, commencing his service in the Red Army Air Force.

At first Lt. (JG) Grigoriy Dol'nikov was an ordinary pilot in the 100th GvIAP of the 9th GvIAD (by then the regiment was entirely equipped with Airacobras, having transferred its P-40s to another unit). Soon, however, he was appointed the leader of a flight, and then the unit's deputy CO in charge of aerial gunnery. On 30 September 1943 he scored his third 'kill,' but this achievement nearly cost him his life. On that day, in his fifty-fifth sortie, Dol'nikov (by then promoted to Guards lieutenant senior grade) participated in a huge free-for-all in which a squadron of Airacobras was up against nearly seventy Luftwaffe aircraft. Having run out of ammunition in the heat of the battle, he rammed and destroyed a German bomber, but his aircraft caught fire and he was wounded. Bailing out over enemy-held territory, Dol'nikov was captured and taken to a prison camp. Miraculously avoiding execution after an

RIGHT AND ABOVE RIGHT: Lt. Grigoriy U. Dol'nikov, 100th GvIAP ace, Guards (*centre, with the fur-lined ushanka cap*) poses with his P-39N-BE 42-9033 ('01 White'), in the spring of 1945. The aircraft was previously the mount of another Soviet ace, Ivan I. Babak, until the latter was transferred to the 16th GvIAP in early 1945. Note the inscription Ot shkol'nikov Mariupolya (From the schoolchildren of Mariupol'); the aircraft had been presented to Babak by the said schoolchildren, who had raised money to pay for it. Dol'nikov had his fighter emblazoned Za Vanyu Babaka (Revenge for Vanya Babak) on the port side and Za Petyu Guchka (Revenge for Petya Guchok) on the starboard side to commemorate his buddies who had been shot down shortly before and presumed dead (Ivan Babak survived the shootdown on 16 March but became a prisoner of war and was liberated by US troops on 24 April, while Pyotr I. Guchok was indeed killed in action on 18 April). Note the P-39Q-25 or -30 (with a four-bladed propeller) in the background.

unsuccessful attempt at escaping, he managed to kill the German sentry and escape from a train while being transported to another concentration camp on 3 November. Locals took him to a partisan detachment and he fought in the ranks of this outfit until the area was liberated by the advancing Red Army in April 1944, which allowed him to return to his unit. Even though he served with distinction after this, he was still treated with suspicion because he had been a POW.

When his close friend Ivan I. Babak was transferred to the 16th GvIAP, becoming its CO in early 1945, Grigoriy Dol'nikov 'inherited' his aircraft (P-39N-BE 42-9033), which he flew until the end of the hostilities. He ended the war as an ace with fifteen individual 'kills' and one shared 'kill' in 160 sorties and forty-two engagements, serving on after the war; he graduated from the air force academy in 1955 and from the general staff academy in 1968, holding high posts in the air force. His combat score made him

FAR LEFT: 100th GvIAP pilots Grigoriy U. Dol'nikov (*left*) and Pyotr I. Guchok at one of the unit's airfields.

LEFT: Lt. Grigoriy U. Dol'nikov wearing his two Orders of the Red Banner of Combat.

ABOVE RIGHT: 102nd GvIAP CO maj. Aleksandr G. Pronin poses with his mount, a P-39 coded '96 White.'

RIGHT: Here, Aleksandr Pronin climbs into his aircraft for another sortie.

LEFT: 102nd GvIAP officers pose with one of the unit's P-39s ('55 White') parked in a hangar. *Left to right*: the unit's executive officer, Maj. A. S. Shoostov; deputy CO, Maj. Sergey S, Bukhteyev; Capt. Aleksandr G. Pronin (probably a squadron commander); and Lt. (SG) Nikolay I. Tsisarenko (probably a deputy squadron commander).

96

96

Lt. (SG) Pavel I. Orlov, North Fleet air arm pilot, with his Airacobra I.

eligible for the Hero of the Soviet Union title, but because of his POW experience and the resulting extensive cross-check, the well-earned award was not conferred upon him until 21 February 1977. By then Grigoriy Dol'nikov was a lieutenant-general and was waging his third war, being one of the Soviet military advisors to Ethiopia, which was fighting back the Somalian aggression (the Ogaden War); previously, in 1970, he had been an advisor to the Egyptian air force, helping to organise the defence of Egypt against Israeli air raids. He retired in 1987 as a colonel-general from the post of the Soviet air force's deputy commander in chief (military educational establishments). He died on 23 March 1996 at the age of seventy-two.

Aleksandr G. Pronin (1917–1992)

Aleksandr Gheorgiyevich Pronin was born on 23 April 1917 in Moscow in a worker's family. He was drafted into the Red Army in 1937. In 1938 he graduated from the 2nd military flying school in Borisoglebsk and was assigned to an air unit in the Transbaikal Military District. Pronin took part in the fighting during the Nomonhan Incident with Japan and the Soviet-Finnish war of 1939–40 (the Winter War). When the war with Germany broke out he was serving with the 124th IAP (later reorganised as the 102nd GvIAP). During the war he initially flew I-16, I-15*bis*, and MiG-3 fighters.

In 1943 the squadron commanded by Captain Aleksandr Pronin ferried P-39 Airacobra fighters from Krasnoyarsk to the Leningrad Front over a distance of more than 5,000 km (3,107 miles) and conducted conversion training of other squadrons of the regiment. Rising in the ranks, Pronin became the commander of the 102nd GvIAP in June 1943; he held this post until December 1947. The regiment took part in the action at the Karelian Isthmus.

In the course of the war Aleksandr Pronin flew more than 310 combat sorties, repelling air raids, escorting bombers, and conducting ground attack missions. He took part in thirty-one group aerial engagements in which he scored six aerial victories (two individual 'kills' and four shared 'kills').

After the war Aleksandr Pronin served in the fighter element of the air defence force and rose in the ranks, holding the posts of regiment CO, deputy division CO, division CO (in two different fighter divisions), and deputy chief of Tactical Aviation's famous 4th Combat Training & Aircrew Conversion Centre in Lipetsk. He retired in 1973 in the rank of air major-general. He died on 27 July 1992. Aleksandr Pronin did not earn the HSU title, but he was decorated with many prestigious orders, including the Order of the Red Banner (three times).

Pavel I. Orlov (1914–1943)

Pavel Ivanovich Orlov was born in1914 in the village of Solntsevo, of the present-day Tambov Region, in a peasant family. In 1933 he entered the Yeisk naval flying school and successfully graduated from it, becoming an instructor pilot in this school.

From October 1941 Pavel Orlov took up frontline service in the ranks of the 72nd Composite Air Regiment of the North Fleet air arm (renamed as 2nd GvIAP in March 1942). Initially he flew an I-16 fighter. Later he exchanged it for a Hawker Hurricane IIb, then for a P-40E Kittyhawk, and, finally, an Airacobra.

By March 1943, as deputy squadron commander of the 2nd GvIAP Guards, Captain P. I. Orlov had made 276 combat sorties, flying different types of missions: ground attack, bomber escort, reconnaissance, and interception of enemy aircraft. In twenty-four aerial engagements he shot down eleven aircraft. His skill and cold-blooded behaviour in combat earned him a reputation as an 'expert in head-on attacks.'

Pavel Orlov was killed in action on 15 March 1943, being shot down in a dogfight with German fighters near Lake Urd-Ozero on the Kola Peninsula. By that time he had made 342 combat sorties, conducted thirty-two aerial engagements, and shot down twelve enemy aircraft (Mikhail Bykov's research produces the figure of nine confirmed individual victories plus one 'probable'). The aircraft shot down by him include the following types: Bf 109, Ju 87, Ju 88, and Fw 189.

On 24 July 1943 Pavel Orlov was awarded the title of Hero of the Soviet Union posthumously.

CHAPTER 6

P-63 Kingcobra in the Soviet Air Force

Bell P-63 Kingcobra Tactical Fighter and Fighter-Bomber

The Bell P-63 Kingcobra was conceived as an improved version of the P-39 Airacobra. Actually it had its origins in the experimental XP-39E (Bell Model 23, later redesignated XP-76) first flown in February 1942, which embodied new wings of greater span and area with squared-off tips and new airfoils, a revised tail unit (all three prototypes had differently shaped vertical tails), and a V-1710-47 (V-1710-E11) engine that was longer, necessitating a 0.83 m (1 ft. 9 in.) fuselage stretch. Eventually, despite having better high-altitude performance, the XP-76 was deemed inferior to the basic Airacobra in some respects, and production was cancelled. Still, many of the changes introduced on this aircraft led to the emergence of a new production fighter that for all its external similarity to the Airacobra was virtually a new design.

While retaining the general layout and basic appearance of its predecessor, the P-63 (Bell Model 25) was bigger and featured new wings and tail surfaces. The wings had greater span and area; the rear fuselage was lengthened and considerably reinforced, carrying a recontoured, taller vertical tail of greater area (the

Lt.-Col. B. I. Frolov, 3rd Ferry Air Regiment CO, gives instructions to his pilots beside a row of brand-new P-63s.

269239

LEFT: Row upon row of P-63As await the ferrying flight to the USSR at Ladd Field as a Soviet Li-2 carrying their pilots arrives.

BELOW LEFT: P-63A-8-BE 42-69239 undergoes a preflight check amid a row of sister aircraft.

ABOVE: Eight P-63As fitted with two drop tanks each fly along the ALSIB route, with a B-25J bomber as the lead ship.

RIGHT AND BELOW RIGHT: Two more views of a mixed B-25/P-63 formation over the rugged and featureless terrain found along much of the route.

rudder had a characteristically straight trailing edge and angular lower end). The centre fuselage housed a V-1710-93 (V-1710-E21) engine rated at 1,325 hp (versus the 1,100–1,325 hp versions that powered the P-39) driving a new four-blade propeller. This engine was almost identical to the V-1710-47 of the XP-39E, offering improved high-altitude performance thanks to the provision of a two-stage supercharger (an additional centrifugal supercharger). The V-1710-93 also had a five-minute contingency rating of 1,500 hp; the use of this rating enabled the P-63 to attain a speed of 657 km/h (408 mph). Taking into account the combat experience accumulated with the P-39, from the outset the new fighter was intended primarily for use as a close-support aircraft.

Design work on the P-63 began in February 1941; the first XP-63 prototype (41-19511) performed its maiden flight on 7 December 1942. The development work was conducted with the participation of Soviet specialists, since it was clear from the start that the fighter would be largely intended for deliveries to the Soviet air force. Soviet specialists were sent to the US to help in the

development work, and teams of Bell's specialists worked in the Soviet Union on the same tasks.

Probably no other US warplane was influenced by Soviet pilots and engineers to a greater degree. The testing was completed in less than twelve months, and the first production version, the P-63A-1-BE (Bell Model 24), began leaving the assembly line in late 1943. A limited number of these aircraft were introduced into service with the USAAF; however, the latter found the P-63 to be inferior to the North American P-51 Mustang. (Ironically, the P-63 was originally intended to be powered by the 1,280 hp Packard V-1650-3 Merlin [licence-built Rolls-Royce Merlin 63] but never

TOP: P-63A-7-BE 42-69188 was subjected to trials at NII VVS. Here the aircraft is seen in original guise with delivery markings; note the faired underwing hardpoints.

ABOVE: The same aircraft with a Venturi tube added on the port cowling panel as part of the test instrumentation.

ABOVE RIGHT: 42-69188 with drop tanks attached.

RIGHT: A NII VVS technician installs control surface travel sensors on 42-69188 before the stability and handling tests.

received it because of priority deliveries of the Packard Merlin for the Mustang!)

Soviet Participation in the P-63's Tests

At an early stage it became obvious that the type would be used primarily by the Soviet air force. Having received detailed information on the P-63 from the Bell Aircraft Corporation, the Soviet authorities decided that it would be prudent to test the P-63A prior to the start of large-scale deliveries of this aircraft to the USSR. For this purpose two experienced test pilots from NII VVS, Andrey G. Kochetkov and Fyodor P. Suproon were sent to the US in February 1944 (Fyodor Suproon was also an engineer). The testing revealed that the P-63 had inherited the Airacobra's vicious spin characteristics. On 28–29 April the Soviet pilots made two test flights in P-63A-6-BE 42-68939, studying the aircraft's spinning characteristics at two CG positions (normal and full aft). The first flight went smoothly. The following day the ammunition was removed from the nose bay for the second flight. It was well known that most accidents with the Airacobra happened when the ammo was used up and the CG shifted aft. How would the Kingcobra behave in similar circumstances?

After doing three turns in a left spin, Kochetkov did all he could to recover but the P-63 ignored his inputs, doing more than twenty turns before the pilot bailed out. Kochetkov acted coolly in this complicated situation, managing to leave the cockpit without making contact with the stabiliser.

Kochetkov expected to be reprimanded for the loss of the brand-new aircraft; to his surprise, instead he received thanks for the job he had done. The same evening, a debriefing was held at which Bell Aircraft Company vice president Ray P. Whitman was present. Kochetkov gave a detailed description of the P-63's behaviour in a flat spin. All those present agreed that the Kingcobra's maximum aft CG had to be moved forward. Thus, Kochetkov succeeded in convincing the Bell Aircraft Company that the Kingcobra's spin characteristics needed improving; subsequently the Bell designers introduced some modification partially alleviating this deficiency.

Interestingly, Kochetkov received a commendation from the Irving Parachute Company, whose parachute saved his life.

In parallel with the development work in the US, Soviet specialists at TsAGI, NII VVS, and LII NKAP (***Lyot**no-is**sle**dovatel'skiy institoot Narodnovo komissari**ah**ta aviatsi**on**noy pro**mysh**lennosti*; Flight Research Institute of the People's Commissariat of Aircraft Industry) made their contribution to perfecting the new aircraft. Between the end of 1944 and March 1945 the P-63s from the A-1, A-5, A-7, and A-10 blocks were consecutively flight-tested at NII VVS and LII NKAP. A P-63A-8-BE serialled 42-69261

ABOVE AND LEFT: Here, P-63A-7-BE 42-69188 is depicted after more modifications; prominent stiffening ribs have been added to the upper rear fuselage sides to prevent structural deformation during sharp manoeuvres. Note that the insignia on the fuselage (but not on the wings) have been revised.

BELOW LEFT: A P-63A seen during one of the stages of the delivery flight.

ABOVE RIGHT: P-63A-7-BE 42-69178 awaits delivery at Ladd Field. The red stars appear almost invisible on the strongly reflective white background (the one on the wing underside is barely discernible).

RIGHT: Six Kingcobras, with P-63A-9-BE 42-69596 nearest, seen at one of the staging points on the ALSIB route. The aircraft are fitted with two 75 US gal. drop tanks.

was subjected to testing in TsAGI's gigantic T-101 wind tunnel and to static structural-strength tests. Its engine was test-run in all possible modes. The information obtained was immediately sent to the US, where Bell engineers and workers promptly made the necessary modifications.

The Soviet input in the development of the P-63 was significant. The Bell Aircraft Company was quick to implement suggestions coming from the Soviet side. The vast majority of changes in the P-63A subvariants were a direct result of Soviet inputs; for example, increased pilot armour and the fuselage hardpoint on the P-63A-5, two underwing hardpoints and extra fuel tanks on the P-63A-6, and so on. Soviet P-63s had two unique features as compared to versions used by the USAAF: a direction finder loop aerial and a nub on the propeller spinner, which was, in fact, a starter dog. The cold in Siberia would often cause battery failure, and this attachment allowed a Hucks starter based on an army truck to ground-start the engine.

Deliveries to the USSR

In accordance with the III Protocol on deliveries of war materiel, the P-63s were to be despatched to the USSR starting in the first half of 1944. In June 1944 the first Kingcobras started arriving

LEFT AND BELOW: 42-69683, another P-63A-9-BE, over the white wilderness of the ALSIB. These photos show to advantage the Kingcobra's more elongated fuselage, reshaped vertical tail, and dorsal (rather than ventral) DF loop aerial.

RIGHT: An unidentified Soviet technician poses with one of the Kingcobras undergoing acceptance by the Red Army Air Force.

BELOW RIGHT AND FAR RIGHT: The same technician in the aircraft's cockpit.

at Fairbanks, Alaska, where Soviet pilots started receiving conversion training. Only squadron leaders from the Ferry Air Division were trained in Alaska; the rest of the pilots took conversion training for the new type at the home bases of their regiments. Virtually all the Kingcobras supplied to the Soviet Union were delivered by ferrying along the ALSIB route. The deliveries proceeded in parallel with the continuing flow of the P-39 Airacobras; by the end of 1944 the P-63s already outnumbered their older stablemates on the ALSIB. By 9 May 1945, operational units had 1,148 Kingcobras on strength, including 1,050 in tactical fighter units.

After a check flight at Bell's factory in Buffalo, New York, the Kingcobras were flown to Great Falls, Montana. There they were checked and adapted for operations in the cold climate, whereupon they were ferried to Ladd Field (Fairbanks, Alaska) to be turned over to the Soviet acceptance mission. As often as not, the final check performed there revealed various deficiencies that had to be rectified on the spot. One of the first batches was entirely rejected by the Soviet acceptance personnel. On 7 October 1944, all the Kingcobras on the ALCAN route were grounded because structural deformation of the rear fuselage had been discovered on some examples. Hundreds of mechanics from Great Falls and

LEFT: P-63A-7-BE 42-69136 seen somewhere on the delivery route.

BELOW LEFT: P-63A-8-BE 42-69213, with an aerial mast aft of the cockpit instead of the DF loop.

RIGHT: Soviet and American ferry pilots pose for a joint commemorative photo (probably at Ladd Field) with five Kingcobras, including P-63A-7-BE 42-69130.

BELOW RIGHT: Another photo of Soviet and US airmen together, commemorating the days when the two nations were allies fighting against a common enemy.

BELOW: This Kingcobra (apparently a P-63A-7-BE) became the 5,000th Lend-Lease aircraft delivered to the USSR over the ALSIB route. Here, USAAF and Soviet air force representatives pose with the aircraft at Ladd Field on 16 September 1944. Regrettably the serial has been scratched out by the military censor.

from nearby airports were mobilised to perform the urgent work of modifying the grounded machines. In all, 223 fighters had their airframes reinforced. The aircraft that had already crossed the border were subsequently modified at the Soviet air force repair facilities in accordance with recommendations evolved at TsAGI.

Numbers Delivered, Totals

Immediately after the surrender of Japan on 2 September 1945 the US side stopped submitting fighters for acceptance by the Soviet mission at Fairbanks. By that time the Soviet side had received 2,400 Kingcobras of the 2,450 ordered under the terms of the IV Protocol. Of these, 2,397 were delivered via Alaska and only three arrived by sea to Murmansk. Yet, the movement on the ALSIB continued for almost a month. The final Kingcobra was delivered to Yelizovo airfield near Petropavlovsk-Kamchatskiy on the Kamchatka Peninsula on 29 September 1945.

Note that in this case the figure of 2,400 is given as the exact number, while in some sources it is regarded as an approximate

number ('more than 2,400' in a US source). This tallies with the statement of historian William Green, who wrote that *'No less than 2,421 Kingcobras of the total of 3,303 machines of this type built were supplied to the Soviet Union under Lend-Lease'* [according to US sources, twenty-one P-63s crashed during delivery].

P-63s were supplied to the Soviet air force in several successive versions, which passed testing at NII VVS as they became available. A brief review of these variants, along with modifications effected in the Soviet Union, is given below.

P-63A (A-1, A-5, A-7, A-8, A-9, A-10)

Initial deliveries of the P-63 comprised different subtypes of the P-63A (Model 25), including the A-5, A-6, A-7, and A-10 production blocks. The P-63s in this range of subtypes were powered by the Allison V-1710-93 engine, rated at 1,325 hp. Introduction of

these fighters into service was accompanied by thorough testing of the mentioned subtypes at NII VVS and LII. The overall appraisal of the P-63 was positive (more about this below). Examples tested at NII VVS included P-63A-7-BE 42-69188.

Let us take a look at the development of the A subtypes, which was largely undertaken in response to recommendations and requests from the Soviet side.

The P-63A-5-BE differed from the P-63A-1-BE in having the weight of the armour plating increased from 40 kg (88 lb.) to 81 kg (179 lb.); a hardpoint for the carriage of a 227 kg (500 lb.) bomb was added under the fuselage. Only three of the twenty Block 5 aircraft (42-68911 to 42-68913) were delivered to the USSR under the Lend-Lease programme.

The P-63A-1 and P-63A-5 deserve special attention because they became the object of an interesting document issued by BNT NKAP in 1945: Technical description No. 269, titled 'General description and layout of the Bell P-63A Kingcobra: Performance and aerodynamic characteristics.' The document was based on information sourced from US manuals and on the results of tests conducted at NII VVS (presumably the machine tested was a P-63A-5 mentioned in the document). Of special interest are the performance characteristics determined in these tests, and the appraisal of the P-63 by Soviet specialists.

To begin with, Soviet specialists noted with approval various features of the Kingcobra's design that gave it an advantage over other fighter types. Thanks to the laminar-flow airfoil the drag

ABOVE AND ABOVE LEFT: Two aspects of P-63A-9-BE 42-69721 during a predelivery test flight at Buffalo, New York, with Bell Aircraft test pilot Jay Deeming at the controls.

LEFT: P-63A-9-BE 42-69778, seen here on one of the legs of the delivery route, has had nose art chalked on by the Americans.

ANOTHER EXAMPLE OF NOSE ART: This P-63A bears the legend Katya iz Klondaika ('Katya from Klondike') in Russian (Katya is the pet form of the Russian name Yekaterina, equivalent to Catherine). This is not just wartime humour—this aircraft was bought for the war effort by donations from Russian settlers living in Alaska, who felt they should not sit idle when their historic homeland was in danger.

of the P-63's wings was reduced by 11 percent as compared to that of the P-39. Placing the engine amidships was deemed advantageous in many respects. Among other things, it was noted that in the event of an engine fire, the flames did not penetrate into the cockpit, thus enabling the pilot to make a forced landing or to bail out. The final part of the conclusions in the BNT document deserves to be quoted verbatim:

'8. Judging by its aerodynamic characteristics, the Bell P-63A represents a more refined aircraft design in comparison with US and German fighters built earlier:

a) in its performance it is inferior to the German Me-109G4 fighter [sic; should be Bf 109G-4] *as regards maximum speed at a specified altitude by 9 km/h* [6 mph], *which is merely some 1.5%; as regards vertical speed, the rate of climb at an altitude of 5,000 m* [16,400 ft.] *is 2 m/sec* [790 ft./min.] *less, which is equivalent to 14%;*

b) as regards manoeuvrability in the vertical plane at the altitude of 5,000 m, it is also inferior to the Me-109G4. . . .

Better performance of the Me-109G4 as regards speed and manoeuvre in the vertical plane is due to the considerably greater [available] *engine power and lower AUW. The engine power of the Me-109G4 at 6,000 m* [19,680 ft.] *is 1,360 hp, while the engine power of the P-63A at 6,850 m* [22,470 ft.] *is 1,150 hp. Should the*

LEFT: P-63A-8-BE 42-69332 became the 10,000th fighter manufactured by the Bell Aircraft Company. Here it is ceremonially handed over to the Soviet side, with the company's president, Lawrence D. Bell (*rightmost*), Soviet test pilot Andrey G. Kochetkov (*second from right*), and officials in attendance.

BELOW LEFT: Lawrence Bell demonstrates the aircraft to Kochetkov, who is sitting in the cockpit.

RIGHT: Here, Kochetkov is seen in the cockpit of a different Kingcobra, P-63A-6-BE 42-68939, on 29 April 1944.

BELOW RIGHT: Test pilots Andrey Kochetkov and Fyodor P. Suproon discuss the Kingcobra.

P-63A be equipped with an engine delivering 1,360 hp, its maximum speed would exceed that of the Me-109G4 by 4.5%, and the [Bf 109's] *vertical speed would be exceeded by 7%.*

c) as regards manoeuvrability in the horizontal plane and the diving speed, the P-63A has higher performance in comparison with the Me-109G4.

d) With regard to both flight performance and manoeuvrability characteristics the P-63A is superior to the German Focke-Wulf Fw-190A4 fighter' [again, the rendition in the document is a bit inaccurate and should be Fw 190A-4].

The BNT document quoted the following performance figures for the P-63A on the basis of the manufacturer's specifications:

- Maximum speed at military power, 657 km/h (408 mph)
- Landing speed, 130 km/h (81 mph)
- Time to 6,100 m (20,000 ft.), 5.4 minutes
- Service ceiling, 11,900 m (39,040 ft.)
- Range with 380 litres (83.6. imp. gal.) of fuel, 870 km (541 miles)
- Range with 800 litres (176 imp. gal.) of fuel, 1,620 km (1,007 miles)

RIGHT: The wreckage of P-63A-6-BE 42-68939, which crashed at Buffalo after suffering in-flight structural failure during an aerobatics session with Andrey Kochetkov at the controls. Kochetkov bailed out successfully, and his report proved instrumental in refining the P-63, leading the Bell Aircraft Co. to reinforce the structure. After this experience Kochetkov officially became the second Soviet member of the Caterpillar Club, and Lawrence Bell invited the Soviet test pilots to dinner.

Lawrence Bell stands on the wing of P-63A-8-BE 42-69332 during the 10,000th fighter's rollout and handover ceremony.

RIGHT: Factory-fresh P-63A-10-BEs on the Bell Aircraft Company's preflight and delivery line at Niagara Falls (Buffalo, New York).

BELOW RIGHT: Another view of the same flight line. As these photos show, the use of the white circle background for the ferry markings of aircraft built for the USSR under the Lend-Lease programme was discontinued at some point when the P-63A-10 entered production.

At the same time, the document featured a very detailed table of performance characteristics as determined by tests at NII VVS, the figures in which differed from those quoted above (see page 194).

Coming back to the subsequent production blocks of the P-63A, it may be noted that the P-63A-6 and subsequent models received a further two 'wet' hardpoints under the wings for two 227 kg bombs or 284-litre (62.48 imp. gal.; 75 US gal.) drop tanks. The latter were indispensible during the delivery flight.

Two examples of the P-63A were used (reportedly in response to a Soviet suggestion) for experiments with ski undercarriage, which, however, did not gain acceptance. Available pictures show a P-63A-1-BE (42-68887) and another machine serialled 42-68931 (the first P-63A-6-BE) fitted with retractable skis. The tests were started with 42-68931 in Canada in 1944. The behaviour of the machine was studied both during taxiing and in flight. After a pause the tests continued in the winter of 1944–45, this time in Buffalo, New York, and the example used was 42-68887. No

P-63A-9-BE 42-69721 in delivery colours, with stars on a white background.

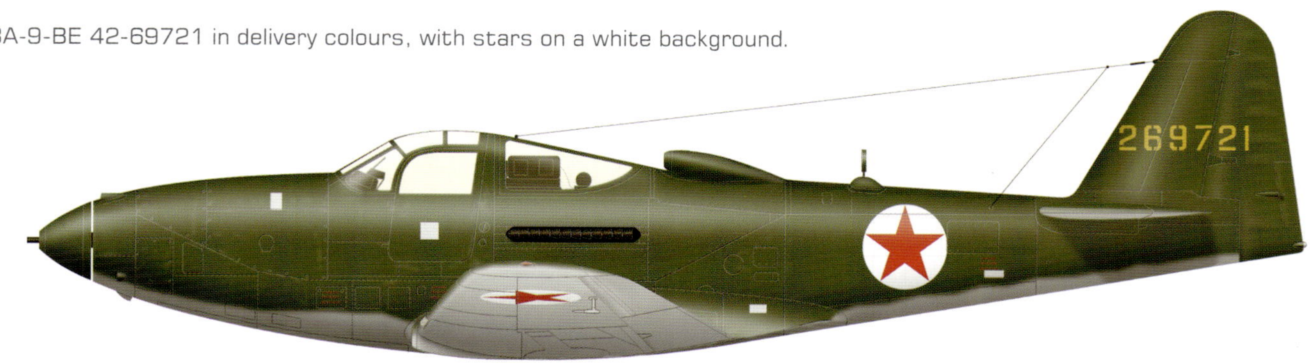

P-63A-10-BE 42-70468 with standard Soviet insignia (as built).

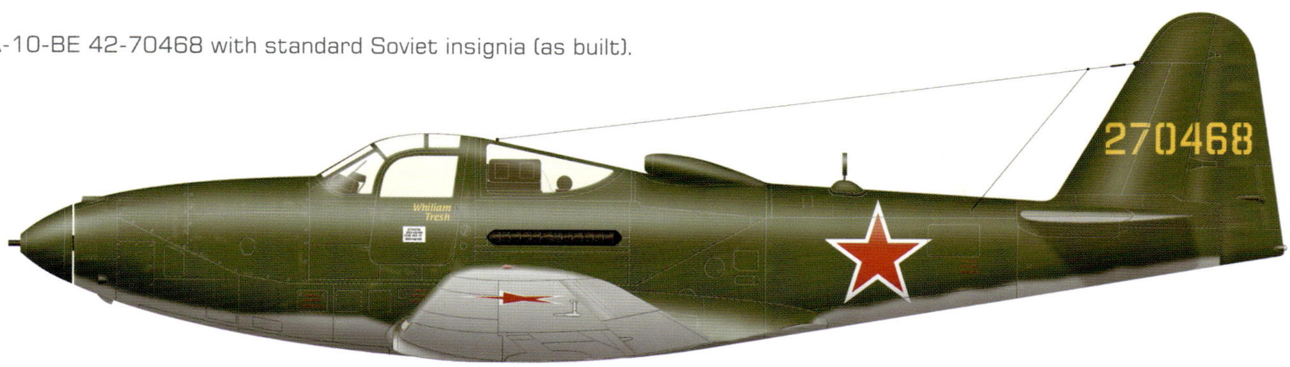

270396
270468

270290
270289

270115
270052

ABOVE: P-63A-10-BE 42-70628 with drop tanks in place sits at Fairbanks, Alaska, awaiting favourable weather for crossing the Bering Strait into Soviet territory. Note the cloth covers on the wings, preventing ice and snow building up on the wings in snowy weather and jamming the ailerons.

RIGHT: This view of 42-70525 shows that the elevators were similarly protected.

RIGHT: A P-63A makes a predelivery check flight from Buffalo. The faired wing hardpoints (empty in this instance) are visible.

ABOVE LEFT: An engineer gives instructions to a test pilot preparing to take a brand-new P-63 on a check flight at Buffalo.

LEFT: P-63A-10-BEs 42-70052 and 42-70115 cruise along the ALSIB route.

P-63A-10-BE 42-70610 has had the name Little Toots bestowed by the US technicians.

P-63A-10-BE 42-70478 is prepared for engine starting, with a compressed air cylinder and a fire extinguisher at the ready.

information is available on the results of the tests, but the two machines remained the sole examples of the P-63 to be fitted with skis.

The machine serialled 42-68931 was photographed at Wright Field, Ohio (later known as Wright-Patterson AFB) in October 1945. The ski kit was being shown as part of an open house at the base for nearby civilians.

The P-63A-7-BE was the first Kingcobra version to be supplied in quantity to the Soviet air force. According to Phil Butler, the examples delivered to the USSR (mostly on the UK Lend-Lease account) were serialled 42-69076, 42-69078, 42-69081, 42-69088, 42-69091, 42-69094, 42-69101, 42-69104, 42-69109 to 42-69111, 42-69116, 42-69119, 42-69120, 42-69122, 42-69124 to 42-69129, 42-69132, 42-69136, 42-69138 to 42-69140, 42-69142 to 42-69149, and 42-69151 to 42-69210. Joe Baugher also includes 42-69141 but omits 42-69104 and 42-69129, stating '42-69124 to 42-69128.'

On the P-63A-7-BE, longitudinal stability was improved by introducing a new horizontal tail with a higher aspect ratio and a counterbalance in the elevator control linkage. This model also featured reinforcements to the wings and rear fuselage, with thicker skins, coupled with reinforced wing internal structural members, to cure the skin buckling observed on the A-1, A-5, and A-6 subtypes. However, the reinforcements made by Bell turned out to be insufficient. During static tests held at TsAGI, the rear fuselage failed at two-thirds of the nominal load. In late October 1944, TsAGI developed a reinforcement kit that was retrofitted to P-63A-7s already in service. It included two external stiffening ribs high on the rear fuselage sides, which can be seen in some pictures.

An example of the P-63A-7-BE (42-69188) was tested at NII VVS. The importance of this version version is emphasised by the fact that in 1946 the Bureau of New Technology (BNT) issued a detailed technical description of the P-63A-7.

The P-63A-8-BE featured an improved propeller and additional armour, whose total weight rose to 85.5 kg (189 lb.). Block 8 (42-69211 to 42-69410) was delivered to the Soviet Union almost entirely, except one aircraft (42-69215).

The P-63A-9-BE featured a further 5 kg (11 lb.) increase in the armour plating. More importantly, in response to a requirement from the Soviet air force the cannon was moved forward, with a resulting shift of the CG, and its ammunition load was increased from thirty to fifty-eight rounds. This subvariant was supplied in huge numbers. Known Soviet examples are 42-69414 to 42-69416, 42-69418 to 42-69420, 42-69424, 42-69428, 42-69429, 42-69433, 42-69435, 42-69437, 42-69448, 42-69451, 42-69454, 42-69457, 42-69459, 42-69463, 42-69466, 42-69469, 42-69470, 42-69476, 42-69480, 42-69484, 42-69485, 42-69488, 42-69491, 42-69494, 42-69497, 42-69500, 42-69503, 42-69506, 42-69510, 42-69511, 42-69513 to 42-69516, 42-69518, 42-69519, 42-69524 to 42-69526, 42-69528, 42-69529, 42-69531 to 42-69533, 42-69535, 42-69536, 42-69538, 42-69541, 42-69542, 42-69544 to 42-69546, 42-69549, 42-69551, 42-69556, 42-69559, 42-69562, 42-69565, 42-69566, 42-69568, 42-69569, 42-69571, 42-69572, 42-69574, 42-69575, 42-69577 to 42-69581, 42-69583, 42-69584, 42-69586, 42-69587, 42-69589, 42-69590, 42-69592, 42-69593, 42-69595 to 42-69599, 42-69601, 42-69602, 42-69604, 42-69605, 42-69607, 42-69608, 42-69610, 42-69611, 42-69613 to 42-69617, 42-69619, 42-69622, 42-69624, 42-69625, 42-69628, 42-69630, 42-69631, 42-69637, 42-69640, 42-69641, 42-69643, 42-69646, 42-69649, 42-69651, 42-69652, 42-69655, 42-69657 to 42-69661, 42-69664, 42-69666, 42-69667, 42-69670, 42-69672, 42-69673, 42-69675, 42-69676, 42-69679, 42-69681 to 42-69685, 42-69687, 42-69688, 42-69691, 42-69692, 42-69694, 42-69695, 42-69697 to 42-69700, 42-69702, 42-69703, 42-69705 to 42-69768, 42-69770, 42-69772 to 42-69800, and 42-69802 to 42-69860 (Joe Baugher, however, does not include 42-69837 in the above list).

The P-63A-10-BE had its armour weight increased to 107 kg (236 lb.). It could be identified externally by the air intake of the additional supercharger, which was relocated from the starboard side panel of the engine bay to the port side of the upper cowling panel. Some sources state that the A-10 subtype could be armed with three air-to-ground rocket projectiles under each wing.

According to Phil Butler, the examples destined for the USSR were serialled 42-69861 to 42-69879, 42-69975 to 42-70246, 42-70248 to 42-70254, 42-70256 to 42-70454, 42-70457 to 42-70470, 42-70472 to 42-70617, 42-70619, 42-70621 to 42-70651, and 42-70653 to 42-70685. Joe Baugher gives slightly different data, omitting 42-69879 but including 42-70247, 42-70455, 42-70456, 42-70471, 42-70618, and 42-70620 in the list.

Not all the above aircraft actually reached the USSR, several being lost en route. For example, on 23 November 1944, P-63A-10-BE 42-70412, temporarily operated by the 3rd Ferrying Group, collided with an unidentified sister ship when coming in to land at Great Falls, Montana. Both fighters crashed 8 km (5 miles) east of the airfield; the pilot of 42-70412 suffered severe burns and died in the hospital, but the other pilot survived. 42-70159 was similarly lost in a fatal midair collision with another P-63 near Onaway (Alberta, Canada) on 14 February 1945.

P-63A-10-BE 42-70640 underwent comprehensive testing at NII VVS, with Vladimir Ye. Golofastov as project test pilot and Izrael' G. Rabkin as engineer in charge. Powered by a V-1710-93 optimised for high altitudes, the fighter performed well at 7,000–9,000 m (22,965–29,530 ft.). Yet, it was up to 90 km/h (56 mph) slower than a production Lavochkin La-7 at low level, despite the fact that the Soviet fighter was powered by a bulky radial engine, with an attendant increase in frontal area.

The various versions of the P-63 in Soviet service were armed with the 37 mm Browning M4 cannon—the same weapon that was used on the P-39. As noted above in the chapters dealing with the P-39, the Soviet pilots appreciated the M4's potent punch but criticised its relatively low rate of fire and the small ammunition complement (thirty rounds). The same assessment must have been applicable to the M4-armed Kingcobras. In the case of the Airacobras, the low rate of fire was not considered a major drawback because the prevalent tactics in air combat were based on opening fire at very short range, when even a single hit of a 37 mm round was often enough to destroy the target.

The M4 fired M54 high-explosive rounds and M80 armour-piercing rounds; however, the latter were not supplied under the Lend-Lease agreement. Yet, tests conducted in the US showed that a standard M54 shell could pierce 20 mm (25/32 in.) steel armour plate at a distance of 460 m (1,510 ft.).

A few sources claim that starting with the P-63A-9 version, the Kingcobras supplied to the Soviet Union were armed with the

270640

270640

LEFT AND BELOW LEFT: P-63A-10-BE 42-70640 was another A model Kingcobra subjected to trials at NII VVS. The trials took place in March 1945.

ABOVE: Another view of the same aircraft. The shiny patch on the fin is a nonstandard feature and may be associated with a test equipment sensor.

37 mm Browning M10 cannon, identifiable by its muzzle protruding from the spinner. The M10, an improved derivative of the M4, differed from the latter in having a greater rate of fire—165 rpm instead of 140 rpm, but, more importantly, the bulky magazine was replaced by belt feed with disintegrating metal links, almost doubling the ammunition capacity (from thirty to fifty-eight rounds).

A Soviet maintenance and flight manual for the P-63 contains a brief reference to the operation of the armament. It literally repeats a similar sentence from the P-39 manuals: *'The machine guns should be fired in bursts of not more than 10–15 rounds; the bursts of cannon fire must not exceed two or three rounds.'*

The passage quoted above is taken from a manual endorsed on 30 November 1944; it is applicable to versions *'powered by the Allison V-1710-93 (E11) engine'* [sic]—that is, the P-63A model (Blocks A-1, A-5, A-6, A-7, A-8, A-9, and A-10 are mentioned, as well as the P-63C not covered by the V-1710-E11 engine)—and may be presumed to incorporate the results of the testing of Kingcobras at NII VVS mentioned above [Note: The manufacturer's designation of the engine quoted on the title page of the manual does not match the actual service designation; in reality V-1710-E11 equals the service designation V-1710-47, whereas the V-1710-93 equals V-1710-E21]. It is of interest to quote some assessments and recommendations from this document.

The manual notes that the P-63 has the same general layout as the P-39. *'Bearing in mind the aft location of the CG which results from this layout, errors in the piloting techniques are accompanied by high G-loads, especially when performing vertical manoeuvres and during recovery from a dive,'* the manual says, and goes on: *'In the USAAF training centres there were cases when pilots flying the P-63A-1, A-5 and A-6 subjected the aircraft to high G-loads which resulted in permanent structural deformation of the wing skin (buckling, waviness and skin dents). Starting with the P-63A-7, the Bell Company reinforced the wings by increasing the skin thickness and introducing reinforcing angle brackets.*

To reduce the longitudinal instability of the P-63A, starting with Block 7, a counterbalance is introduced into the system of elevator linkages and the size of the stabiliser is increased. These measures have considerably improved longitudinal stability, but not to the point of completely eliminating the aircraft's instability during recovery from a dive and at the moments when the aircraft enters vertical manoeuvres.

The flying personnel must take into account the abovementioned peculiarities of the P-63 and comply with the following prescriptions:

1. It is forbidden to perform the recovery from a dive and initiate vertical manoeuvres in an abrupt manner, so as to avoid [subjecting the airframe to] *high G-loads.*

2. Aerobatic manoeuvres shall be performed by smooth control inputs.

Flight performance of the P-63A (data based on the tests at NII VVS, with an AUW of 3,738 kg/8,242 lb)					
Altitude, m (ft)	**Maximum level flight speed, km/h (mph)**	**Rate of climb, m/sec (ft/min)**	**Time to altitude, minutes**	**Indicated airspeed during climb, km/h (mph)**	**Engine power mode**
0	483 (300)	n.a.	n.a.	n.a.	Continuous power rating (1,000 hp)
1,000 (3,280)	n.a.	11.0 (2,164)	1.5	260 (162)	
3,000 (9,840)	n.a.	11.0 (2,164)	4.6	251 (156)	
5,000 (16,400)	557 (346)	11.0 (2,164)	7.6	246 (153)	
7,000 (22,960)	n.a.	11.0 (2,164)	10.6	235 (146)	
9,000 (29,530)	n.a.	8.1 (1,574)	14.0	222 (138)	
11,000 (36,090)	n.a.	3.8 (747)	20.0	200 (124)	
12,500 (41,000)	n.a.	0.5 (98)	34.7	176 (109)	
8,600 (28,210)	612 (380)	n.a.	n.a.	n.a.	
0	514 (319)	n.a.	n.a.	n.a.	15-minute military power (1,150 hp)
1,000 (3,280)	n.a.	14.6 (2,873)	1.2	260 (162)	
3,000 (9,840)	n.a.	14.6 (2,873)	3.5	254 (158)	
5,000 (16,400)	588 (365)	14.6 (2,873)	5.8	246 (153)	
6,000 (19,680)	n.a.	14.6 (2,873)	6.9	240 (149)	
7,250 (23,780)	620 (385) *	n.a.	n.a.	n.a.	
0	n.a.	n.a.	n.a.	n.a.	5-minute contingency rating (1,500 hp)
1,000 (3,280)	530 (329)	18.2 (3,581)	0.9	260 (162)	
3,000 (9,840)	n.a.	16.8 (3,306)	2.8	254 (158)	
5,000 (16,400)	597 (371)	15.3 (3,011)	4.0	246 (153)	
6,000 (19,680)	n.a.	14.6 (2,873)	6.0	240 (149)	

Service ceiling, 12,500 m (41,000 ft)
Landing speed with a 50% fuel load and expended ammunition, 139 km/h (86 mph)
* According to US official sources the P-63A has a maximum speed of 657 km/h (408 mph) at an altitude of 7,450 m (24,440 ft) with an AUW of 3,487.5 kg (7,690 lb)

3. It is forbidden to perform piloting for training purposes and, especially, the spin without the ammunition or a balance of equal weight in the fuselage nose, because the longitudinal stability of the P-63 deteriorates as the ammunition is depleted.'

The abovementioned flight and maintenance manual on the P-63 powered by the Allison V-1710-93 (that is, P-63A models), which was issued on 30 November 1944, contains interesting information on the P-63's range and endurance in different flight modes (apparently based on the tests conducted in the Soviet Union).

Without drop tanks, and with a full internal fuel load of 136 US gallons (515 litres), range was as follows:

In maximum speed mode with the carburettor set to 'Auto Rich' mode, the technical range (that is, with full consumption of the fuel) reached a maximum of 500 km (310 miles) at an altitude of 1,000 m (3,280 ft.) and 520 km (323 miles) at 5,000 m (16,400 ft.), the endurance being 1 hr. 1 min. and 55 min., respectively.

At high indicated airspeeds reduced to a more economical level, (again, in 'Auto Rich' mode), the range and endurance varied from 800 km (497 miles) and 1 hr. 48 min. at 1,000 m (3,280 ft.) and 440 km/h (273 mph) to 970 km (603 miles) and 1 hr. 43 min. at 9,000 m (29,530 ft.) and 370 km/h (230 mph).

At best economy cruising power with the carburettor set to 'Auto Lean' mode and an indicated airspeed of 290 km/h (180 mph), the range and endurance varied from 1,240 km (771 miles) and 4 hr. 15 min. at 1,000 m (3,280 ft.) to 1,230 km (764 miles) and 3 hr. 5 min. at 7,000 m (22,965 ft.).

With two drop tanks of 75 US gallons each and a full fuel load of 286 US gallons (1,082 litres), the following results were obtained:

In maximum speed mode the technical range reached a maximum of 1,010 km (628 miles) at 1,000 m (3,280 ft.) and 1,120 km (745 miles) at 5,000 m (16,400 ft.), the endurance being 2 hr. 12 min. and 2 hr. 7 min., respectively.

At high indicated airspeeds reduced to a more economical level, the range and endurance varied from 1,550 km (963 miles) and 3 hr. 45 min. at 1,000 m (3,280 ft.) and 410 km/h (255 mph) to 1,760 km (1,093 miles) at 7,000 m (22,960 ft.) and 370 km/h (230 mph).

ABOVE RIGHT: New P-63C-5-BEs (including 43-11133) await delivery at the Bell Aircraft factory.

RIGHT: A P-63C with drop tanks seen during the delivery flight; note the number '2' chalked on the nose.

311133

2

270708

LEFT AND ABOVE LEFT: P-63C-1-BE 42-70708 was delivered to NII VVS for trials. It is seen here on a very wet hardstand at Chkalovskaya AB.

ABOVE: Here the same aircraft is seen in a winter setting.

At best economy cruising power and an indicated airspeed of 290 km/h (180 mph), the range and endurance varied from 2,480 km (1,541 miles) and 8 hr. 25 min. at 1,000 m (3,280 ft.) to 2,410 km (1,498 miles) and 6 hr. 45 min. at 5,000 m (16,400 ft.).

For comparison, the last Soviet piston-engined fighters—the Lavochkin La-9 and La-11—had a practical range of 1,735 km (1,078 miles) and 2,235 km (1,389 miles), respectively

There was no P-63B; this projected version powered by the 1,400-hp V-1650-5 (Packard Merlin) failed to materialise for the reason stated earlier.

P-63C (C-1, C-5)

The P-63C (Bell Model 33) was powered by the new Allison V-1710-117 (V-1710-E27) engine, with the same normal rating as the V-1710-93 but with a combat rating of 1,500 hp (according to some sources, its output could be raised to 1,800 hp by means of water injection). The C model also featured an internal fuel capacity increased from 378 to 405 litres (from 83.16 to 89.1 imp. gal.), an altered supercharger air intake and a ventral fin (the latter was also retrofitted to some of the late-model Kingcobras already manufactured, including the P-63A-10s, which caused some delays in the deliveries).

The P-63C-1-BEs delivered to the USSR were serialled 42-70686 to 42-70860 and 43-10893 to 43-10932, amounting to 215 aircraft. One of them (42-70708) was tested at NII VVS. The test report said that *'the imported P-63C-1 aircraft . . . is inferior to production La-7, Yak-9U and Yak-3 fighters in top speed, rate of climb and manoeuvrability but superior in service ceiling and range.'*

851 P-63C-5-BEs were allocated for the USSR. According to Phil Butler, they were serialled 43-11133 to 43-11542, 43-11544 to 43-11565, 43-11568 to 43-51573, 43-11576 to 43-11581, 43-11584 to 43-11589, 43-11592 to 43-11597, 43-11600 to 43-11605, 43-11608 to 43-11613, 43-11616 to 43-11621, 43-11624 to 43-11628, 43-11631 to 43-11635, 43-11638 to 43-11643, 43-11646 to 43-11649, 43-11652 to 43-11657, 43-11660 to 43-11665, 43-11668 to 43-11673, 43-11676 to 43-11681, 43-11684 to 43-11688, 43-11692 to 43-11695, 43-11700 to 43-11705, 43-11708 to 43-11713, 43-11716, 43-11717, 44-4001 to 44-4003, 44-4007 to 44-4011, 44-4015 to 44-4019, 44-4023 to 44-4027, 44-4031 to 44-4035, 44-4039 to 44-4043, 44-4047 to 44-4051, 44-4055 to 44-4059, 44-4063 to 44-4067, 44-4071 to 44-4075, 44-4079 to 44-4083, 44-4087 to 44-4091, 44-4095 to 44-4099, 44-4103 to 44-4107, 44-4111 to 44-4116, 44-4119 to 44-4124, 44-4127 to 44-4132, 44-4135 to 44-4140, 44-4143 to 44-4148, 44-4151 to 44-4156, 44-4159 to 44-4164, 44-4167 to 44-4172, 44-4175 to 44-4177, 44-4179, 44-4180, 44-4183 to 44-4188, 44-4191 to 44-4196, 44-4199 to 44-4204, 44-4207 to 44-4212, 44-4215 to 44-4226, 44-4228 to 44-4271, 44-4273 to 44-4279, 44-4281 to 44-4288, 44-4290 to 44-4296, 44-4298 to 44-4312, 44-4314 to 44-4320, 44-4322 to 44-4329, 44-4331 to 44-4338, 44-4340 to 44-4347, 44-4349 to 44-4356, 44-4358 to 44-4365, 44-4367 to 44-4374, 44-4376 to 44-4383, 44-4385 to

ABOVE AND ABOVE LEFT: 42-70763 has suffered the attentions of the local wits while awaiting delivery, sporting the names Mabel's Boy and Ohio Kid (the nicknames of the test pilot, Lt. B. L. Brown), a shark's mouth, and 'kill' markings! Interestingly, the information panel on the port side mentions the USSR as the recipient of the fighter.

LEFT: P-63C 43-11676 has been christened Bell Booby Trap!

RIGHT: An American ferry pilot poses with a P-63 temporarily bearing the name Delma X.

OPPOSITE PAGE, BOTTOM LEFT: Col. Il'ya P. Mazurook (*right*) in the HQ of the ferry air regiment with Chief Political Officer Pushkarevskiy (*centre*) and Executive Officer I. Pryanishnikov.

OPPOSITE, BELOW RIGHT: Ferry squadron commander I. P. Drozdov on the wing of a P-63.

OPPOSITE, BOTTOM RIGHT: I. P. Drozdov and his crew chief Vladimir A. Likhod'kin.

BELOW: USAAF technicians crank the engine of a P-63 at Ladd Field.

44-4392, 44-4394 to 44-4401, and 44-4403 to 44-4422. Joe Baugher further includes 44-4125 and some of the intervening serials (44-4178, 44-4297, and 44-4313).

Interestingly, with the exception of the first two batches (which consisted of 410 and 22 aircraft, respectively), the P-63C-5-BEs contracted in fiscal year 1943 that were earmarked for the USSR were almost invariably allocated in batches of six, while the ones contracted in FY 1944 initially mostly came in fives, then in sixes and ultimately in eights.

Again, not all of the P-63C-5s reached their destination. In particular, three P-63C-5-BEs from the 7th Ferry Group (43-11498, 43-11578, and 43-11589) were damaged beyond repair on 20 April 1945, losing their way on the ALCAN section of the delivery route and making off-field forced landings at Lesser Slave Lake, Alberta; a further (43-11203) crash-landed at Watson Lake (Yukon Territories, Canada) and was declared a total loss five days later. Interestingly, P-63C-5-BE 44-4178, which also crash-landed at Watson Lake, was repaired and returned to the US instead of going to the Soviet Union, subsequently becoming a civilian unlimited racing aircraft registered NX67115.

P-63E

This was the 'production' version of the P-63D. The sole example of the latter differed from the P-63A in having a sliding bubble canopy without doors, an uprated V-1710-109 (V-1710-E22) engine delivering 1,425 hp, and a wing span increased by 25.4 cm (10 in.). The P-63E (Bell Model 41) reverted to the standard canopy but retained the uprated engine and the increased wing span. It

had the ventral fin of the C model. The P-63E was intended for deliveries to the Soviet Union but came too late. Only thirteen P-63E-1-BEs were built. Of these, at least one was painted in Soviet air force colours but remained in the US. Serialled 43-11727 and bearing the tactical code '8' on the fuselage, this machine was flown to Davis-Monthan AFB, where it remained in storage until sold to the Honduran air force in 1948 together with four other examples. In 1960 this particular aircraft was sold back to the US; after sitting in storage at several locations in Arizona until 1973, it was put on display at the USAF Museum (Wright-Patterson AFB, Dayton, Ohio). It is now on loan to the Pima Air & Space Museum in Tucson, Arizona.

TP-63A-10 Trainer

The Bell Aircraft Company had plans for producing a two-seat version of the Kingcobra. The proposed trainer variant was designated TP-63A-10 (Bell Model 38). It was basically inspired by the two-seat TP-39 Airacobra conversion; a new cockpit was grafted on to the nose ahead of the existing cockpit, with a canopy hinged to starboard. All armament was removed, and a ventral fin was fitted to compensate for the added area ahead of the CG. The basic idea was for the company to build conversion kits for existing P-63A-10 aircraft. However, none were actually built at the Bell factory, so the TP-63A-10 remained a paper project—even though some sources claim that 24 TP-63As and one TP-63C were built.

Nevertheless, the statement in one source that *'at least one TP-63A ended up in the USSR and was tested at NII VVS'* is erroneous. The machine tested was a conversion undertaken in the USSR (*see below*), presumably with no direct link to the Bell project. The same must be the case with the three two-seat P-63s completed in the Soviet Union for which serial numbers are cited (42-69304, 42-70503, and 43-11334).

Soviet Two-Seat Conversions of the Kingcobra (P-63U; P-63V, UTI P-63)

Many P-63 Kingcobras in Soviet service were converted into two-seat trainers in a fashion similar to the two-seat TP-39s. At first this work was performed in a makeshift way at different places. This was in particular the case with the P-63 converted to a two-seat version in the 6th IAD, based at Tiraspol', Moldavia.

Logically enough, the two-seat version was dubbed UTI P-63 (*oochebno-trenirovochnyy* ***i****strebitel'*; fighter-trainer) by analogy with the UTI P-39. In Soviet documents the designation was rendered as 'УТN P-63,' with a mix of Cyrillic and Roman characters.

ABOVE AND ABOVE LEFT: Two views of the flight line at Ladd Field in the winter, with dozens of P-63Cs destined for the Soviet Union waiting for the weather to improve. The fighters are placed under wraps to keep the snow out. The examples visible here include P-63C-1-BE 42-70716, P-63C-5-BEs 43-11291, 43-11317, 43-11460, and so on.

LEFT: P-63C-5-BEs for the Soviet air force and the Free French air force await delivery at Niagara Falls. The Soviet machines wear standard olive-drab/light-grey colours; the French ones are unpainted.

RIGHT: The rear end of P-63C-1-BE 42-70717, showing the deep ventral fin of the C model.

311459
311457

LEFT: Three P-63C-5-BEs (43-11457, 43-11459, and 43-11465) fly over Niagara Parkway on the Canadian side of the Niagara River for a photo shoot, with Niagara Falls (which gave the Bell factory in Buffalo its name) visible on the right.

ABOVE: A pair of P-63Cs in Soviet markings approaches Horseshoe Falls, the most iconic part of Niagara Falls.

RIGHT: 'The one that got away.' P-63C-5-BE 44-4178 force-landed at Watson Lake en route to the USSR and was never delivered. Later it was recovered and returned to airworthy status; after the war it became an unlimited racing aircraft registered NX67115.

TOP LEFT: A snowbound P-63 at a staging point on the ALSIB route. The flaps are marked 'No step' in English and in Russian.

MIDDLE LEFT: P-63C-5-BE 43-11498 has made a wheels-up forced landing during the ferry flight, but the jacks and tool-boxes in the foreground show that not all is lost.

BOTTOM LEFT: 43-11589, another P-63C that came to grief in Alaska under similar circumstances but also appears to have a good chance of returning to service.

ABOVE RIGHT: These P-63As are pictured at an airfield on the Soviet side during the delivery flight, with the hills of the Soviet Far East as a backdrop. The fighters appear to have had tactical codes applied.

BOTTOM RIGHT: P-63Cs with drop tanks seen at a staging point on the ALSIB route.

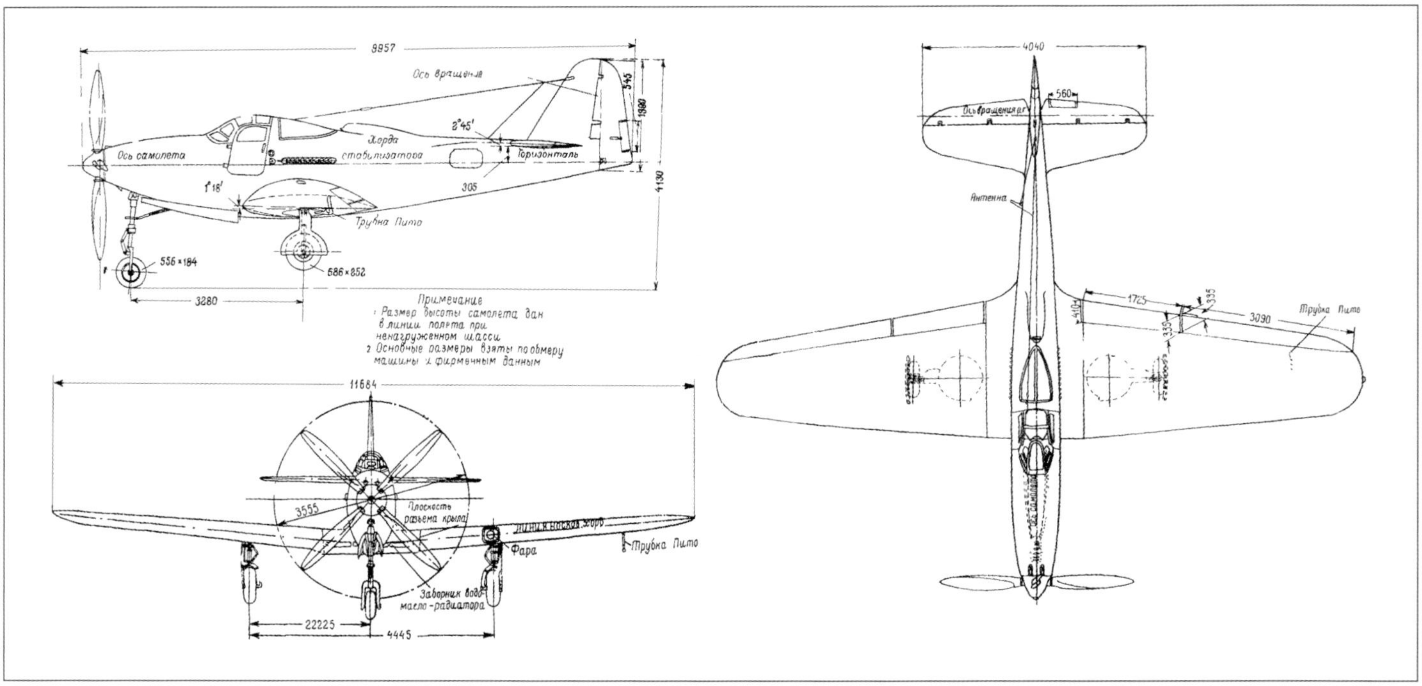
9957
Ось вращения
Ось самолета
Хорда стабилизатора
Горизонталь
Трубка Пито
556×184
586×852
3280
4130
Примечание
1 Размер высоты самолета дан в линии полета при ненагруженном шасси
2 Основные размеры взяты по обмеру машины и фирменным данным
11684
3555
Плоскость разъема крыла
Фара
Трубка Пито
Заборник воды масло-радиатора
22225
4445
4040
560
Антенна
Трубка Пито

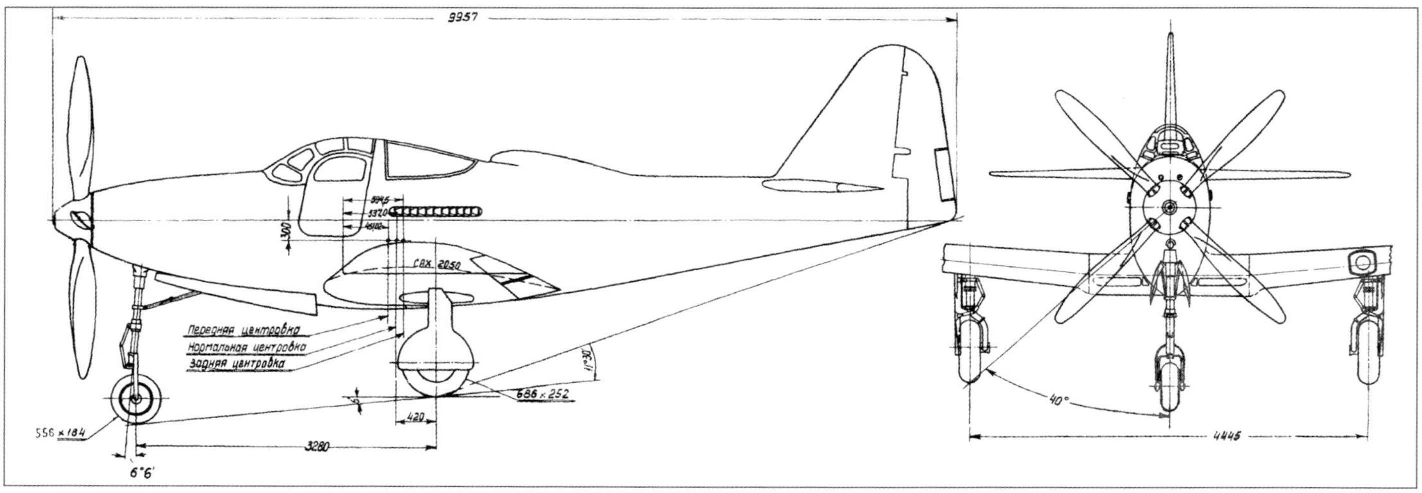
9957
САХ 2050
Передняя центровка
Нормальная центровка
Задняя центровка
586×252
556×184
420
3280
6°6'
40°
4445

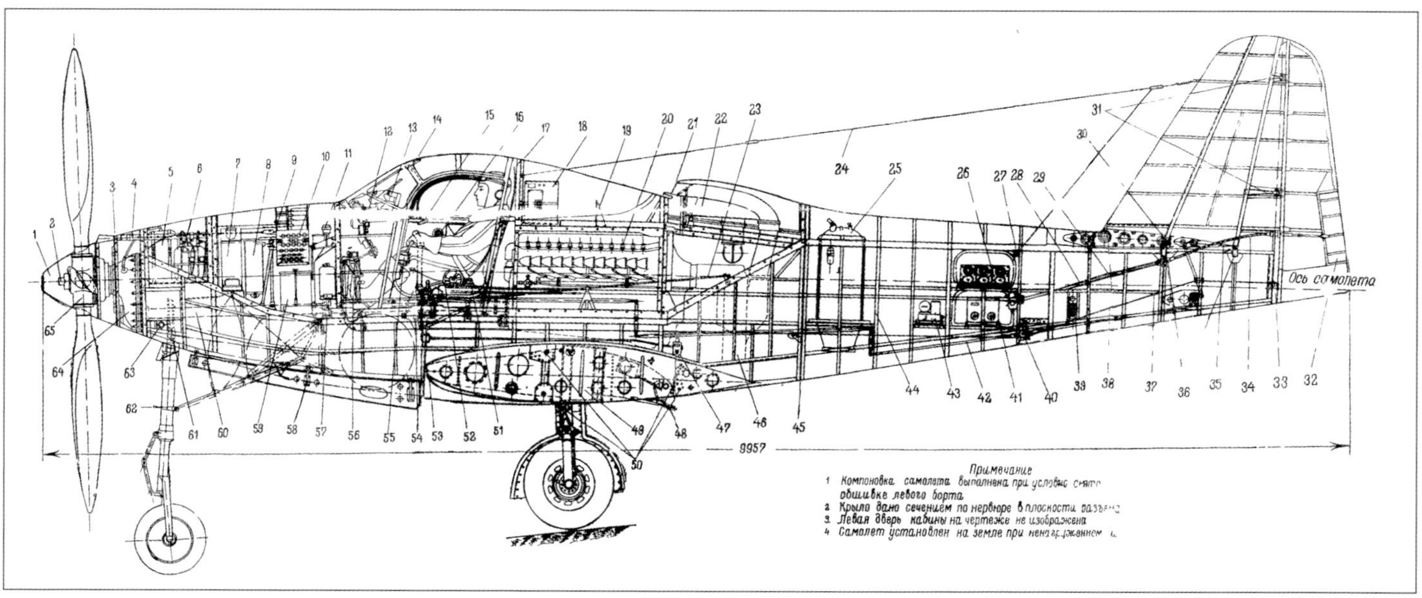
Ось самолета
9957
Примечание
1 Компоновка самолета выполнена при условии снятой обшивки левого борта
2 Крыло дано сечением по нервюре в плоскости разъема
3 Левая дверь кабины на чертеже не изображена
4 Самолет установлен на земле при ненагруженном

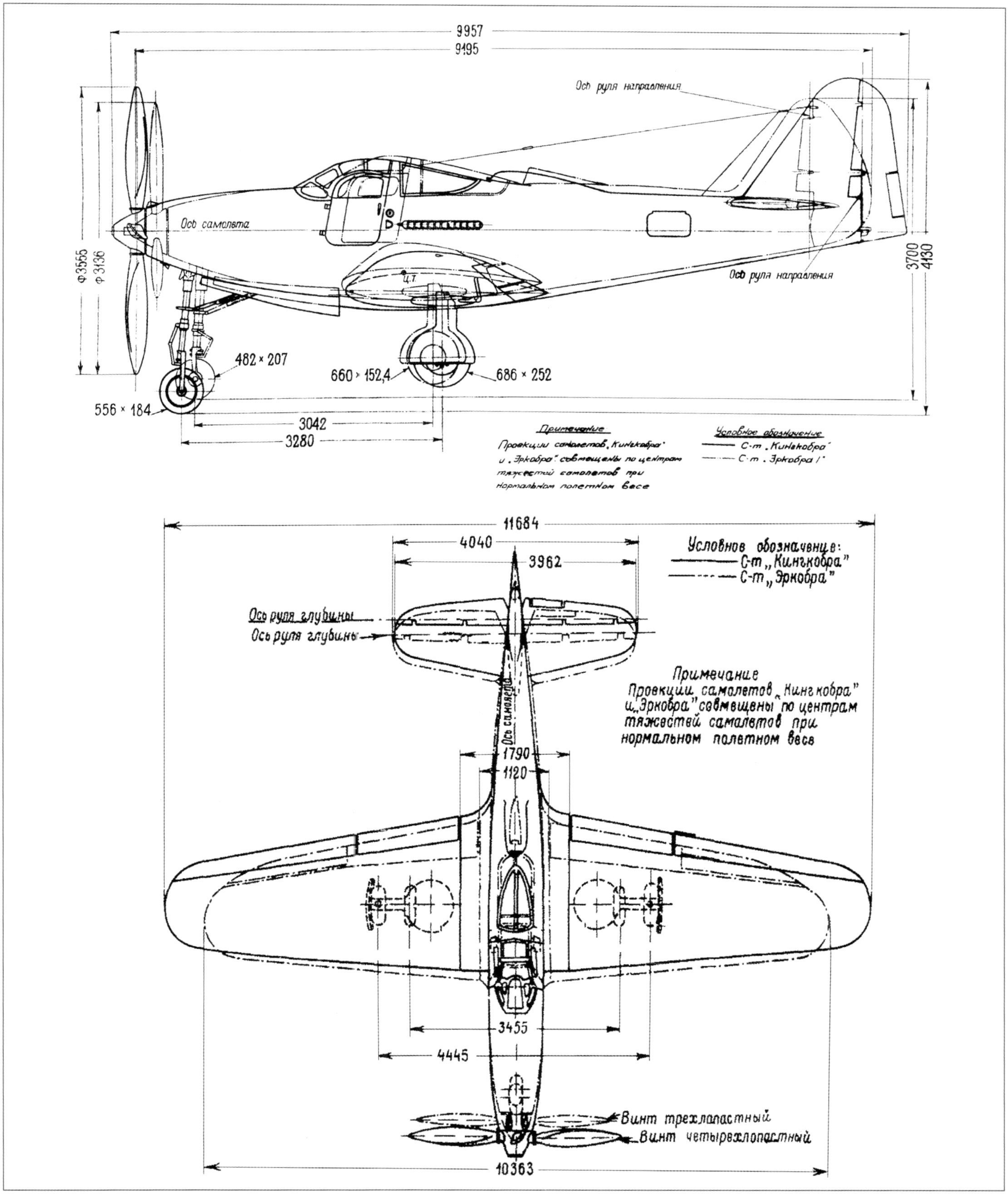

TOP LEFT AND MIDDLE LEFT: These drawings of the P-63 come from Soviet manuals prepared by NII VVS.

BOTTOM LEFT: A cutaway drawing of the P-63 from a Soviet manual.

ABOVE: This drawing from a Soviet manual gives a graphic comparison of the P-39 and the P-63A.

An example of the UTI P-63 was modified from P-63A-8-BE 42-69304 by the 321st Aircraft Repair Shop at Kubinka, west of Moscow (this is now the Russian air force's 121st Aircraft Repair Plant) in late 1946. The trainer was tested at NII VVS in November that year (the date of 21 November is mentioned in some sources). Another example of the UTI P-63, also tested at NII VVS in November 1946, was converted from a P-63A-10-BE (42-70502).

In 1948 TsNEB VVS (the Sovoet air force's central scientific and experimental base) developed a set of modifications that were recommended as a standard for conversions of this kind. The trainer version of the P-63 featured a second cockpit located in front of the usual one, supplanting the armament bay. One of the nose-mounted machine guns was retained for gunnery practice. The original cockpit was used by the instructor, with the trainee occupying the front cockpit. A further P-63-10-BE (42-70503) converted to a UTI P-63 two-seater underwent state acceptance trials at NII VVS between 28 December 1948 and 30 April 1949, with Vladimir Ye. Golofastov as project test pilot. The testing revealed that the change in the CG position had improved the aircraft's spin characteristics. The test programme also included

LEFT AND ABOVE LEFT: UTI P-63C 42-69304 seen at Chkalovskaya AB during trials at NII VVS. Note the different style of the Soviet insignia on the wings and the fuselage.

ABOVE: This side view of 42-69304 shows the canopy shape, the P-63C-style ventral strake, and the reinforcement ribs on the rear fuselage.

RIGHT: The front cockpit of the same aircraft with the canopy open.

ABOVE: UTI P-63 42-70503, which was converted by the 321st Aircraft Repair Shop and tested by Vladimir Ye. Golofastov at NII VVS between 29 December 1948 and 30 April 1949.

BELOW AND BELOW RIGHT: A meeting of the personnel of a Soviet ferry air regiment delivering P-63Cs in the first days after the war. The banner's last line reads S Pobedoy, tovarishchi! (Congratulations on the Victory, comrades!).

ABOVE: The personnel of a Soviet unit line up to receive instructions next to the P-63s being ferried.

LEFT: A Soviet pilot poses with his P-63A-10-BE 42-70xxx, wearing the code '40 White.'

BELOW: The flight line of a Soviet unit with in-service Kingcobras; P-63A-10-BE 42-7043 . . . / '42 White' is second from camera.

evaluating the emergency jettison system of the front cockpit canopy and assessing the ease of bailing out in an emergency; parachute jumps were performed from the forward cockpit in order to show that the trainee could bail out safely. This was done by Vasiliy G. Romanyuk, well known for his role in testing parachutes and parachuting techniques. Golofastov made eleven flights, with encouraging results.

Upon successful completion of the NII VVS trials, a go-ahead was given for the conversion of a substantial number of P-63s at the repair facilities of the Soviet air force's air armies and navy fleets. For example, the repair facility of the 3rd Air Army, located at Siauliai (in the then Soviet Lithuania), converted 25 P-63s into a two-seat version that was designated P-63U (*oo**cheb**nyy*: for training); again this was rendered in paperwork as a strange combination of Roman and Cyrillic characters—'P-63У'). A similar version built at a repair shop in Tbilisi was known locally as the P-63V (*vyvoznoy*: for familiarisation; again, the suffix was a Cyrillic letter, the designation being rendered misleadingly as

Another Kingcobra pilot poses with his mount coded '2 White.' The serial ends '314' but the preceding digits are unfortunately illegible.

'P-63B'). Several hundred machines were converted in this way. A photo taken in 1949 shows an UTI P-63 with the serial 43-11334, converted from the second P-63C-5-BE built.

At least one P-63 underwent a field conversion into a two-seat variant in the 6th IAD (based at Tiraspol' in the then Soviet Moldavia). The conversion proved less then successful, the machine being beset with all sorts of defects and vices.

Wartime Operational Service with the Soviet Air Force

The Kingcobras delivered in the course of 1944 and 1945 were eventually distributed between various air force units, but not among those engaged in combat. According to the generally accepted view of the events, the Kingcobras were not committed to action on the Soviet-German front.

Some sources have it that *'by a 1943 agreement, P-63s were disallowed for Soviet use against Germany and were supposed to be concentrated in the Soviet Far East for an eventual attack on Japan.'* However, the same source states that *'there are many unconfirmed reports from both the Soviet and German side that P-63s did indeed see service against the Luftwaffe. Most notably, one of Pokryshkin's pilots reports in his memoirs published in the 1990s that the entire 4th GvIAP (Guards Fighter Air Regiment) was secretly converted to P-63s in 1944, while officially still flying P-39s. One account states that they were in action at Königsberg* [now Kaliningrad, Russia], *in Poland, and in the final assault on*

P-63 '32 White' sports a strange white circle over the exhaust stubs.

LEFT: P-63C 43-11387 is caught by the camera on final approach, showing the unit markings on the nose and tail.

BELOW: The pilots of an operational P-63 unit pose with one of the regiment's aircraft wearing the code '47 White.'

OPPOSITE PAGE, ABOVE: A Soviet P-63A sitting partly under wraps at an unidentified airfield.

OPPOSITE PAGE, BELOW: Two sergeants (obviously from the ground crew) pose with P-63s and Polikarpov U-2 liaison aircraft as a backdrop. The nearest P-63 appears to have the star on the tail superimposed on a red flag!

Berlin. There are German reports of P-63s shot down by both fighters and flak.'

Of interest is an anonymous comment that appeared at a Russian forum site dealing with the history of the Second World War. The author (hiding behind an assumed name) contested the generally accepted belief that the P-63s had not seen action on the Soviet-German front. His grandfather, a wartime fighter pilot, claimed that his fighter regiment had converted to the P-63 *'by early February 1945'* (obviously a misprint—it should be 1944) and then took part in the operations against the German group of troops in Courland (part of Latvia). Later, the air regiment *'was redeployed to the territory of Czechoslovakia, where operations involving the use of aviation went on until August.'* The regiment reportedly operated the P-63A-6-BE version (which, in fact, was not delivered to the USSR!); they were equipped with compact aerial cameras in flush-fitting pods under the wing centre section. The grandfather, the author of the comment writes, spoke very highly of the Kingcobra's performance and piloting qualities and asserted that no P-63s of his regiment were shot down in air combat. He considered the Kingcobra to be the best fighter he had flown.

Nevertheless, all Soviet records show nothing but P-39s on the Soviet-German front. Given the lack of positive proof that the P-63 was used against Germany, we shall stick to the generally accepted story.

Russian aviation historians Konstantin Yu Kosminkov and Yevgeniy Pavlov wrote in a magazine article in 1986: *'The authors have failed to find information concerning the Kingcobra's performance in air combat. At the end of the war, when the P-63s were taken on strength by the Soviet air force, their use directly at the front was not a vital necessity because indigenous fighters were manufactured in sufficient numbers. At the same time, conversion to a new type and its maintenance under field conditions would pose certain difficulties. The Kingcobras were assigned to regiments and squadrons that were not directly involved in combat; for example, to Moscow air defence units. They also served with the flights intended to provide cover for frontline airfields.'*

From the spring of 1945 some first-line units of the air defence force began converting to the Kingcobra. This decision must have been prompted by the good high-altitude performance of the P-63. At altitudes above 7,500 m (24,610 ft.) it had a better turn of speed compared both to the Spitfire IX and the La-7. The Kingcobra's navigation equipment also gave it an advantage. All P-63s were fitted as standard with the MN-26Y direction finder, which was a valuable aid to nighttime navigation and flights in the clouds.

Moreover, one P-63A-10-BE delivered in early 1945 was even equipped with a radar—not an aerial intercept radar, though, but a tail warning radar.

In the spring and summer of 1945 the P-63s were in service with the PVO fighter regiments deployed around Moscow—the 7th, 821st, and 39th IAPs.

The summer of 1945 was also the time when the P-63s began to be distributed to air force regiments. It was the Soviet air force units redeployed to the Far East for the purpose of participating in the war against Japan that were equipped with P-63s. This led to a change in the delivery route: new Kingcobras arrived at Petropavlovsk-Kamchatskiy and in the Baikal region of East Siberia. The 190th IAD under Col.-Gen Vasiliy V. Fokin, which reported to the 12th VA, was probably the first unit to receive them, completing conversion training by early August 1945.

P-63A-9-BE 42-69775 / '91 White' with a ventral fin retrofitted.

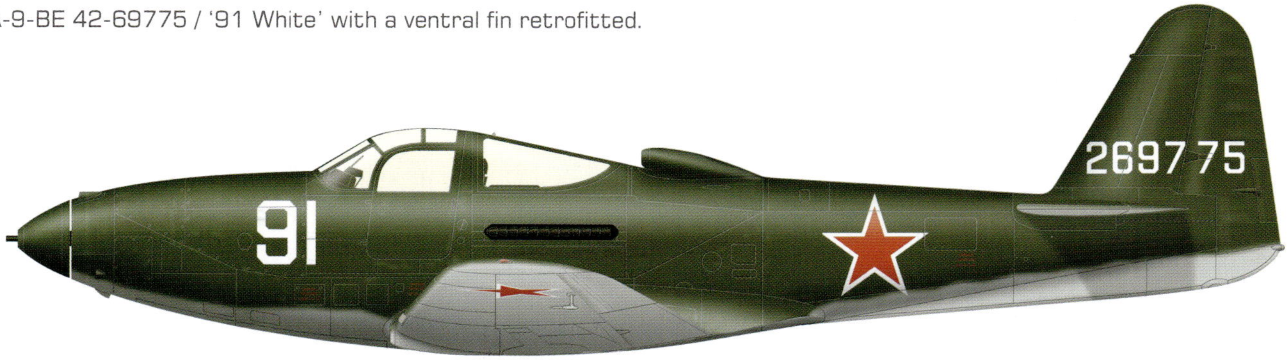

P-63C-5-BE 43-11332 / '41 White' with a yellow spinner and yellow fin cap as unit markings.

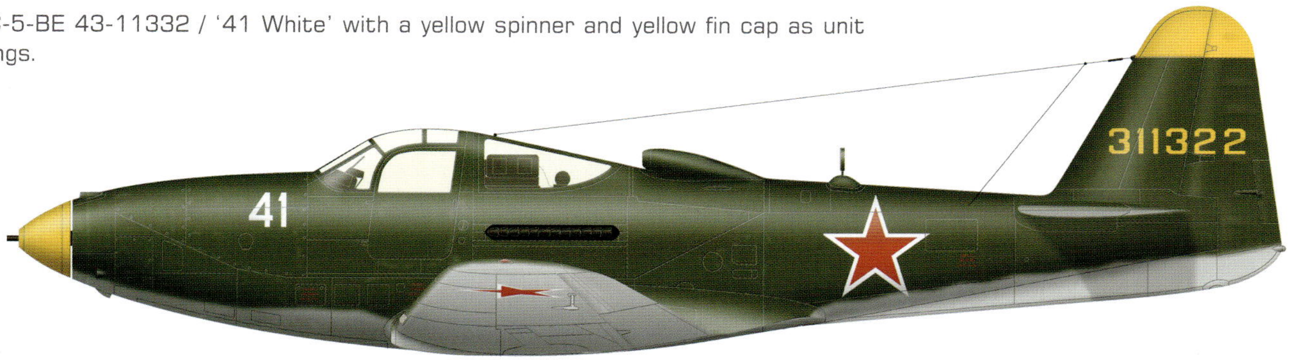

P-63C-5-BE 43-11387 / '41 White,' 16 GvIAP.

P-63C-5-BE 44-4011 / '08 White' as restored after the war, with the serial incorrectly presented as 44-44011.

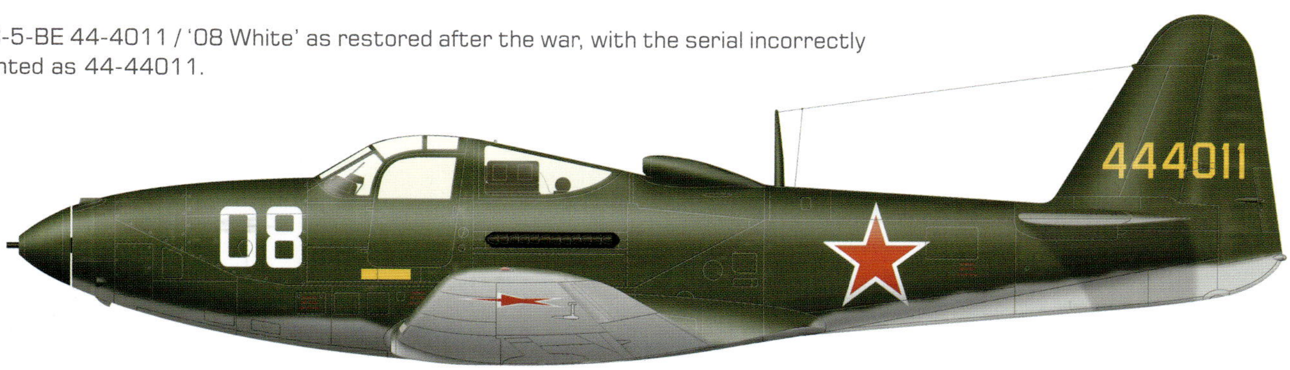

The pilots of a Soviet fighter unit pose for a group photo with one of the unit's aircraft; the tactical code is applied in red on a white circle like a racing number. The two pilots on the right are rather relaxed! P-63C-5-BE 44-43xx wears unit markings in the form of a vertical stripe on the rudder, which partly obscures the serial.

Another group photo of the flying personnel in a different Kingcobra unit (in less formal dress). The aircraft's tactical code appears to be '68 White.'

The pilots and crew chiefs of a Soviet air force unit operating Kingcobras in winter attire.

The P-63s are known to have operated against Japanese forces from air bases codenamed 'Ural' and 'Leningrad.' There was practically no opposition in the air, so there was no chance to build up a score in air combat. Yet, on 15 August the Soviet P-63s scored their first 'kill.' Lt. I. F. Miroshnichenko of the 17th IAP/190th IAD, flying air cover for transport aircraft coming in to land, shot down an elderly Nakajima Ki-43 Hayabusa ('Oscar') Imperial Japanese army fighter.

In the Pacific theatre of operations, the P-63 had a variety of tasks—escorting bombers and reconnaissance aircraft, providing air cover for ground troops and ships, and, of course, strafing and bombing Japanese positions. William Green wrote: *'The Russian pilots used the Kingcobra primarily for close support and ground strafing, making full use of the fighter's relatively good low-altitude performance and surprising ability to absorb battle damage and remain in the air.'* Presumably, this statement refers to the use of Kingcobras against Japan.

P-63s acted as escort for Soviet bombers. For example, fifty Kingcobras provided escort for a group of forty Ilyushin Il-4 bombers that attacked the Choochow (Zhuzhou) defensive region in Manchuria on 10 August 1945, the second day after hostilities started. The P-63s flown by pilots of the 245th IAD escorted transport aircraft flying supply missions for Soviet ground troops.

The P-63s were committed to action in the course of the assault operation on the Kuril Islands (the capture of the islands of Shumshu and Paramushir), which took place between 18 August and 1 September 1945. The landing of Soviet ground troops on Shumshu was to be supported by the 128th SAD (***smesh**annaya* ***a**viadi**vee**ziya*; Composite Air Division), comprising a bomber regiment (the 903th BAP) equipped with Douglas A-20s and two fighter regiments (the 888th IAP and the 410th IAP), of which the former was to play the main role.

The 888th IAP, formed in June 1942, was based at Yelizovo airfield, in Petropavlovsk-Kamchatskiy on the Kamchatka Peninsula, and initially had borne the name Kamchatka fighter regiment. It was equipped with obsolete I-15 and I-16 fighters, converting to modern materiel shortly before the operation. From 27 July 1945 it began to receive P-63 fighters, which had to be mastered by the pilots in all haste. By 8 August 1945 the regiment had in its inventory thirty-three Kingcobras and five surviving I-16s. Its participation in the Soviet-Japanese hostilities took place between 9 August and 3 September 1945, the last day of the war.

As for the 410th IAP, it had its origins in the 75th ShAP (*shtoormovoy* ***a**via**polk***; Attack Air Regiment), deployed in the Far East and equipped with Il-2 *shturmoviks*. In October 1944 the regiment was renumbered as the 410th ShAP; on 19 January 1945 it was transferred (without aircraft) to Yelizovo AB on Kamchatka and included into the 128th SAD. Together with the division it was included into the 10th Air Army of the 2nd Far Eastern Front. On 9 August the regiment was officially committed to active duty, albeit it joined combat somewhat later. On 13 August, just five days before the operation, the regiment received thirty-four Kingcobras and started conversion training. In fact, sorties over the Kuril Islands were flown by only six pilots who had mastered the new machines well enough. On 14 August 1945 the regiment was renamed as the 410th IAP.

In accordance with the plan of the operation, the 128th SAD, with its fifty-eight aircraft, was tasked with providing top cover for the assault troops during their sea passage, landing and fighting at the captured bridgehead. Ten Beriyev MBR-2 flying boats from the 2nd Independent Naval Bomber Border Guard Air Regiment conducted reconnaissance and other auxiliary missions (actual participation was reduced to forty-two and six machines, respectively).

At 0200 hrs. on 18 August the A-20s of the 903rd BAP and Kingcobras of the 888th IAP scrambled for their mission, designed to provide support to the advanced detachment of the assault troops. There was no aerial opposition because the Japanese had transferred all their aircraft from the Kuril Islands to the main parts of the country and to Manchuria. Soviet aircraft bombed and strafed Japanese positions and ammunition depots on Shumshu and safely returned to base. The second mission was flown already in daytime. Strong ground fire from the Japanese caused no losses, but one of the pilots of the 888th IAP, Ivan Dergachov, lost his life when his Kingcobra hit the slope of a volcano. His remains were discovered in 1980 and given a dignified burial at Yelizovo.

On 20 August, bombers and fighters of the 128th SAD dealt a powerful blow against Japanese naval bases of Kataoka and Kashiwabara and against concentrations of troops and materiel. Despite fierce resistance, Soviet troops succeeded in capturing the islands of Shumshu and Paramushir, as well as the rest of archipelago.

The participation of the 410th IAP in the action turned out to be purely nominal. It was limited to a mere twelve combat sorties, of which nine were flown into the area of Shumshu and Paramushir. There were no encounters with enemy aircraft, but one aircraft was lost to ground fire, the pilot bailing out safely.

The contribution of the 128th SAD to the defeat of Japan received due recognition from the Supreme Command; the division was granted the honorary appellation *Kuril'skaya* ('the Kuril division'), and all pilots of the 888th IAP were decorated.

On the whole, the Kingcobras gave a good account of themselves with the Soviet air force. Pilots and commanders appreciated their high speed, good manoeuvrability, and heavy armament; the aircraft was reliable and free from bugs.

After the surrender of Japan on 2 September 1945, signifying the end of the Second World War, the Bell P-63s and P-39s remained in the arsenal of the Soviet air force for quite some time. The postwar story of these types in Soviet service is traced in chapter 7.

CHAPTER 7

Postwar Years: End of the Bell Fighters' 'Soviet Career'

After the end of the Second World War some of the P-39s remaining on the strength of the Soviet air force were scrapped (all P-39Ds through P-39Q-5s were disposed of in 1946), while late-model examples (from the P-39Q-10 onwards) soldiered on until the early 1950s, albeit they were gradually replaced by P-63 Kingcobras. The Soviet reluctance to part with this aircraft is illustrated by the following facts: the 574th RAP (*razvedyvatel'nyy aviapolk*; Reconnaissance Air Regiment) of the North Fleet air arm started converting from the Yak-9 and P-40 to the P-39 in May 1946, while the 18th PVO Air Regiment, based at Khabarovsk in the Far East, converted from the Yak-9P to the P-39 and P-63 as late as June 1950. The 28th GvIAP retained the P-39s in its inventory until August 1948. The 68th GvIAP did the same until March 1947, when it was disbanded. The 67th GvIAP had eleven Airacobras in its inventory on 1 January 1947; the regiment was disbanded on 10 March 1947.

The Airacobras remained in the inventory of some Soviet air units stationed abroad. For example, the 129th GvIAP, deployed in Austria (at Tulln an der Donau between 28 June and 25 July1945 and at Stockerau between 25 July 1945 and the beginning of 1946),

The personnel of the 66th IAP read newspapers during a deployment to Ashkhabad-Voyennyy (= Military) airfield, Turkmen Soviet Socialist Republic, after the war. The fighters include 42-70685 / '5 Red,' the last P-63A-10-BE delivered to the USSR.

P-39 4*-*671 / '9 White' of the Black Sea Fleet's 6th GvIAP is pictured here at Yevpatoriya on the Crimea Peninsula in 1947.

RIGHT: A curious mix of types at a Soviet airbase in the early postwar days; P-63s share the flight line with a pair of U-2 biplanes, a Yak-11 trainer (*third from left*), and a North American AT-6C Texan (*fourth from left*).

BELOW RIGHT: UTI P-63 '2 White,' converted from P-63C-5-BE 43-11334, was operated by a Soviet air force unit temporarily stationed in Austria after the war. Here the ground crew reports to the aircraft's crew chief P. Ye. Vikulin (*left*) that the trainer is serviceable.

was equipped with P-39s; this was preceded by a brief deployment in Germany in May–June 1945. The 21st GvIAP, equipped with Airacobras, was also stationed in Austria; this deployment took place between 11 May 1945 and 1 March 1947, when the regiment reporting to the 23rd GvIAD was disbanded. The Airacobras of the 54th GvIAP were stationed in Germany for a brief period after the Victory (July 1945 is specifically mentioned). In January 1946 they were deployed to the Baltic Military District (initially termed Special Military District, since it encompassed a part of East Prussia later integrated into the USSR as the Kaliningrad Region); they were replaced by Kingcobras during 1946. Likewise, the Airacobras of the 69th GvIAP were stationed in Austria between 11 May 1945 and 12 March 1947, when the regiment was disbanded. A similar story concerns the 72nd GvIAP, whose Airacobras soldiered on until the end of 1947, when they were superseded by other types. The 104th GvIAP with its P-39s was stationed in Germany (Grossenhain and Riesa) in May and early June 1945, then it was redeployed to Austria (Absdorf and Münchendorf) and retained the Airacobras until at least July 1946.

Airacobras were supplied to several flying schools. For example, a single P-39 was in the inventory of the naval flying school named after Iosif V. Stalin, which was based in Yeisk (Krasnodar Territory, southern Russia), on the shore of the Sea of Azov; five Airacobras formed part of the inventory of the higher aviation courses for officers. Six P-39s were transferred to the naval aviation's 65th APON (*aviapolk osobovo naznacheniya*; Special Mission Air Regiment), alternatively rendered in some sources as the 65th OAPSN (*otdel'nyy aviapolk spetsiahl'novo naznacheniya*; Independent Special Mission Air Regiment), a unit performing both transport duties and research work. This unit was based at Izmaïlovo AB, located immediately east of Moscow, which was notable for its role in the Soviet copying of the Boeing B-29 bomber as the Tupolev Tu-4—the Superfortresses that fell into Soviet hands arrived there from the Far East, and one of them (B-29-15-BW, '358 Black,' ex-USAAF 42-6358) was stored there for a while. (Today, Izmaïlovo is a residential area of Moscow, and the base is long gone. The airfield used to be where the present-day Sirenevyy Blvd. ('Lilac Boulevard') is, between the present-day tube stations Pervomaïskaya and Shcholkovskaya.)

Interestingly, a single P-39Q from Soviet air force stocks came to serve for a while with the Polish air force in the first postwar years. It was the personal 'hack' of Col.-Gen. Fyodor P. Polynin Soviet air force, who commanded the Polish air force (reborn on Soviet soil during the war) in 1944–47 (and, as such, also had the Polish rank *General Broni*, the second-highest generals grade in the Polish army). The command structure of the Polish air force was formed on the basis of the Soviet 6th Air Army's command structure on 31 October 1944. The P-39Q bearing Polish insignia and the code '01' on the rudder was operated by the 2nd Independent Air Squadron of the Polish air force between 1944 and 1948. Then it was withdrawn from service and turned over to an aviation technical school as a ground instructional airframe. One more P-39 was used in Poland for the same purpose; this machine, retaining Soviet insignia (the identity is unknown), became a teaching aid at the *Szkoła Wawelberga i Rotwanda* (the mechanical-technical school named after Hipolit Wawelberg and Stanisław Rotwand) in Warsaw.

The P-63 Kingcobra, as distinct from its progenitor, occupied a more prominent place in the postwar activities of the Soviet air force and Soviet naval aviation. As noted elsewhere, the P-63s assigned to the Soviet air force units took part in the final phase of the Second World War—the war against Japan. Kingcobras were introduced into the inventory of the Soviet naval aviation in the summer of 1945. The 7th IAD of the Pacific Fleet air arm succeeded in obtaining ten P-63s immediately before the Soviet Union's entry into the war with Japan; a further several dozen machines joined them in the course of August 1945. However, they could not reach operational capability immediately and thus did not take part in the hostilities.

As mentioned earlier, immediately after the surrender of Japan the delivery of US fighters to the Soviet mission in Fairbanks stopped. By that time the Soviet side had received 2,400 of the 2,500 Kingcobras that had been ordered in accordance with the 6th Protocol. In total, 2,397 of them had been ferried via ALSIB, and only three reached the Soviet Union by sea through Murmansk. The final P-63 delivered to the Soviet Union reached Yelizovo airfield, in Petropavlovsk-Kamchatskiy, on 29 September 1945.

By September 1945 a large number of newly delivered P-63s had been amassed at Krasnoyarsk and Ukurey (Chita Region); so large, indeed, that it took almost a year to collect them and ferry them to recipients—the various air force units. Many of these units were located in the Far East, but they were by no means the only 'beneficiaries'—the Kingcobras were also distributed in the European part of the Soviet Union. They were supplied to the 5th GvIAD, deployed in the Baltic Sea area, and to the 269th IAD, in

DANGER
PLANE ON

LEFT: A former Soviet air force P-63 that has been returned to the US after the war undergoes a brake and tyre inspection at Great Falls, Montana, in June 1945.

BELOW LEFT: One of two ex-Soviet Airacobras that ended up in Poland became an instructional airframe at the Wawelberg & Rotwand technical school in Warsaw.

RIGHT AND ABOVE RIGHT: An Airacobra or Kingcobra used as a cutaway teaching aid at the Kazan' aviation institute.

Armenia. In 1946 the 101st GvIAP, stationed in Siberia, was also equipped with Kingcobras. In June 1946 the 28th GvIAP undertook conversion training to the P-63, but in the same month the new aircraft were transferred to the 57th GvIAP. This regiment retained the P-63s in its inventory up to 1950; in 1949–50 it was assigned to the Moscow Air Defence District. In June 1946 the 31st GvIAP, stationed in the Odessa Military District, started converting to the Kingcobras, which it retained until early 1952.

In January 1946 the 66th IAP, deployed in Poland, converted from the P-39 to the P-63 and was transferred to the Turkestan Military District (central Asia). After 1949 it was assigned to the air defence force and redeployed to the Baku Air Defence District. In 1946–49 the P-63s forming the inventory of the 54th GvIAP were deployed at unspecified airbases in the Baltic Military District. The 57th GvIAP converted to the P-63 in August 1946. The Kingcobras also made their appearance in the inventory of the 72nd GvIAP, where they served in the Moscow Air Defence District between January 1948 and the beginning of 1950, to be supplanted by MiG-15s. The 85th GvIAP started converting to the P-63s in June 1946 and operated them until late October 1951.

The P-63s from Lend-Lease deliveries were also supplied to the Soviet air force units based abroad—in Germany, Austria, and China. For example, they equipped the regiments of the 1st GvIAD, stationed at Neuhausen in East Prussia (in 1946 this became Goor'yevsk in the Kaliningrad Region of the USSR), and of the 83rd IAK, stationed at Port-Arthur (China). In December 1945 the P-63s, together with the P-39s, were in the inventory of the 67th GvIAP, assigned to the 22nd GvIAD, 2nd VA. On 1 January 1947 the regiment had twenty-three Kingcobras. In 1946 the Kingcobras served with the 129th GvIAP, also assigned to the

22nd GvIAD and stationed at Parndorf, Austria; this service ended when the regiment was disbanded on 12 March 1947. In July 1946 the 73rd GvIAP, assigned to the Odessa Military District, started conversion training on the P-63s, replacing the Yak-9s; in October 1951 it was redeployed to East Germany (airbase unknown), only to start conversion training on the MiG-15 jet fighter in November of that year.

In January 1949, the 100th GvIAP, stationed at Trausdorf in Germany, was reequipped with P-63s (in February 1949 the regiment was renamed as the 789th GvIAP of the 237th GvIAD). The 104th GvIAP, stationed in Austria (consecutively at Absdorf, Münchendorf, and Wiener-Neustadt), replaced its P-39s with Kingcobras in 1946.

The units of the Baltic Fleet air arm (the 314th GvIAP and the 246th GvIAP) and the Black Sea Fleet air arm (the 6th GvIAP and the 11th GvIAP) also had Kingcobras at their disposal.

At the end of the Second World War the P-63 was obviously regarded as a valuable asset for the Soviet air force. Initially the Kingcobras were intended to share the fate of many Soviet combat aircraft that were doomed to be scrapped after the end of the war, but in the case of the P-63 this decision was reversed. The machines received were retained in the air force inventory and were operated until the mid-1950s. The type was even given the NATO reporting name *Fred*. However, with the first deliveries of jet fighters starting in 1947, the P-63s lost their importance and were relegated to a secondary role. Their value lay in the fact that they had a tricycle undercarriage—a feature they shared with the new jet fighters. Hence they could help familiarise pilots with the takeoff and landing techniques of aircraft with a tricycle undercarriage. Fighter regiments converting to jet aircraft retained two or three Kingcobras in their inventory specifically for the purpose of this training. Sometimes the training procedures were specially altered to emulate the peculiarities of the MiG-15's landing techniques—the landing approach was to be performed at a speed of 400–500 km/h (248–310 mph), with the flaps retracted. For the purpose of such training it was considered expedient to have a two-seat dual-control version of the P-63. No such version had been produced by Bell, so it was decided to build a trainer version locally.

The P-63s were completely phased out from the operational units by the end of 1953. Of the regiments equipped with these fighters, the 57th GvIAP converted to the MiG-15 in 1950; the 246th GvIAP did the same in May 1951, and the 314th IAP followed suit exactly a year later, in May 1952. The 789th GvIAP, previously stationed in Germany, was redeployed to the Kaliningrad Region and was assigned to the Baltic Fleet air force; in October 1952 it converted from the P-63 to the MiG-15. The 104th GvIAP, stationed in Austria, did the same in 1951. The 5th RAP, based in the Far East, replaced its P-63s with La-11 fighters in May 1950. The Kingcobras soldiered on with the 307th and 308th IAPs, based on the Kuril Islands until 1951. A little later the P-63s were sent into retirement by the regiments of the Pacific Fleet.

The Kingcobras based in the Far East remained there long enough to see the beginning of the Korean War, when the Soviet air force units stationed in that region were placed on combat alert. On 8 October 1950, shortly after the outbreak of the war, a pair of USAF Lockheed F-80 Shooting Stars of the 49th Fighter Group strafed—either by mistake or intentionally—the Soviet airbase Sukhaya Rechka ('Dry River'), located close to the border with North Korea, fairly deep (about 60 nm) inside the USSR's Primor'ye Territory near the junction of the Soviet, Chinese, and North Korean borders. According to a Western report, at that time this airbase was used by the Soviet air force's 821st IAP, a Kingcobra unit. The F-80s (again, according to a Western report) made two strafing runs on the airfield. One P-63 was destroyed, three were heavily damaged, and another three suffered minor damage. There were no personnel losses because the pilots were in their barracks. According to the Soviet version of the story, eight P-63s, which were withdrawn from use and lined up at the edge of the airfield, were damaged by gunfire. Less the one that blew up, all the damaged Kingcobras were later repaired.

The US claimed that the attack was accidental. The F-80 pilots had been assigned to strafe Chonjin airbase in North Korea, about 64 km (40 miles) away from the Soviet border and 109 km (68 miles) southwest of Sukhaya Rechka. The pilots said later that they became disoriented when climbing above a cloud bank in strong winds. The Soviet Union filed a diplomatic protest; the US accepted the responsibility and promised that the pilots would be court-martialled. A court-martial was indeed held later, with the pilots being quietly acquitted.

Some American pilots claimed to encounter P-63s in service with North Korea during the Korean War, but such statements remain unconfirmed. This was obviously a case of mistaken identity, and the fighters in question were obviously Yak-9Ps, which were operated by the Korean People's army air force in considerable numbers. Moreover, some Western researchers state directly that the P-63 did not take part in air combat in Korea. They find it somewhat surprising and wonder whether political reasons could be a possible explanation. However, the more plausible reason may be that the P-63s, with their worn-out engines, would have had no chances against the P-80 jet fighters sent by the US to Korea, to say nothing of the F-86.

Possibly the longest-serving Kingcobras were to be found in the 66th IAP, reporting to the 238th IAD PVO (*istre**bi**tel'naya aviadi**vee**ziya **Pro**tivovoz**dooshnoy** obo**ro**ny*; Air Defence Fighter Division). The regiment parted company with its P-63s in December 1953, converting to the MiG-15.

After the war an attempt was made to utilise demilitarised Kingcobras for civilian duties. An idea was floated of using these high-speed aircraft as mailplanes—specifically, for delivering matrices of the principal Moscow-published newspapers to other cities where they were to be printed from these matrices. The former gun bay was to house the payload. A special group of pilots were selected for this purpose. There is no information as to the implementation of the project.

CHAPTER 8

Soviet Clones of the Airacobra

Soviet Fighters à la Airacobra

The unorthodox and fascinating layout chosen by Bell for the P-39 Airacobra obviously captured the imagination of some Soviet aircraft designers, who set about projecting fighters based broadly on the Airacobra concept. The designers in question were Mikhail I. Gudkov, Viktor N. Belyayev, and Pavel O. Sukhoi. The results of their efforts are briefly described below.

Gudkov Gu-1 Fighter

Mikhail Ivanovich Gudkov, best known for his participation in the development of the LaGG-1/LaGG-3 fighter together with Semyon A. Lavochkin and Vladimir P. Gorbunov, decided to try his hand at designing a fighter entirely on his own. On 15 October 1940 he wrote to Kliment Ye. Voroshilov, chairman of the government's defence committee, proposing the construction of a prototype fighter with a potent weapons complement. The armament comprised a PTB-23 cannon (***push**ka **Ta**ubina i Ba**boorina***; 23 mm cannon designed by Yakov G. Taubin and Mikhail N. Baboorin at OKB-16), two 12.7 mm machine guns, and four 7.62 mm ShKAS machine guns (*[poole**myot**] Shpi**tal**'novo i **Ko**ma**rits**kovo, aviatsi**on**nyy, skoro**strel**'nyy*; fast-firing aircraft machine gun designed by Boris G. Shpital'nyy and Irinarkh A. Komaritskiy). In its layout the fighter copied the P-39 Airacobra, featuring the same engine location amidships, with a long extension shaft to the propeller reduction gearbox and a tricycle undercarriage. Gudkov made no secret of his source of inspiration—he directly referred to his project as the 'Soviet Airacobra,' and this name was even used in the correspondence relating to the Gudkov fighter, which later came to be officially designated Gu-1.

Gudkov's proposal met with a positive response. On 31 October 1940 the defence committee adopted a resolution calling for the construction of a prototype. Somewhat later a decision was taken to equip the Gu-1 with a Shpital'nyy Sh-37 cannon (a.k.a. ShFK-37, *[**push**ka] Shpi**tal**'novo **f**yuze**lyazh**no-**k**ryl'ye**va**ya*; 37 mm Shpital'nyy cannon suitable for fuselage or wing installation) firing through the propeller hub. However, the actual prototype was armed with two synchronised 20 mm ShVAK cannons (*[**push**ka] Shpi**tal**'novo i **V**la**dim**irova, aviatsi**on**naya, kroopnoka**li**bernaya*; large-calibre aircraft cannon designed by Shpital'nyy and Semyon V. Vladimirov).

A recently discovered photo showing a full-size mockup of the Gudkov Gu-2 attack aircraft.

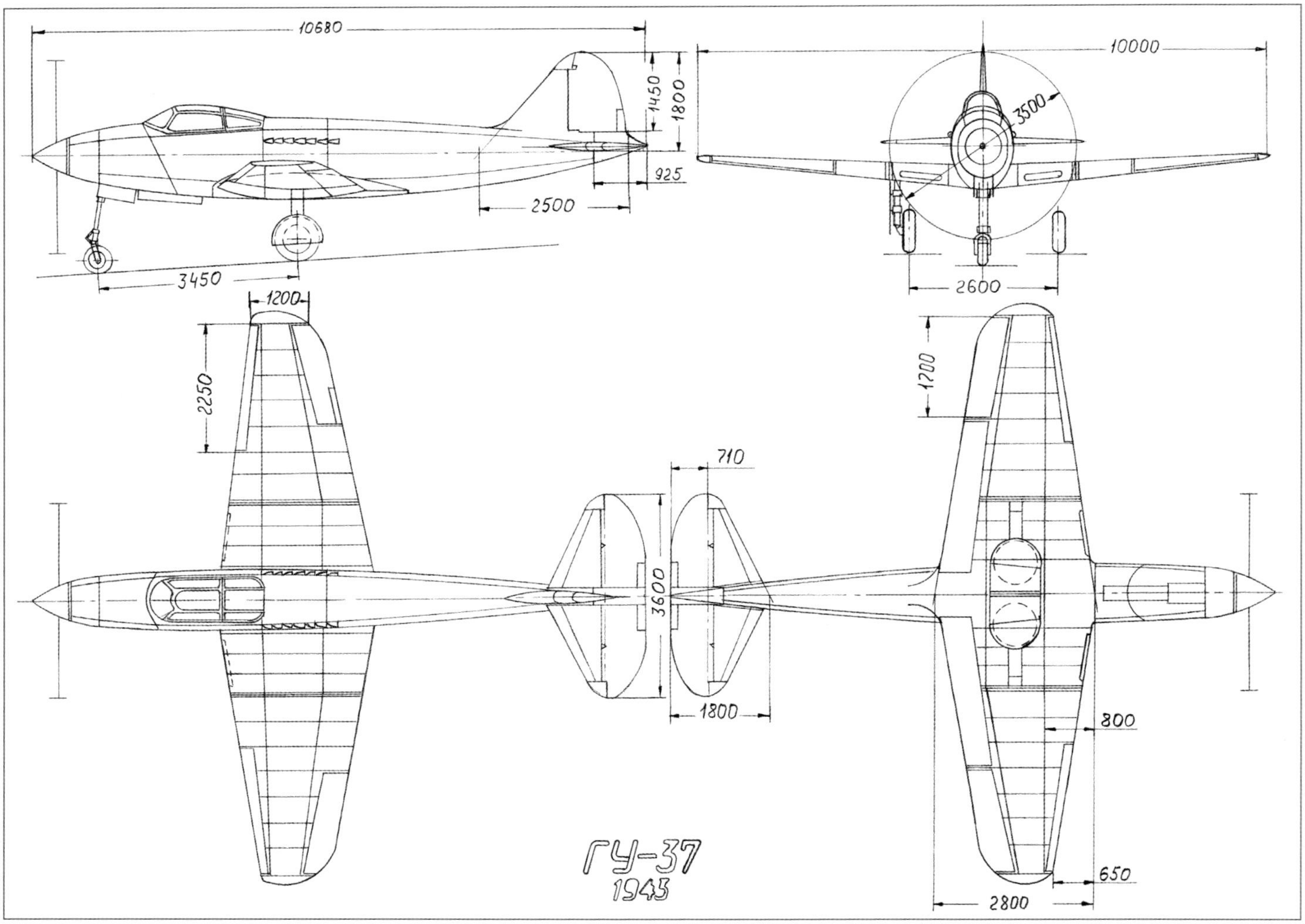

The Moscow-based OKB-24 engine design bureau, headed by Aleksandr A. Mikulin, undertook to develop for this fighter a special version of the new 1,400 hp AM-37 V-12 liquid-cooled engine featuring an extension shaft (the AM-37UV; the suffix stood for *oodlin**nyon**nyy vahl*: extension shaft). However, the work on the AM-37UV was discontinued in favour of a similar version of the 1,800 hp AM-39 (also a V-12 liquid-cooled engine); the AM-39UV was later renamed AM-41. It was the AM-41 that was eventually installed in the Gu-1 prototype.

(In parallel, the OKB-26 engine design bureau, headed by Vladimir Ya. Klimov and based in Rybinsk [Yaroslavl' Region] at the time, was tasked with developing an engine for the Gu-1

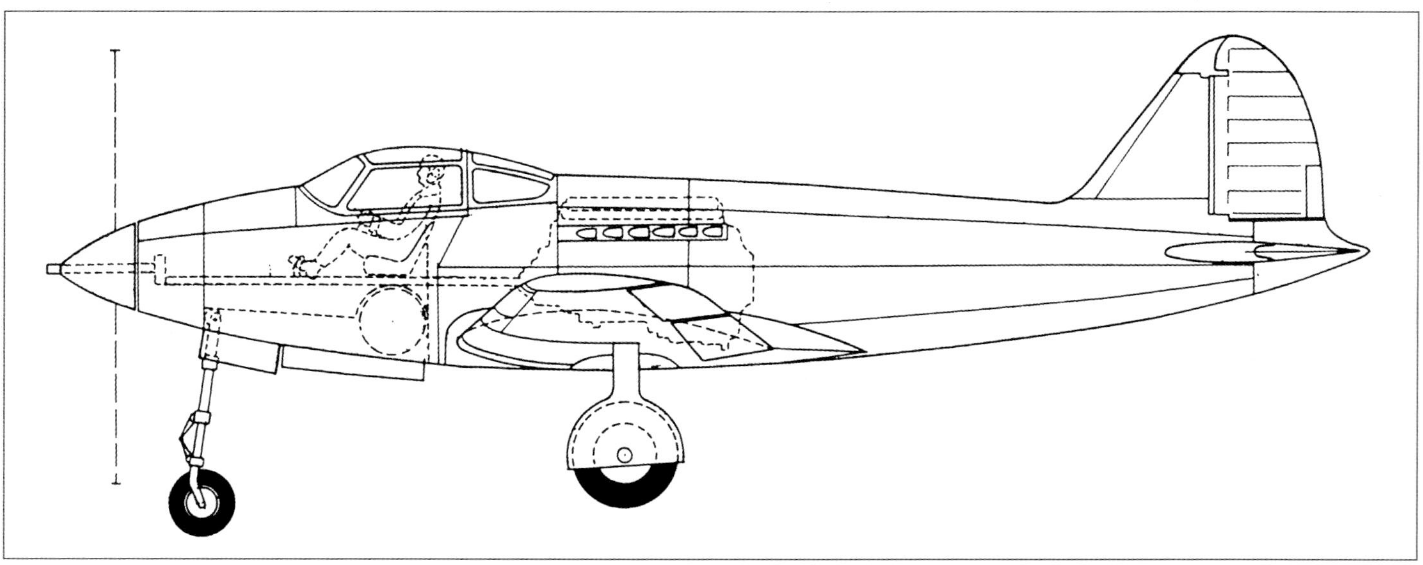

LEFT: A four-view drawing of the Gu-1 fighter (a.k.a. Gu-37).

BELOW LEFT: A cutaway drawing of the Gu-1 showing the midengine layout, the propeller drive shaft, and reduction gearbox.

RIGHT: A provisional three-view drawing of the Gu-1, differing from the one on the opposite page. In particular, the cockpit is located farther aft, making more room for the armament in the nose, and the wings feature dorsal outlet gills for the water radiators and oil coolers buried in the wing roots. Note also the twin engine inlet air scoops aft of the canopy.

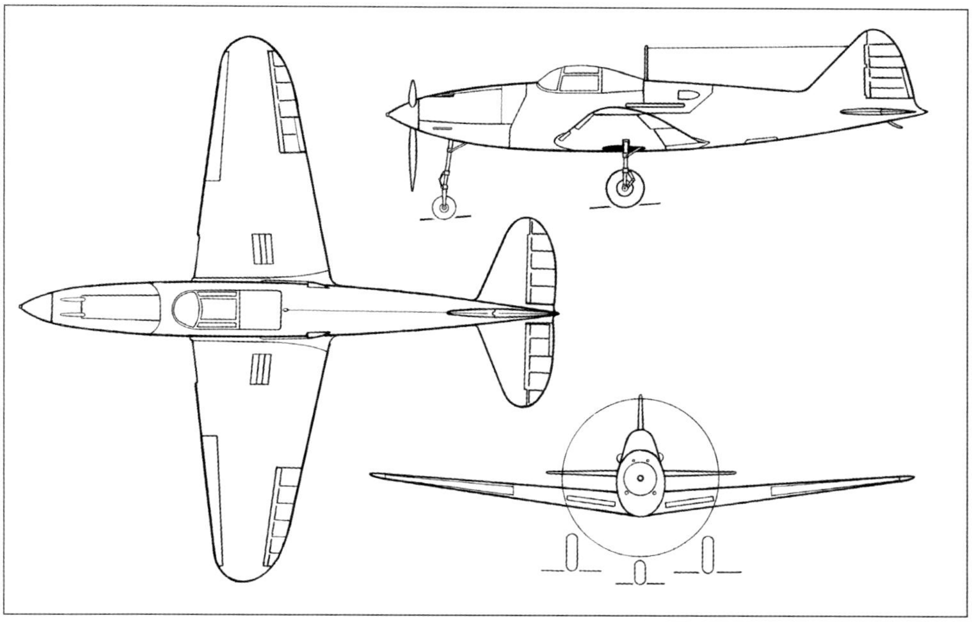

fighter. OKB-26 proposed a version of its M-120 liquid-cooled engine with a design takeoff rating of 1,800 hp. Developed in 1939, this was an unconventional inverted-Y eighteen-cylinder engine based on the components of Klimov's production V-12 engines—initially the 960 hp M-103 and later the 1,100 hp M-105. The M-120UV version customised for amidships installation featured an extension shaft; hence again the UV suffix. Eventually, however, pressure of more urgent work on refining the production models caused Klimov to abandon the M-120UV.)

The 'Soviet Airacobra' project was also known under the designation Gu-37, in which the '37' might refer either to the cannon calibre or to the engine type. This designation was also used alternatively for Gudkov's K-37 fighter, which was an LaGG-3 fitted with Shpital'nyy's 37 mm cannon.

After the outbreak of the war in June 1941, the Gu-1 project was temporarily shelved by NKAP in favour of more urgent work on LaGG-3 modifications; it was revived in the second part of 1942. The prototype was ready by March of 1943. Small hops during taxiing runs showed that with an AUW of 4,350 kg (9,600 lb.), the Gu-1 could lift off after a run of 570 m (1,870 ft.), which was deemed acceptable. The go-ahead was given to start flight tests; the preparations for these were conducted in great haste and, in fact, were not quite completed. The Gu-1 made its maiden flight from Moscow's central airfield, named after Mikhail V. Frunze (a.k.a. Moscow-Khodynka), on 12 June 1943, piloted by Lt.-Col. Aleksey I. Nikashin, an NII VVS test pilot. The very first flight ended in disaster. After a long takeoff run the fighter became airborne with difficulty and barely managed to climb to 200 m (660 ft.), flying with the gear and flaps down. Then, as Nikashin initiated a gentle left turn, the Gu-1 stalled, entered a spin, and crashed on the grounds of Troitskoye-Lykovo estate, 10 km (6.21 miles) west of the airfield, killing the pilot. The accident investigation panel came to the somewhat controversial conclusion that the crash was caused by poor aerodynamic properties of the wings on account of the large radiator air intakes in the leading edge. The experts also laid the blame on the designer for excessive structural weight, high wing loading, and poor lift/drag ratio. Mikhail I. Gudkov contested these conclusions and insisted that the true reasons for the crash be verified by subjecting the second prototype to wind tunnel tests; however, his protests went unheeded. Eyewitness reports suggest that propeller overspeeding may have been the true cause of the crash, but this possibility was not even considered by the panel.

Gudkov Gu-2 Attack Aircraft (Project)

As a further development of the Gu-1, Mikhail I. Gudkov produced a design of a heavy fighter that he submitted to the attention of Stalin in a letter dated 15 May 1941 (together with two other designs based on the LaGG-3). This new project, later known as the Gu-2 and classified in some sources as an attack aircraft, featured an even more potent gun complement. It comprised a 45 mm Shpital'nyy Sh-45 cannon with forty rounds firing through the propeller hub, two 20 mm synchronised ShVAK cannons with forty rounds per gun, two synchronised 12.7 mm Berezin BS machine guns with 220 rpg and two 7.62 mm ShKAS machine guns with 500 rpg (synchronised ShKAS guns are mentioned in one source, but an available drawing of the Gu-2 shows two ShKAS machine guns as installed in the wings to fire outside the propeller disc). Design performance included a maximum speed of 700 km/h (435 mph) at 7,500 m (24,600 ft.) and 560km/h (348 mph) at sea level. The range at 0.8 maximum speed was 1,000 km (621 miles). How this very high performance was to be attained by a heavy fighter is not known (the AUW and engine power rating are not available).

In maximum AUW configuration the aircraft could carry two FAB-100 or FAB-250 high-explosive bombs of 100 kg (220 lb.) or 250 kg (551 lb.) calibre, respectively, and the abovementioned two wing-mounted ShKAS machine guns with 500 rpg.

The Gu-2 was to have the following basic dimensions: length 10.38 m (34 ft. 2$\frac{1}{32}$ in.), wing span 10.0 m (32 ft. 9$\frac{45}{64}$ in.), horizontal tail span 3.8 m (12 ft. 5$\frac{39}{64}$ in.), and height on ground 3.225 m (10 ft. 6$\frac{31}{32}$ in.)—though some sources quote it as 3.285 m (10 ft. 9$\frac{21}{64}$ in.). The wheel track was to be 2.73 m (8 ft. 11$\frac{31}{64}$ in.), but no figures are quoted for the wheelbase. The three-blade propeller was to have a diameter of 3.1 m (10 ft. 2$\frac{3}{64}$ in.).

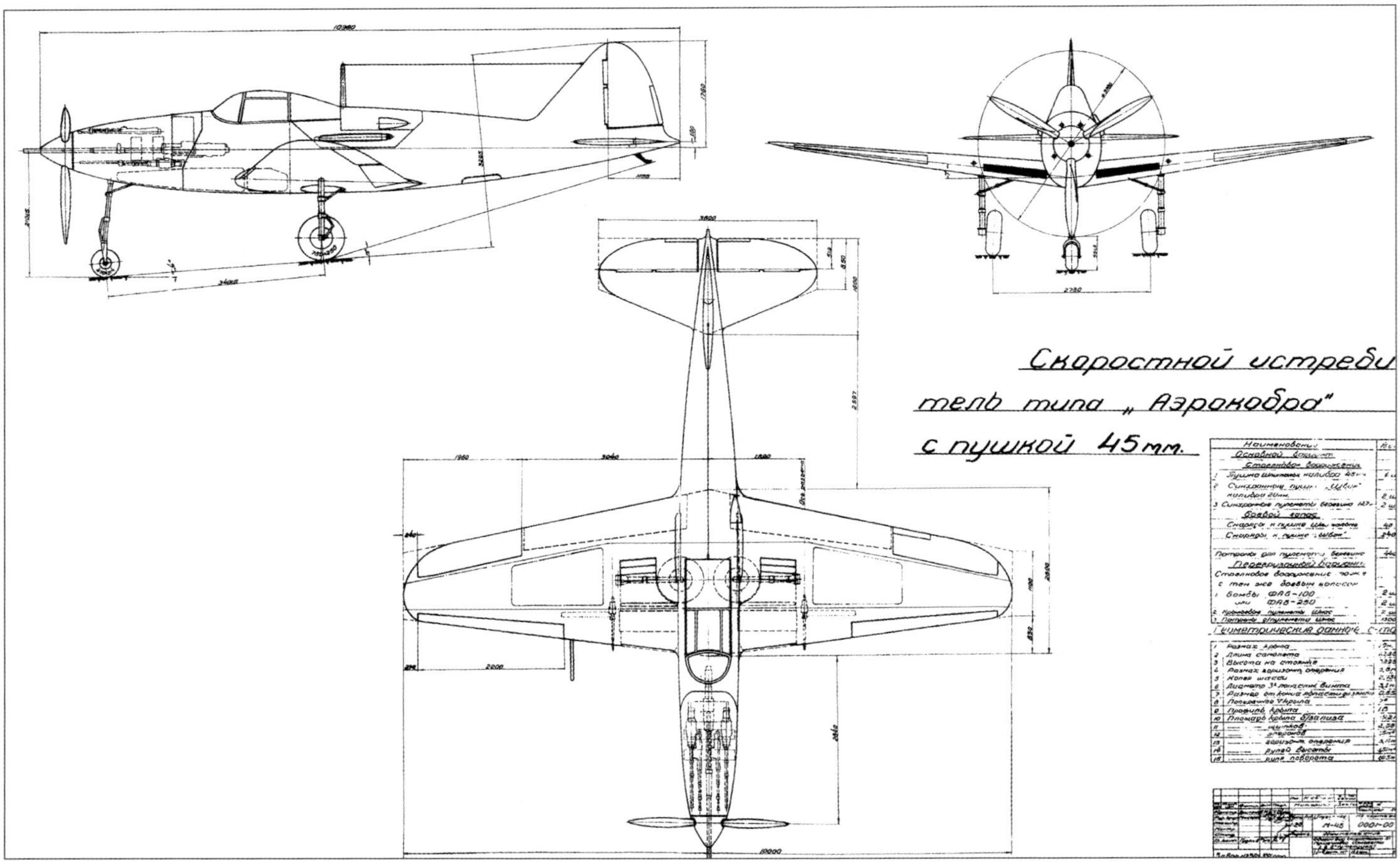

A three-view drawing of the Gu-2 from the project documents (titled 'Airacobra-type high-speed fighter with a 45 mm cannon').

The project did not progress further than the drawing board. Interestingly, design bureau drawings of the Gu-2 carry the inscription 'Airacobra-type high-speed fighter with a 45 mm cannon.' The fighter looked strikingly similar to the P-39 in general outline (as did the Gu-1), but, of course, there was no structural commonality in either case. Notably, instead of the Airacobra's car-type doors, a traditional cockpit with a sliding canopy was used.

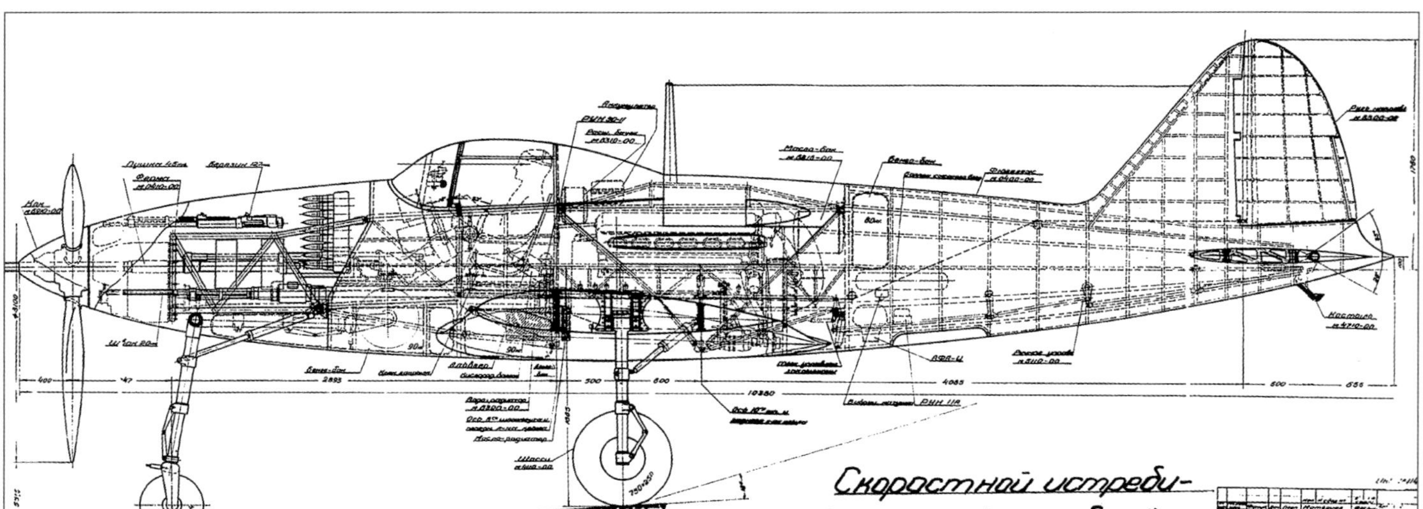

A cutaway drawing of the Gu-2 from the project documents; note the pairs of machine guns above and below the cannon.

Belyayev OI-2 Twin-Engined Fighter (Project)

Viktor Nikolayevich Belyayev was a prominent specialist in aerodynamics who, in parallel with his scientific activities, was engaged in practical aircraft design in the second half of the 1930s. He is probably best known for the unorthodox DB-LK twin-engined bomber of 1940, featuring a twin-fuselage layout (*dahl'niy bombardirovshchik-letayushcheye krylo*; 'flying wing'-type long-range bomber). Yet, he authored several unbuilt projects that were just as unusual.

The North American F-82 Twin Mustang fighter is well known, and you may have heard of the experimental Messerschmitt Bf 109Z Zwilling ('twins') having a similar layout. But can you imagine a 'Twin Airacobra'? In early 1941 Belyayev developed and submitted to NII VVS a preliminary project of the OI-2 single-seat, twin-engined fighter whose layout anticipated that of the later Twin Mustang. OI presumably stands for *odnomesnyy istrebitel'*: single-seat fighter. The figure 2 denotes the second project, the first one being the EOI (*eksperimentahl'nyy odnomotornyy istrebitel'*; experimental single-engined fighter), Belyayev's previous design.

The OI-2 was a low-wing cantilever monoplane having two nearly identical fuselages, each of which was, in fact, closely modelled on the fuselage of the P-39 Airacobra, with the same midfuselage location of the engine, except that the carburettor air intakes were located on the outboard side rather than dorsally. Only the starboard fuselage was provided with a cockpit enclosed by a teardrop canopy. Interestingly, Belyayev copied even the distinctive feature of the Bell machine—the car-type entry door of the cockpit (except that there was only one door, on the starboard side). The two fuselages were joined by a constant-chord wing centre section, while the outer wings were tapered, with rounded tips. The outer wings were provided with leading-edge slats and featured large water radiator / oil cooler air intakes built into the leading edge (the air outlets were located ventrally). At the rear the fuselages were similarly joined by a stabiliser with a full-span elevator (the horizontal tail did not extend on the outboard sides). Interestingly, the rudders terminated at the horizontal tail level instead of taking up the full height of the vertical tails, as on the Twin Mustang. The fighter had a quad undercarriage comprising inward-retracting mainwheels on the inboard sides of the oleo struts (one under each fuselage) and aft-retracting nosewheels; the mainwheel track was barely wider than the nosewheel track. The nose gear struts were inclined forward, again in Airacobra fashion. A pair of tail bumpers were provided to protect the fuselages in the event of a tail-down landing.

The aircraft was to be powered by two Klimov M-120UV liquid-cooled engines with a design rating of 1,800 hp apiece. The armament comprised two 23 mm Taubin cannons with 81 rpg firing through the propeller hubs, four 12.7 mm synchronised machine guns in the port fuselage, with 250 rpg, and four nonsynchronised ShKAS machine guns in the wing centre section, with 500 rpg. In addition, the fighter could carry bombs in various combinations either internally in the wing centre section or externally under it, to a total weight of some 500 kg (1,100 lb.).

The OI-2 was to have a wing area of 34.0 m² (365.97 sq. ft.) and a wing loading of 200 kg/m² (41 lb. / sq. ft.). The all-up weight

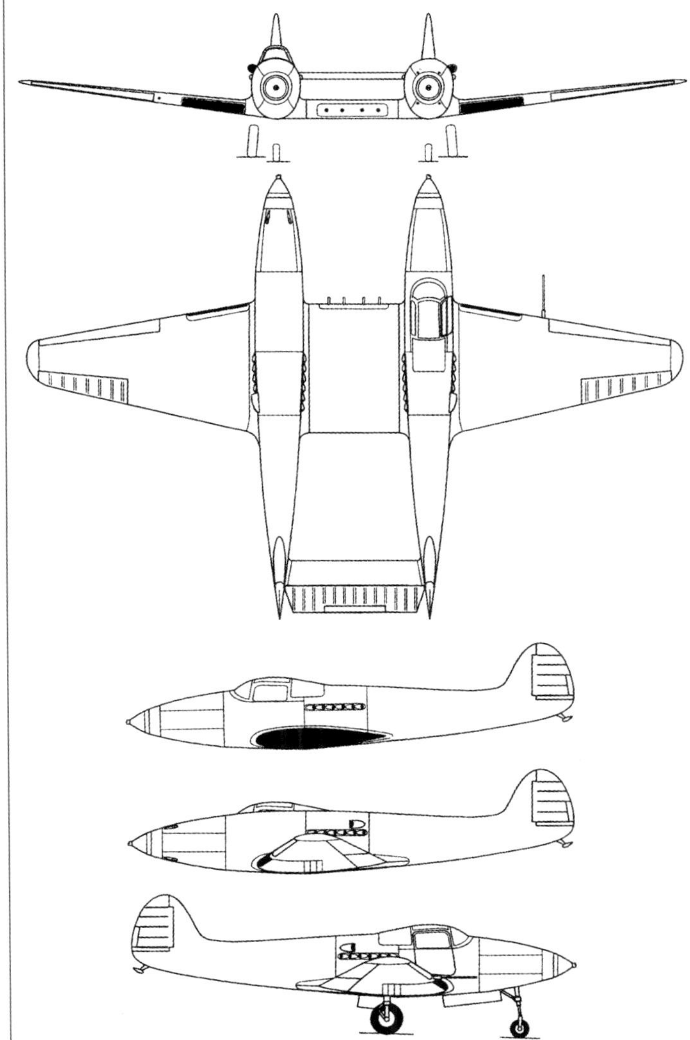

A provisional four-view drawing of the Belyayev OI-2 fighter, with a scrap view showing the inboard side of the starboard fuselage.

was 6,800 kg (15,010 lb.). Design performance included an ambitious maximum-speed target figure of 780 km/h (485 mph) at 7,500 m (24,600 ft.). The landing speed was to be 125 km/h (78 mph). Normal range was 1,000 km (621 miles), increasing to a maximum of 1,400 km (870 miles) in overload (maximum AUW) configuration.

The well-known Russian researcher Oleg Rastrenin has unearthed interesting facts about the story behind Belyayev's fighter. This project was studied with much interest at NII VVS, eliciting various suggestions as to possible improvements. For example, it was suggested that the pilot's cockpit be transferred to the port fuselage in order to improve the pilot's view during the landing approach. NII VVS specialists also expressed the wish that the fighter's range be augmented to 2,000 km (1,242 miles) at 80 percent maximum speed. This apparently reflected the intention to use the OI-2 primarily as an escort fighter.

Despite the favourable comments from NII VVS specialists, the OI-2 project failed to progress further that the drawing board. One of the reasons was the Klimov OKB's development problems

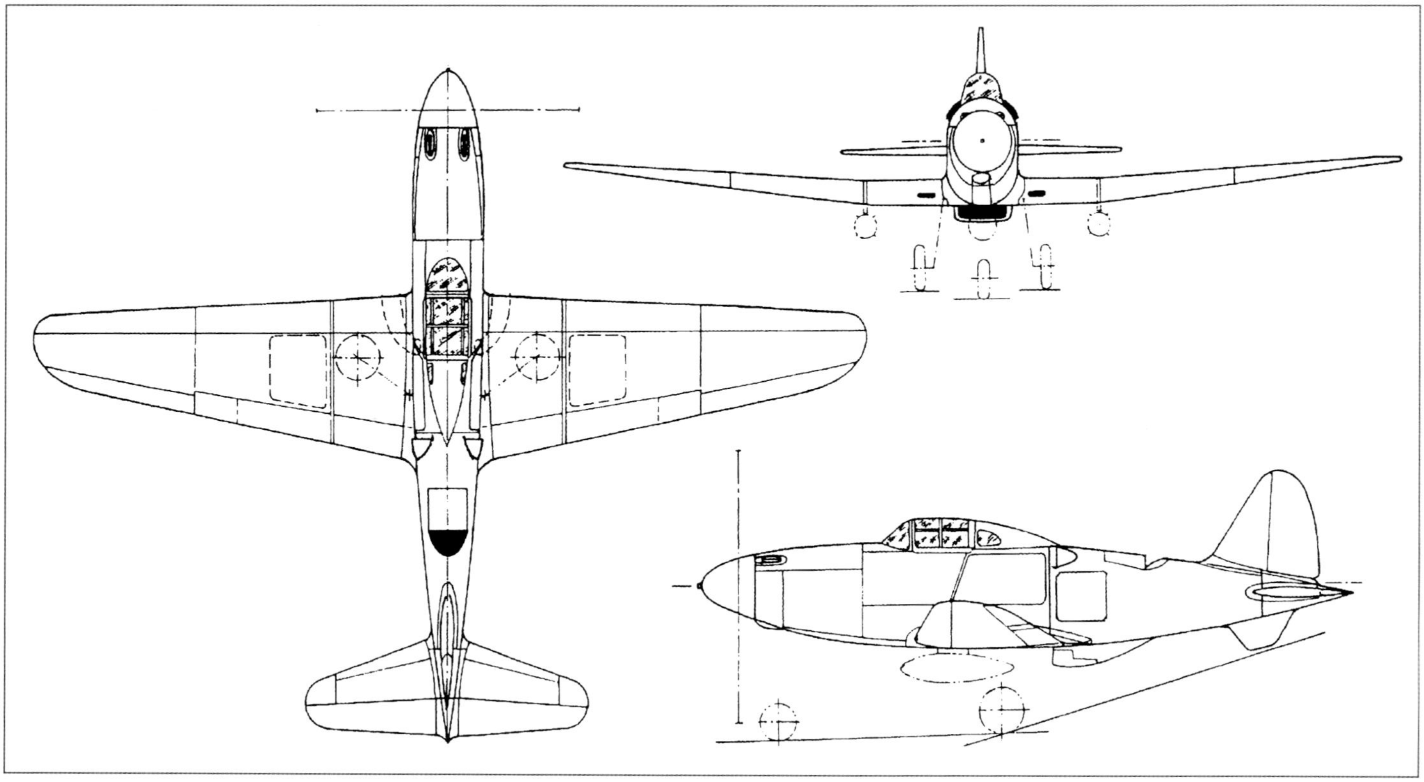

A provisional drawing of a Sukhoi fighter project with an M-120 engine. The narrow track of the outward/forward-retracting main gear units is noteworthy.

with the M-120 engine, whose output and reliability were unsatisfactory (no more than 1,500–1,600 hp could be obtained, and the programme was eventually cancelled in 1942). After the outbreak of the war in June 1941, Belyayev's design bureau (one of the several minor design bureaus stationed at aircraft plant no. 156) was closed down.

Sukhoi Fighter, Airacobra-Style (Project)

An interesting project of a fighter featuring the Aircobra layout was developed by Pavel Osipovich Sukhoi; no specific designation has been quoted. The project was submitted to NII VVS in the second half of 1939. The fighter was to be powered by a Klimov M-120UV engine provided with a turbocharger. The basic feature

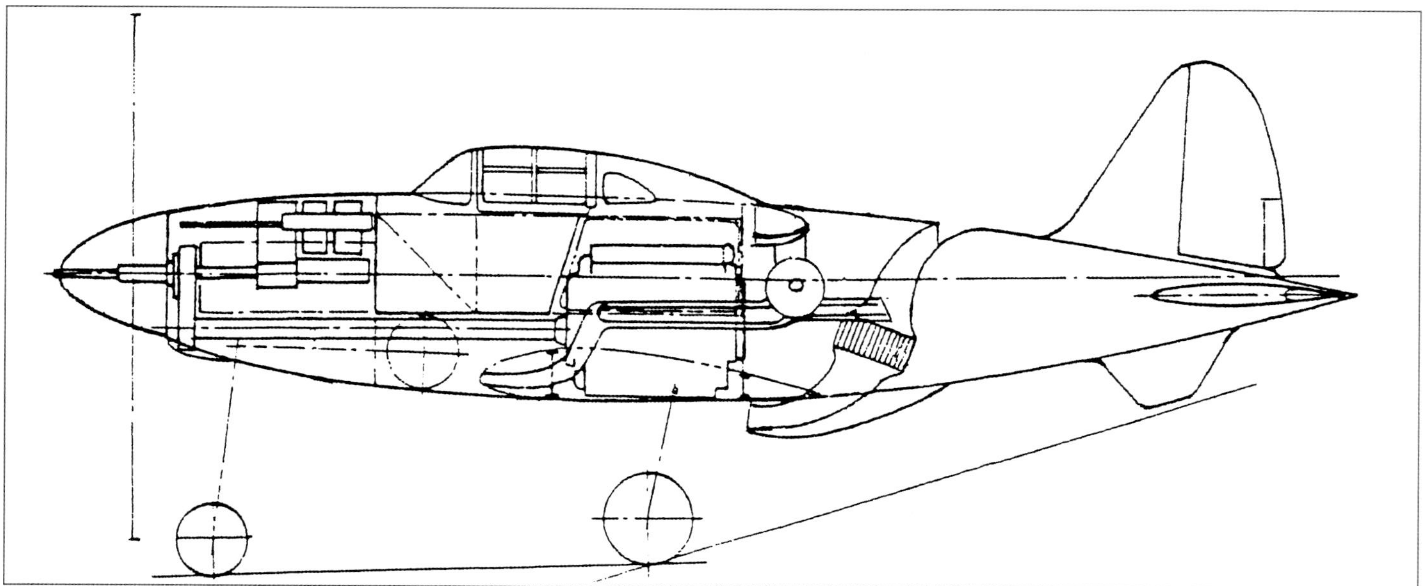

A provisional cutaway drawing of the Sukhoi 'Airacobra-style' fighter, showing the supercharger, the wing root air intakes for the exhaust manifolds' air ejectors, and the S-duct housing the water radiator and oil cooler.

borrowed from the P-39 was the location of the engine amidships behind the pilot's seat, with an extension shaft to the propeller. In fact, this part of the fuselage closely resembled the P-39, except that the cockpit canopy had a conventional design instead of the car-type doors. Other similar points included the weapons arrangement in the nose and the forward location of the cockpit, which, in combination with the tricycle undercarriage, gave the pilot an excellent view in flight and on the ground. The outline of the rear fuselage, on the other hand, was distinctly different from that of the P-39. Patterned on Sukhoi's Su-1 and Su-3 fighter prototypes, it incorporated the coolant radiator with a prominent air scoop below the fuselage (the radiator was housed in an S-duct with a dorsal air outlet) and had a tailcone protruding behind the rudder. A ventral fin complemented the picture. Another difference was the layout of the main undercarriage units, which had a narrow wheel track, retracting outward and forward into the wing centre section.

In October 1939, NII VVS gave its approval to the preliminary design project submitted by Pavel O. Sukhoi. The project was deemed to be realistic and capable of ensuring a leap in performance in comparison with the existing Soviet and foreign fighters. The potent armament (one 23 mm cannon firing through the propeller hub and two 12.7 mm machine guns) and good forward view from the cockpit were also noted. NII VVS recommended the prototype construction with some amendments, including the provision of two turbosuperchargers for the M-120 engine and increasing the top speed to 750 km/h (466 mph)—which, with the benefit of hindsight, seems to be an overly optimistic assessment.

On 4 November 1939, chief of the Red Army Air Force Yakov V. Smushkevich endorsed the preliminary design project, adding a remark: *'The range is to be increased to 1,000 km* [621 miles].*'*

Sukhoi's design bureau, which was then based at Plant No. 135 in Khar'kov, the Ukraine, started the detail design. In January 1940 Pavel Sukhoi wrote to Deputy People's commissar of aircraft industry, Aleksandr S. Yakovlev, expressing a request that his design bureau be transferred to Moscow because the Khar'kov plant could not ensure the required quality of prototype construction.

Unfortunately, the plan for prototype aircraft construction endorsed by the state defence committee on 4 March 1940 did not include the Sukhoi fighter powered by the M-120 engine. Most probably this was due to delays in the development of this engine (its first flight-cleared examples fitted with superchargers did not appear before 1942). Thus, the project failed to materialise.

Here are some further particulars of the design. The forward fuselage incorporating the cockpit, and the engine was a welded truss-type structure made of Chromansil steel tubes, with easily detachable skin panels made of duralumin and *elektron* magnesium alloy. The rear fuselage was a duralumin monocoque structure. The M-120 engine, with a design rating of 1,500 hp, was an assembly comprising three six-cylinder blocks of the M-103 engine in an inverted-Y pattern (one block facing up and two blocks below). The turbosuperchargers were located inside the fuselage on both sides of the engine. Exhaust gases from the engine were ducted into the superchargers, and from these into ducts behind the water radiator. Furthermore, the exhaust manifolds were shrouded by housings that were purged by air from intakes in the wing root leading edges. The warmed-up purged air went into the duct behind the radiator and created a small amount of thrust.

The aircraft was to have a wing area of 18.0 m^2 (193.75 sq. ft.), an empty weight of 2,452 kg (5,407 lb.), and an AUW of 3,300 kg (7,276 lb.)—a figure corrected to 3,425 kg (7,552 lb.) by NII VVS.

Design performance was as follows. According to the design bureau's estimates, maximum speed was to be 540–550 km/h (336–342 mph) at sea level and 730–740 km/h (454–460 mph) at 10,000 m (32,840 ft.). The fighter was to reach an altitude of 8,000 m (26,250 ft.) in 6.8 minutes (7.3 minutes*) and 10,000 m (32,810 ft.) in nine minutes (ten minutes*) flat. The time of a full-circle turn at 1,500 m (4,920 ft.) was estimated as 20.1 seconds (25.0 seconds*). The service ceiling was to be 13,000/12,500* m (42,640/41,000* ft.). Range at an altitude of 10,000 m and 90 percent maximum speed was 610/600* km (379/373*miles) on internal fuel, increasing to 1,000/900* km (621/559* miles) with a drop tank. The takeoff run was to be 180/250* m (590/820* ft.), and the landing run was to be 130/300* m (426/984* ft.). The figures marked '*' were calculated by NII VVS specialists.

Transformable Biplane/Monoplane Fighter with a Fuselage à la XP-39 (Pavel Ya. Kozlov's Project)

In January 1940 a group of engineers of aircraft plant no. 18 (then located in Voronezh) submitted a highly unusual project for an aircraft intended for a speed record attempt and for use as a fighter. The group led by Pavel Yakovlevich Kozlov proposed an aircraft that featured a transformable wing layout: a biplane for takeoff and landing and a monoplane for cruise flight. The transformation was based on splitting the wings along the chord, so that in its monoplane configuration each wing consisted of two superimposed wings with conformal sections, pressed together. On takeoff and landing the upper section of the low-set wing was to be elevated by a special mechanism to the level of the upper fuselage contour, thus forming a biplane structure with nearly twice the wing area.

Of interest is the following aspect of the project: its authors envisioned *'an aircraft of the XP-39 type featuring a normal monoplane layout, but having a 2,000 hp engine and wings with only half the area of those of the current XP-39.'* Such an aircraft, they claimed, would be able to reach a maximum speed of 850 km/h (528 mph) while retaining a modest landing speed thanks to transformation into a biplane (unfortunately, no illustration of the general arrangement is available).

The project was, in fact, little more than a general concept requiring lengthy studies; it failed to impress the aviation authorities and did not receive the go-ahead. One of the reasons for rejection was the existence of the experimental IS-1 transformable biplane/monoplane fighter designed by Vladimir V. Shevchenko and Vasiliy V. Nikitin, which was already in hardware form at the time.

Appendix

Preserved Examples of the P-39 Airacobra and P-63 Kingcobra

Russia had a chance of preserving at least one genuine Airacobra intact to this day. An Airacobra I in RAF markings serialled AH725 (c/n 14-156) was displayed at the BNT (Bureau of New Technology) in 1943, partly stripped down to facilitate inspection of its design features. The BNT collection, created for practical purposes, later became in fact TsAGI's corporate museum, featuring quite a few interesting aircraft. Alas, the opportunity was wasted—the museum was closed in the early 1950s, and the exhibits were scrapped on the grounds that 'the country needed metal'!

An example of the P-39 (subtype unknown), rather crudely restored, is preserved in the North Fleet Air Arm Museum in Safonovo (Murmansk Region). The upper contour of the cockpit glazing is obviously inaccurate, and the rear part of the cockpit glazing is apparently replaced by sheet metal and painted over! Into the bargain, the propeller blades are missing.

A P-39Q-10-BE (42-20613) restored from wreckage found in Siberia was placed on a plinth in Yakutsk, a stone's throw from Tuimaada airport, as a memorial to the pilots who lost their lives while ferrying Lend-Lease aircraft along the ALSIB route (Yakutsk housed the headquarters of this route). Actually, it should be regarded as a full-scale replica using some original parts. The memorial was inaugurated in November 2002. The Airacobra in question had been flown by Major Pavel Morozov (whose remains were found near the wreckage and whose name was presumably traced through documents related to the machine found).

In the summer of 2004, a P-39Q-15-BE, 44-2911 / '23 White,' was recovered from the waters of Lake Mart-Yavr on the Kola Peninsula. Flown by pilot Baranovskiy of the 773rd IAP, it had been lost on 19 November 1944. As it became clear later, the pilot had made a forced landing on the surface of the frozen lake but had been killed by the impact. His remains were still in the cockpit when the aircraft was raised from the water, and he was buried with full military honours. As for the remarkably well-preserved aircraft, in 2005 it was exported to Britain for resale and eventual restoration. In 2009 it was acquired by the Ira G. Ross Aerospace Museum (a.k.a. Niagara Aerospace Museum), in Buffalo, New York. There it was known as 'Miss Lend-Lease.' Restoration work on this aircraft was undertaken during August 2010; the engine and other components were removed for repair and preservation work (the current status is unknown to the authors).

Three Airacobras from the Leningrad PVO's 2nd GvIAK (P-39Q-15-BE 44-2092 / '20 White' and P-39Q-20-BE 44-3255 / '25 White' from the 102nd GvIAP and P-39Q-15-BE 44-2664 / '26

White' from the 103rd GvIAP) had been captured by the Finns after force-landing in southeastern Finland on 17 June 1944, obviously after getting lost and running out of fuel—although one source claims they were shot down. In 1995, after lengthy storage in dismantled condition, it was decided to restore one Airacobra as a static exhibit at the Aviation Museum of Central Finland (*Keski-Suomen Ilmailumuseo*), in Tikkakoski. Probably due to the condition of the three aircraft, the restorers chose to fashion together a composite airframe, using the fuselage of 44-2664 and the wings of 44-3255, so that the end result was neither P-39Q-15 nor P-39Q-20. The painstaking restoration lasted five years; finally, on 6 March 2000, the Airacobra was put on display, painted as the original '26 White.' Sometime between 2006 and 2009 the aircraft was moved to a new home—the Anti-Aircraft Defence Museum (*Ilmatorjunta Museo*), in Hyrylä, becoming the only full-size aircraft in its collection.

It may be of interest to the reader that in 1993 the Russian company NPP Antares (*na**ooch**no-proiz**vod**stvennoye predpri**ya**htiye*; Research & Production Enterprise), headed by Vladimir I. Voronin and based in Ivanovo, the one-time 'Cobra City' (seat of the 22nd ZAP), built a three-quarters scale Airacobra replica, with a view to manufacturing 'production' kits for homebuilders. The aircraft was of wooden construction with a glassfibre skin and was powered by a 100 hp Samson 760 two-cylinder, two-strike, water-cooled engine (which was housed in the nose, not aft of the cockpit). The prototype was accurately painted to represent P-39N-0-BE 42-9033 / '01 White,' a 100th GvIAP aircraft that was originally flown by ace Ivan I. Babak, then by ace Grigoriy U. Dol'nikov, and eventually had crashed on 16 March

OPPOSITE PAGE: The Airacobra in the North Fleet Air Arm Museum is an unfortunate example of a botched restoration job.

ABOVE AND BELOW: P-39Q-10-BE 42-20613 on display in Yakutsk creates a much more favourable impression.

ABOVE AND BELOW: Close-ups of the P-39Q in Yakutsk.

ABOVE RIGHT: The replica in the Pokryshkin Memorial Museum in Novosibirsk, representing P-39N-5-BE 42-19158 with Aleksandr I. Pokryshkin's code '100.'

BELOW RIGHT: P-39Q-15-BE 44-2664 / '26 White,' on display in the Aviation Museum of Central Finland.

100

26

1945 after suffering an in-flight engine fire. The replica was displayed statically at the MAKS-93 airshow in Zhukovskiy (31 August–5 September 1993). Both Ivan Babak and Grigoriy Dol'nikov attended the show and experienced an emotional moment, seeing a likeness of the very fighter they had once flown, and of course they were allowed to sit in the cockpit. Unfortunately, the three-quarters-scale Airacobra was never flown—the American customer who had commissioned the replica's development vanished into thin air, NPP Antares went bankrupt, and the subsequent legal disputes between the former partners made flight tests impossible. This aircraft's last public appearance was in rather sad circumstances. According to one of the members of the design team, on 18 May 2001, preparations were in hand to celebrate the eighty-fifth birthday of Aleksey P.

LEFT: P-63A-9-BE 42-69775, coded '91 White,' in the open-air display of the Central Russian Air Force Museum in Monino.

BELOW LEFT: In 2005 the P-63 was briefly wheeled outside the museum grounds and used as part of an improvised 'frontline airfield' during the Flying Legends festival at Monino.

RIGHT: P-63C-5-BE 44-4011, coded '08 White,' at the Great Patriotic War Museum in Moscow.

BELOW: Another view of the same exhibit. The serial is incorrectly applied to appear as '44-44011,' which was actually an unbuilt B-24 bomber from a cancelled order.

Mares'yev (HSU)—a legendary Soviet fighter pilot who, after being shot down in April 1942 and losing both feet, returned to active duty with prosthetics (he ended the war as an ace with ten 'kills,' seven of which he scored after the shootdown). For the occasion the Airacobra replica was put on stage at the Central House of the Soviet Army (a large concert hall in Moscow). As the audience waited for the war hero to appear, the announcer broke the shocking news that Mares'yev had passed away an hour ago! The Antares P-39N replica is now in storage at the Central Russian Air Force Museum in Monino, near Moscow.

To commemorate the 100th anniversary of the famous ace Aleksandr I. Pokryshkin, which was celebrated in 2013, an exact full-scale replica of his P-39, sporting the code '100' on the fuselage and the serial 42-19158, was placed at the entrance of the Novosibirsk Science and Technology College (in 1932 Pokryshkin graduated from this institution, which at that time was more modestly termed a factory apprenticeship school). Some time later the replica was returned to its owner Vladimir Shumilov, but it was fondly remembered by the students and teachers of the college. In the meantime, a project was started that eventually resulted in

ABOVE AND BELOW: The Airacobra in the museum in Verkhnyaya Pyshma is painted to represent Grigoriy A. Rechkalov's P-39Q-15 44-2547, complete with the pilot's initials, R.G.A. The only jarring note is the P-39D-style small nosewheel instead of the correct large wheel.

ABOVE AND BELOW: The remarkably complete P-39Q-15-BE 44-2911 / '23 White' after being recovered from Lake Mart-Yavr in 2004. This aircraft was subsequently sold to the US for restoration.

The Urals Combat Glory Museum in Verkhnyaya Pyshma also features a P-63C with no markings whatever. It appears that the restorers still had to put the finishing touches to it when this picture was taken.

the creation of the 'Patriot' Historical Memorial Park, associated with the college. A part of this project was the restoration of historical aircraft of the Great Patriotic War; restored examples of the Yak-9 and the Il-10 formed the beginning of this collection. In 2017 these aircraft were joined by Pokryshkin's Airacobra—the replica 'made a comeback' to occupy its place of honour in the park.

In 2017 a new museum piece representing the P-39 was added to the collection of the Urals Combat Glory Military Equipment Museum, which had opened in the town of Verkhnyaya Pyshma (Sverdlovsk Region) in the Urals in 2006. At present this is one of the most prominent military history museums in Russia. The machine acquired by the museum is a copy of the P-39Q-15-BE that was used by one of the most prominent Soviet aces, Grigoriy A. Rechkalov, Twice Hero of the Soviet Union, who, with fifty-six individual victories to his credit, was the third-highest-scoring Soviet fighter ace after Ivan N. Kozhedub and Aleksandr I. Pokryshkin. This museum exhibit was assembled from parts of several P-39s, and its airframe is mostly made up of original subassemblies. It was painted to represent Rechkalov's machine, with the forward fuselage decorated with stars denoting his victories and the rear fuselage sporting the pilot's initials, R.G.A.

Unfortunately, no genuine P-63s have survived in the USSR/Russia. Virtually all retired examples were scrapped. At present, one machine of this type is preserved as an exhibit at the Central Russian Air Force Museum in Monino, near Moscow, supposedly representing P-63A-9-BE 42-69775. Unfortunately, however, it is a strange hybrid of the P-63 and P-39 assembled from parts of the wreckage of several machines that had crashed on the ALSIB route.

Considerably later, another P-63C was restored on the basis of a machine discovered in the Far East, which, likewise, was among those ferried along the ALSIB. The aircraft had made a forced landing and suffered considerable damage. Not later than 2015 the restored machine became an exhibit at the abovementioned Urals Combat Glory Military Equipment Museum in the town of Verkhnyaya Pyshma, becoming a companion to the P-39 that is on display there.

During the first years of the twenty-first century the remains of several Kingcobras were still languishing in the company of a few derelict captured Japanese aircraft at two small airfields on the island of Shumshu—the northernmost island of the Kuril Group. One of these Kingcobras, a P-63C-5-BE serialled 44-4011, was recovered and subjected to restoration. In 2005 the restored machine, which incorporated a large amount of original parts, became an exhibit at the open-air aviation section in the Central Museum of the Great Patriotic War in Moscow. In addition to the USAAF serial on the fin (incorrectly rendered to represent 44-44011, an unbuilt B-24 Liberator), the machine sports the tactical code '08 White' on the forward fuselage.

Interestingly, an example of the P-63 maintained in flying condition as one of the 'warbirds' in the US was painted in Soviet air force colours. Likewise, a P-63 forming part of the collection of the USAF Museum in Arizona wears the Red Star insignia as a tribute to the type's service with the Soviet air force.